ALTERNATIVE
JOURNALISM

Journalism Studies: Key Texts is a new textbook series that systematically maps the crucial connections between theory and practice in journalism. It provides the solid grounding students need in the history, theory, 'real-life' practice and future directions of journalism, while further engaging them in key critical debates. Drawing directly from how journalism is studied and understood today, the series is a full-service resource for students and lecturers alike.

Series Editors: Martin Conboy, David Finkelstein, Bob Franklin

Radio Journalism   Guy Starkey and Andrew Crissell

ALTERNATIVE
JOURNALISM

Journalism Studies:
Key Texts

CHRIS ATTON AND JAMES F. HAMILTON

Los Angeles • London • New Delhi • Singapore • Washington DC

First published 2008

SAGE Publications Ltd
1 Oliver's Yard
55 City Road
London EC1Y 1SP

SAGE Publications Inc.
2455 Teller Road
Thousand Oaks, California 91320

SAGE Publications India Pvt Ltd
B 1/I 1 Mohan Cooperative Industrial Area
Mathura Road
New Delhi 110 044

SAGE Publications Asia-Pacific Pte Ltd
33 Pekin Street #02-01
Far East Square
Singapore 048763

Library of Congress Control Number: 2008921708

British Library Cataloguing in Publication data

A catalogue record for this book is available from
the British Library

ISBN 978-1-4129-4702-2
ISBN 978-1-4129-4703-9 (pbk)

Typeset by C&M Digitals (P) Ltd, Chennai, India
Printed in India by Replika Press Pvt. Ltd
Printed on paper from sustainable resources

For Sue (Chris)
For Cynthia (James)

CONTENTS

ACKNOWLEDGEMENTS

Portions of Chapters 1, 2 and 4 extend arguments made in James Hamilton's *Democratic Communication: Formations, Projects, Possibilities* (Lexington Books, 2008). The section on the ethics of alternative journalism (Chapter 5) is based on Chris Atton's 'Ethical Issues in Alternative Journalism' (*Ethical Space: The International Journal of Communication Ethics* 1(1), 2003: 26–31). In Chapter 6, parts of the radio section are based on Chapter 5 of Atton's *An Alternative Internet* (Edinburgh University Press, 2004). Parts of Chapter 7 are developed from parts of Atton's *Alternative Media* (Sage, 2002) and his article 'Current Issues in Alternative Media Research' (*Sociology Compass* 1, 2008).

We would like to thank the editors of this series for commissioning a book that would have been unlikely to find a publisher even a few years ago. This is due, of course, to the work of our many colleagues in alternative media studies across the world, who have done so much to develop this subject into many university curricula and to argue its importance as part of wider studies in sociology, political communication and cultural and media studies. Our 'personal' editor, David Finkelstein, offered unfailing encouragement and valuable criticism throughout the writing. Rachel Hendrick at Sage clarified much and supported us even more. Finally, we recognize the extraordinary creative energy of countless journalist-activists throughout the world who provide not simply the grist for this book, but more generally the hope and promise for journalism(s) that contribute to a more democratic public life.

INTRODUCTION

The Scope of the Book

What is alternative journalism? For those encountering the term for the first time – and even for those familiar with it – it can appear infuriatingly vague. How does it relate to an array of similar terms such as citizen journalism, citizen's media, community media, democratic media, emancipatory media, radical media and social movement media? When we turn to specific practices, there is an even wider range to consider: newspapers, magazines, radio and television stations; blogs and social networking sites; pamphlets and posters; fanzines and zines; graffiti and street theatre; independent book publishing and even independent record production. These practices are often informed by the desire to provide news, information, comment and analysis to specific, identified communities defined in geographic or socio-cultural terms (such as ethnic minority journalism, gay/lesbian journalism, or community media).

In what is the first academic book-length study of alternative journalism, we argue that what all these concepts and practices share is an emphasis on thinking about journalism in a particular way: in other words, they are primarily informed by a critique of existing ways (the dominant practices) of doing journalism. Alternative journalism proceeds from dissatisfaction not only with the mainstream coverage of certain issues and topics, but also with the epistemology of news. Its critique emphasizes alternatives to, *inter alia*, conventions of news sources and representation; the inverted pyramid of news texts; the hierarchical and capitalized economy of commercial journalism; the professional, elite basis of journalism as a practice; the professional norm of objectivity; and the subordinate role of audience as receiver.

Alternative journalism, at least in its ideal form, is produced outside mainstream media institutions and networks. It 'can include the media of protest groups, dissidents, fringe political organisations, even fans and hobbyists' (Atton, 2004: 3). It tends to be produced not by professionals, but by amateurs who typically have little or no training or professional qualifications as journalists: they write and report from their position as citizens, as members of communities, as activists or as fans. (Though as we shall see, there are examples of alternative journalism where professional journalists and professional techniques are employed, often in ways radically different from their conventional uses.) Much of the work of alternative journalism is concerned with representing the interests, views and needs of under-represented groups in society. As well as being homes for radical content, projects of alternative journalism also tend to be organized in non-mainstream ways, often non-hierarchically or collectively, and almost always on a non-commercial basis. They hope to be independent of the market and immune to institutionalization. Practitioners of alternative journalism also seek to redress what they consider an imbalance of media power in mainstream media, which results in the marginalization (at worst, the demonization) of certain social and cultural groups and movements.

It is this emphasis on media power that we argue lies at the heart of alternative journalism. It is for this reason that, despite all the cognate terms used to refer to its practices, we prefer to call it alternative journalism. This is because, as Nick Couldry and James Curran have argued, it functions as a comparative term to indicate that 'whether indirectly or directly, media power is what is at stake' (Couldry and Curran, 2003b: 7). We develop this argument in detail in Chapter 7, where we explore a range of theories that have been put forward to make sense of alternative media production. These include John Downing's theory of radical media (Downing, 1984; Downing et al., 2001); Clemencia Rodriguez's 'citizens' media' (Rodriguez, 2001) and Hackett and Carroll's (2006) notion of democratic media activism. These studies are undoubtedly extremely useful: they offer valuable insights into the ideologies and practices of non-mainstream media. However, they share a common assumption that alternative media are primarily concerned with radical politics and social empowerment, with what Pippa Norris has called 'critical citizens' (Norris, 1999). Once again we find ourselves in agreement with Couldry and Curran; just as they do in their own work, we wish to explore non-mainstream media that 'may or may not be politically radical or socially empowering' (Couldry and Curran, 2003b: 7).

Alternative journalism, then, becomes both a comparative term and a broader term. Within it, we may place not only the journalisms of politics and empowerment, but those of popular culture and the everyday. Alternative journalism may be home to explorations of individual enthusiasm and subcultural identity just as much as to radical visions of society and the polity. This is one reason why, as we conclude the theory chapter of this book, we apply the field theory of Pierre Bourdieu to alternative journalism, a theory that is capable of dealing with all forms of cultural production, all forms of journalism, whatever the aims and practices of those forms.

It is not enough, of course, simply to answer the question: what is alternative journalism? If media power is indeed at stake in its varied principles and practices, we must also ask such questions as: how does it relate to the dominant practices and ideologies of journalism, as well as those of politics and economics? How is it – and how has it been – culturally and socially significant? How does it manifest itself in different countries and at different times? To hope for a comprehensive set of answers to these questions is quite unrealistic, not least because of the immense historical and geographical sweep this book would need to take. Instead, we have used the structure shared by all the books in this series of *Journalism Studies: Key Texts* to explore alternative journalism by focusing not on the accumulation of microscopic detail but, first, on the identification of broad currents in the field (such as those found in history and political economy) and second, on case studies that illuminate these currents through their ideologies, practices, and specific locales. In this way, we aim to present a study of alternative journalism that is wide-ranging (though with no pretension to comprehensiveness), theoretically coherent and sensitive to the many contexts in which alternative journalism's challenges to media power take place.

The Structure of the Book

The book begins with a history of alternative journalism in the UK and the US (Chapter 1). This historical overview contests the grand narratives of much mainstream media history, which emphasises the development of institutions and the accounts of 'great men' (Hamilton and Atton, 2001). It begins by recounting the emergence of received conceptions of journalism itself, beginning with the rise of Enlightenment positivism, empiricism and their corollaries, not only in Baconian inquiry but also in the appearance of epistolary novels and hybrid forms of reportage prior to the 1700s (Altschull, 1990; Davis, 1983). The subsequent politicization of journalism in the forms of party presses supported by patronage came to be challenged in the Industrial Revolution by the rise of the popular presses (Williams, 1978b) and the industrialization and rationalization of journalism forms in such ways as the inverted pyramid and objectivity as both a prose style and professional creed (Barnhurst and Nerone, 2001). This industrialization was challenged in turn both by the continuation of earlier polemical forms of journalism as well as by the development of new narrative forms in the wake of the modernist critique of empiricism, an example being the 'new journalism' of the 1960s, variations of which have been practised more recently in the service of a variety of new social movements (Reed, 2005). Chapter 1 is developed through an overview of historical developments in other parts of the world, such as varieties of journalistic practice outside of the Western 'objective' mode, the amateur political journalism of Central and South America (Rodriguez, 2001) and the dissident media of Iran and the former Soviet Union.

An understanding of the history of forms of alternative journalism needs to be complemented by an understanding of the political-economic context of their formation and practice. A dominant theme in accounts of media history is the equation of political independence with the growth of democracy, where press freedom is equated with popular freedom (Curran, 2002). Chapter 2 critiques this approach, drawing on studies that show how alternative media have resisted the effects of neoliberal orthodoxy and market 'reforms' to produce journalism that both critiques the prevailing political and economic orthodoxy and at the same time develops its structures and networks of media production and reception in ways that challenge the institutionalized and capitalized methods of mainstream media.

Alternative journalism is a response most generally to capitalism as a social, cultural and economic means of organizing societies, and to imperialism as a global dynamic of domination and consolidation. The practice of capitalism and imperialism enabled the rise of 'liberal' democracies of the West and, later, the socialist revolutions of the twentieth century. It also created the conditions to which subsequent social movements are a response as well as the means of challenge. Resources of challenge include the more immediate, such as new means of manufacture and distribution, new kinds of technologies of reproduction and of infrastructure and distribution, as well as the more general such as the moderation of working hours and the rise of consumer society and institutionalized leisure (Schiller, 1996: 3–38). In particular, the Internet provides a critical point in political-economic examinations of alternative journalism. There is a powerful dialectic here between the use of a neoliberal new technology that is largely in the control of Western economic forces, and its deployment as a radically reforming (if not revolutionary) tool for globalized, social-movement-based activism.

Chapter 3 shifts the focus of the book to specific case studies in its exploration of the social demographics of alternative journalism. There are few surveys of alternative journalists (Harcup, 2005 provides the only one for the UK, for example), and no surveys that pretend to completeness. However, accounts of media practices across a range of alternative journalisms do provide insights into the educational background, professional training, and the gender and ethnic mix of practitioners. Of particular importance here is the relationship between the journalist as writer and the journalist as activist (or enthusiast or fan); for many alternative journalists, the journalism is a secondary activity at the service of a greater goal (in the case of social-movement journalism, the goal might be political reform or revolution). Many such journalists are autodidacts, which brings not only different ways of writing but different approaches to sourcing and ethics (Atton, 2003b; Atton and

Wickenden, 2005). This chapter therefore locates the social demographics of alternative journalists within wider social and political practices.

In particular, it draws on and emphasizes alternative journalism in the context of actual contemporary practices. The chapter examines the wide range of people involved in the production of alternative journalism, including the amateur, the autodidact and the trained journalist. It explores how these various types utilize existing forms of journalism and production techniques and to what extent they innovate. The chapter also explores the relationships between mainstream and alternative journalists, the possibilities for collaboration and their movement from one field to the other.

Chapter 4 is concerned with policy. The community media sector has enduring and active organizations that function in part as policy forums (for example, AMARC – the World Association of Community Broadcasters – and the UK's Community Media Association), and in the UK and the US, much governmental attention is given to community media. By contrast, for alternative journalism there is little or no formal policy discussion at governmental or 'industrial' levels (in a sense there is no industry). Yet there is no shortage of critiques and position papers that could form the basis of policy here. Some of these come from media organizations and their professional organizations, which consider alternative journalism as a form to be incorporated into the dominant practices of journalism. Others represent challenges to dominant practices and seek to reform them: these include proposals such as Journalism That Matters (2007a, 2007b) and the work of the trade association American Alternative Newsweeklies (2007). Finally, the most radical proposals come from groups and individuals who seek to subvert dominant practices and to replace them entirely with new ways of reporting that seem to bear little resemblance to traditional journalism.

Contemporary practices have already been introduced as a factor in the social demographics of alternative journalism; in Chapter 5, they are explored in depth. These practices are broadly divided into two, as relating to two broad divisions of journalistic content: the political and the popular-cultural. The political is explored through media that exhibit specifically radical positions, media allied to social movement activities and ideologies, and the individual contributions of bloggers. The popular-cultural is represented by fanzines, zines and other specialist publications that focus on cultural products, genres, movements and individual artists.

Inevitably, the chapter examines the relationship between alternative and mainstream media practices. Some alternative journalism not only employs populist methods of presentation that resemble the practices of tabloid journalism, it also challenges conventional notions of expertise and authority, particularly in their foregrounding of 'ordinary' people as sources of news. This foregrounding is not without its problems, though: who is to say that these sources might not be used ideologically? Consequently, this chapter

examines issues familiar from studies of mainstream media: ethics, objectivity, representation and sourcing practices, and reliability and credibility.
How do alternative journalists deal with issues such as representation and
objectivity, particularly when they are developed from the structural and
cultural characteristics of alternative journalism, and the radicalizing of
journalistic practices through notions such as 'active witnessing'?

Journalistic practices are, of course, determined to some degree by their
location in differing cultural, social and political contexts. Chapter 6 highlights the comparative significance of specific conditions under which alternative journalism is produced, whether at the local, national, regional or even
international level. As with our survey of social demographics, this chapter
does not attempt to be comprehensive. Instead it employs case studies to draw
attention to the ways in which politics, economics, and social and cultural systems provide specific contexts that contribute to the shaping of a wide range
of journalistic practices. Examples come from the present and from recent
history (the 1980s onwards, thus providing chronological connection with the
historical material in Chapter 1). The survey encompasses alternative journalism in Asia, Eastern Europe, Latin America and Africa, as well as the UK,
the US and Canada. Comparison is emphasized by analysing different uses of
the same medium (radio, television and the Internet) in different countries.

The theoretical arguments in Chapter 7 have their beginnings in critical
media studies, which also act as a site for some types of alternative journalism. Three broad theoretical positions are advanced (as we have already
noted): Downing's theory of radical media; Rodriguez's concept of citizens'
media; and a broader framework for alternative journalism based on media
power and the notion of the native reporter. The chapter examines key texts
that have shaped our theoretical understanding of alternative media, as well
as studies that have addressed alternative journalism itself. Chapter 7 concludes with an appraisal of how Bourdieu's theory of cultural production
might aid our understanding of alternative journalism in all its dimensions:
the political, the economic, the social and the cultural.

The final chapter of the book begins with what is currently the most conspicuous site for alternative journalism, the Internet. In looking for the future
directions of alternative journalism, we question the continuing value and efficacy of a media technology that has been in large part responsible for the massive increase and visibility of alternative forms of journalism. More broadly, we
ask to what extent such practices are sustainable in a media-centric world, especially when some of their aims are so grounded in actual political change. Do
the number and diversity of alternative journalism projects encourage and sustain 'active' citizenship, or do they merely represent another facet of a media-
centric world where lived experience is diminished? Do such journalisms have
a coherent future or is their very pluralism a threat to their effectiveness?

Part 1

1

THE HISTORICIZATION OF ALTERNATIVE JOURNALISM

Many historical accounts of journalism have been criticized for their preoccupation with great men or great technologies. Attention has been drawn to the ways in which such accounts unduly valorize individual exploits and validate the simplistic position that anyone determined (or great) enough to change the world can do so (Hardt, 1990; Hardt and Brennen, 1995). Many historical accounts of alternative journalism also suffer from the same preoccupations, which has created great gaps in understanding (Hamilton and Atton, 2001). While narrowly focused biographies of publishers, writers, journalists, publications or organizations have yielded insights into specific episodes, the resulting patchwork collection of accounts prevents a broader understanding of the general media practices and necessary conditions upon which these individual cases rely.

Accordingly, this chapter provides an historical overview of the emergence of alternative journalism. However, instead of describing a series of specific people and separate projects, it emphasizes general practices and conditions. The key insight of this overview is that alternative journalism is not an unchanging, universal type of journalism, but is an ever-changing effort to respond critically to dominant conceptions of journalism. Alternative journalism is best seen as a kind of activity instead of as a specific, definitive kind of news story, publication or mode of organization. What alternative journalism is at any given moment depends entirely on what it is responding to.

It is in this sense that this chapter is not simply a 'history' of events of the past disconnected from today, but instead is an effort to 'historicize' alternative journalism. This chapter does not present the history of alternative journalism as a neutral, complete set of facts to recount (if only it were so easy!). Rather, it seeks to understand the historicity of alternative journalism – its relational, always changing nature as a response to and a struggle against an equally changing dominant journalism within changing conditions. To adequately grasp alternative journalism in all its complexity, one must constitute and understand it not only in relation to today's conception of the alternative as simply the opposite of the mainstream, but also in relation to its own complex development, which calls into question the viability of such a conceptual map.

We first describe the emergence of bourgeois journalism, which assisted the successful challenge to royal and ecclesiastical authority by a mercantile and later capitalist bourgeoisie. While acknowledging the contributions of many European developments, the chapter focuses on Anglo-America as a centre not only of the emergence of journalism as a mode of writing and public debate, but also of capitalism, which has proven to be such a formative force not only for journalism but for world affairs in the past 400 years. We trace the breakdown of the authority of bourgeois journalism as the accepted form of public debate, which culminates in the development of new forms of journalistic writing and new modes of journalistic organization and practice. The amalgam referred to today as alternative journalism is determined in all its variety by these contexts.

While a single chapter cannot do justice to the depth and complexity of the developments noted here, the purpose is to outline a general framework for understanding the development of alternative journalism in a way that resonates with concerns today. Expanded accounts are given in the many detailed historical studies already available.

The Absorption of the Radical-Popular

Any account of the emergence of alternative journalism that purports to be historical in the sense outlined above must begin by noting a supreme irony, which underscores the necessity of seeing alternative journalism as constituted by its social and historical context. Although disparaged today (and often for good reason), the development of what we refer to today as the 'dominant' or 'mainstream' mode of journalism was initially a critical (dare we say 'alternative'?) response in its day to an earlier dominant.

Raymond Williams's influential reinterpretation of the contours of the historical development of the press in Britain helps explain this irony (Williams, 1970; Williams, 1978a; Williams, 1978b). It may seem baffling at first how a committed socialist such as Williams recognized 'the achievement of the bourgeoisie in the creation of the modern press [... as] a major historical break-through' of great significance for radical-democratic politics (Williams, 1979: 310–311). What explains this seeming contradiction is that, for Williams, no essential, pure types of journalism exist. Rather, journalism – like all forms of popular culture – 'is always an uneasy mixture of two very different elements: the maintenance of an independent popular identity, often linked with political radicalism, resistance to the establishment and movements for social change; and ways of adapting, from disadvantage, to a dominant social order, finding relief and satisfaction or diversion inside it' (Williams, 1970: 22).

Williams's general argument is worth recalling here. In early nineteenth-century England and before the formation of a commercial journalism industry, comparatively clear class antagonisms delineated, on the one hand, independent radical newspapers as the 'popular press' of the day in the sense of their 'staking a new claim, articulating a new voice, in a situation in which otherwise there would have been silence'; on the other hand, 'established newspapers' addressed a narrowly defined readership composed of business and political leaders (Williams, 1970: 17; see also Hollis, 1970; for the case in France, see Skuncke, 2005 and Trinkle, 2002).

This opposition began to collapse as authoritarian repression of the independent radical papers gave way to absorption and incorporation by the emerging commercial popular press. To siphon readers into this new commercial 'popular', the commercial press adopted long-standing popular forms of chapbooks, ballads and pamphlets as well as selected 'radical social and political attitudes'. What enhanced the replacement of the radical-popular by the commercial-popular was the consolidation of the newspaper business into groups and chains and the securing of advertising revenue at a scale unimaginable only a short time previously, both of which gave the commercial-popular a productive capacity that moved it on to a level entirely different from the radical-popular. As a result, 'the control of popular journalism passed into the hands of successful large-scale entrepreneurs, who alone now could reach a majority of the public quickly and attractively and cheaply, on a national scale, but who by their very ability to do this, by their control of resources, were separated from or opposed to the people whom this popular journalism served' (Williams, 1970: 23).

The result of this extremely complex process was that 'what had once been popular, in the political sense, was absorbed or deflected into "popular" in quite other senses', with 'market journalism replac[ing] the journalism of a community or movement' (Williams, 1970: 20–21). What we call in this book 'alternative journalism', then, was not simply repressed or stamped out in England, although clear and sustained efforts were made to do so, as Curran (1978) has described. Today in most countries, and particularly on the Internet, we can indeed find and read 'a press of bewildering variety' (Williams, 1970: 24). However, at the same time, radical-popular journalism (in Williams's terms) or alternative journalism (in our terms) has been effectively isolated from what is taken today to be the 'popular', not only in that it lacks the resources of the commercial-popular but also in cultural terms as now being seen largely as specialized, idiosyncratic, 'sectarian and strange' (Williams, 1970: 22).

The Rise of Bourgeois Journalism

Williams's reinterpretation serves well as a means of further organizing an understanding of the complex development of alternative journalism. Indeed, the accomplishment of this reinterpretation is the greater specificity and complexity granted to the general category of alternative journalism, and an analysis that explains it not by fixing a definition, but by viewing it as entirely determined by its relation to that against which it struggles. Williams's provocative interpretation thus serves well as the link between developments that preceded it and those that followed. Let us first address developments prior to the point at which Williams's account begins.

The Rise of the Bourgeoisie

The 'established' press that Williams refers to can be more overtly linked to its class basis by calling it 'bourgeois journalism'. The term 'bourgeois' or 'bourgeoisie' refers generally to a property-owning class whose resources and influence come not from royal decree or royally granted monopoly but through capital generated by an expanding capitalist economy. What must be addressed first in an account of bourgeois journalism is the rise of the economic system that made this class possible. While one could characterize this new system as simply one in which the amount of goods produced and sold increased dramatically, what was more novel and important was the corresponding, fitful and often contentious reorganization of society from mercantilist to capitalist. Hawkes summarizes the decisive change as the institutionalization of a 'system of production for exchange rather than for use', which the increasing internationalization of finance and production helped bring about and support (Hawkes, 2001: 15).

Assisting the emergence of capitalism was increased state involvement in empire-building and colonialism. By the mid-seventeenth century and the establishment of the Protectorate headed by Cromwell, the government had already become 'a proactive authority in commercial matters', with a good portion of its involvement related to matters of colonization and trade beyond the confines of Europe which, as Loades argues, was where 'the most spectacular changes took place' (2000: 215–219). Such involvement helped lay the groundwork not only for social, political and economic changes in England, but also for the intertwinement of capitalism with colonialism and imperialism in an increasingly worldwide political and economic project that presaged today's intensely globalized and polarized world.

The basis of bourgeois journalism in this new propertied class was significantly different from the royal-religious basis of knowledge and authority. In England and in Europe, sources of authority prior to the rise of capitalism and the bourgeoisie were rooted in combinations of divine right of rule and the word of God. As a result, what we would regard today as arbitrary – if not capricious – rulings and decrees were justified by claims of absolute authority that was seen as beyond the human ability to affect or change. While granting this, however, one should not assume that people of the day accepted such decisions and authority blindly and passively. As Hindle points out concerning early modern England, exercising rule was 'a process in which subjects were intimately involved, one which they learned to manipulate, to criticize, and even to change' (Hindle, 2000: 237). To give just one example, the many rebellions and riots during the reigns of Henry VIII and Elizabeth I alone suggest a far from quiescent populace (Fletcher and MacCulloch, 1997).

However, just as the emergence of capitalism and imperialism initiated growing social and economic inequalities, it also made possible the consolidation of the bourgeoisie, which was a countervailing source of power increasingly outside royal control. While royal monopolies, patronage, licensing and chartering in exchange for a share of revenues and for political support had been key ways of supporting commercial enterprises financially to ensure their political compliance, such controls were gradually superseded as independent commercial centres of finance and investment grew, diversified and internationalized. Thus, economic expansion and change in the context of empire-building helped produce and validate a new class of merchants, traders and financiers who were unbound by class rules of custom and traditional decorum and deference, and enabled through their control of capital.

Bourgeois Journalism as Cultural Form

The production of a social class with sources of power outside direct royal or ecclesiastic control relied upon and enabled the rise of what today we call 'journalism'. Indeed, the emergence of journalism is intimately tied to the emergence of capitalism and the class it both relied on for financing and catered to as readers and buyers. Journalism at this time represented a new kind of authoritative claim to knowledge about the world that was embodied in new kinds of writing.

Journalism as a way of writing and understanding is an amalgam of a number of sources, with one being empiricism. As influentially interpreted by Francis Bacon (Lord Chancellor in the court of James I), empiricism means gathering and cataloguing evidence from which to generalize and test universal cause-and-effect relationships (Farrington, 1964). Far from a process a single person can carry out, Bacon proposed a bureaucratized project whereby a veritable army of assistants would gather data according to Bacon's highly standardized procedures, with the goal of generating knowledge useful to the crown and to industry. Importantly, the dependability of information was directly related to how closely specific rules for gathering data were followed – much like the need for professional journalists today to follow rules such as seeking out more than one side to a story, basing conclusions on multiple sources and setting one's personal views aside.

A second key source was the newly popular form of essays and commentary, in which claims to authority were based not on how much external evidence was gathered in support of a conclusion based on systematically gathered evidence, so much as on an individual writer's own powers of observation, reasoning and writing skill. A third source was reportage, a longstanding practice of hiring agents to travel to distant lands and report back to their benefactors (often diplomats and other government officials) regarding events or situations that had a bearing on their interests (Schneider, 2005; see also Shapiro, 2000: 77–78, 87). In addition to diplomatic reports and private handwritten newsletters, forerunners of reportage included town criers' announcements, broadsides, news pamphlets and manuscript newsletters (Raymond, 1996; Shapiro, 2000: 86).

A fourth source of journalism is found in the evolving standards of legal disputation, which increasingly codified rules for establishing valid evidence and legally sound claims. These rules included using details of time, place and circumstance; identifying and evaluating witnesses and their testimony; and rejecting second-hand accounts in favour of direct testimony and personal observation (Shapiro, 2000: 99–103). Such rules slowly became the standard for other purportedly 'factual' writing such as history, chorography, travel reporting and, of course, early journalism, which emphasized the use of credible sources, impartiality, a clear separation of the fictional from the factual, a distinction between reporting facts and speculation based on those facts, and the use of plain and unadorned prose (Shapiro, 2000: 86, 94; see also Clark, 1983: 99; Davis, 1983; and Raymond, 1996: 130–133). As Shapiro argues about the relationship between these four sources and early journalism, 'news genres ... played a role in transforming "fact" from a category limited to human actions and deeds into one that comprehended both human and natural phenomena' (Shapiro, 2000: 4). In other words, all of these sources combined to help produce a new basis for creating and presenting a truthful and thus authoritative account of the world.

Implications of Bourgeois Journalism

Recalling the great importance Williams attributed to its emergence, the implications of the rise of bourgeois journalism for new forms of political resistance were immense. Together with other changes, bourgeois journalism helped validate plural, secular and individual routes to knowledge; solidify a challenge to the authority of divine rulers and institutionalized clergy; and challenge the monopoly of knowledge enjoyed by court and church (although such a 'monopoly' was never total or conclusively challenged.) As the seventeenth century merged into the eighteenth, it gradually became accepted that authoritative claims to knowledge could be gained through bourgeois journalism, by virtue of its writers' own observation, reasoning and argument. Assessments of the power and abilities of a certain class of readers rose similarly, in that passionately argued cases and detailed descriptions of events addressed readers as capable of evaluating claims and evidence for themselves and of drawing their own conclusions. While acknowledging the often severe limitations on who was allowed to participate (a point to be addressed in more detail below), determining what was plausible if not true became a comparatively more public process of debate – what Jürgen Habermas has influentially called the European bourgeois 'public sphere' (Habermas, 1989; for commentary and critiques, see Calhoun, 1992).

By the mid-eighteenth century, bourgeois journalism was firmly in place as the 'coin of the realm' for public debate in European countries and colonies, one that was employed by all sides that sought to be deemed 'legitimate'. And yet these sides were decidedly one-sided, with barriers of class, property, race, gender and others sifting from societies only those deemed capable or worthy of such participation. Such restrictions help explain the fit of journalism with European colonial expansion. Accounts of the emergence of journalism in a number of non-European areas suggests the degree to which it was a European invention exported to other countries as part of colonial and capitalist expansion. Whether serving a colonial occupation (as for example in India, Indonesia, Nigeria, Hawaii, Spanish colonies in the Americas and South Africa), a transnational capitalist class (such as in Japan), or an indigenous state elite (such as in Egypt), the establishment of journalism in non-European areas was intimately part of the colonial project and thus a European and capitalist effort at control rather than an indigenous effort. (Studies that address the emergence of journalism in non-Western countries include Adam, 1995; Akinfeleye, 1987; de Lange, 1998; Geracimos, 1996; González, 1993; Huffman, 1997; Kendall, 2006; Nair, 1987; Parthasarathy, 1989; Rugh, 2004; and Switzer and Adhikari, 2000.)

This class-based restriction suggests the degree to which bourgeois journalism as a means of public discourse – while indeed crucial for radical-democratic politics and radical-popular journalism in comparison with what had come before – was itself tied to a particular kind of social order, in this case the rising bourgeoisie that supported and worked within the emerging systems of capitalism and imperialism.

The Consolidation of the Commercial-Popular

Like the paradox that today's mainstream journalism is yesterday's critical response to monarchical and ecclesiastical authority, Williams's reinterpretation of how commercial-popular journalism absorbed and then replaced radical-popular journalism identifies a second paradox. On the one hand, commercial-popular journalism can indeed be said to have been more popular in that it extended more deeply into society and thus addressed the concerns and lives of a broader social stratum (although only in particular ways and not into all social strata, as will be discussed). But, on the other hand, it had become the new dominant and thus, less popular. Where bourgeois journalism had been a clear challenge to existing orders but not popular, commercial-popular journalism was more popular in that it engaged broader orders of society, but it no longer constituted a serious challenge.

Williams's account makes clear that what transformed this erstwhile oppositional practice into a dominant one was its fit within burgeoning industrial capitalist societies, with the UK and the United States the harbingers of changes that were also afoot in other countries and regions. It was no accident that the form in which bourgeois journalism became incorporated was the commercial business and, more specifically, commercial companies in urban centres such as the so-called 'penny presses' in the United States which were based in New York City (Barnhurst and Nerone, 2001; Schudson, 1978) and the commercial-popular press in England (Wiener, 1988). This had not always been the case. Newspapers and the journalism they enabled had initially been funded by combinations of subscriptions and patronage, particularly in the form of the political press and, as Williams and others note, of the radical-popular press (Ames, 1972; Hollis, 1970; Smith, 1977).

By the end of the nineteenth century, commercial consolidation corresponded with a second development: the institutionalization of objectivity as both a writing technique and a professional creed (Kaplan, 2002). Far from being a new development, it was an enhancement and further institutionalization of core precepts of bourgeois journalism such as the emphasis on empirical evidence, clear and unadorned prose and judgements drawn from facts. But, in the commercial environment, objectivity had great value in that it enhanced the value and necessity of large-scale, professionalized organizations, which had the requisite resources and training for the authoritative gathering of evidence in the first place, with the United States by the late nineteenth century perhaps the best exemplar of this trend (Salcetti, 1995; Solomon, 1995).

The Rise of Oppositional Journalism

The emergence of the commercial-popular press helped instigate its own resistance, in the form of what we would recognize today as alternative journalism (although this term was not used at the time). The many oppositional presses of the nineteenth century were rooted in differing mixes of labour, foreign-language, suffrage and human rights interests both in the UK and the United States (Ostertag, 2006; Streitmatter, 2001; Tusan, 2005; see also the review of key studies cited in DiCenzo, 2000, Mercer, 2004 and Tusan, 2003).

In addition to movement-based newspapers, community and small-town presses sought increasingly to bolster resistance to what was seen as the onslaught of urban mass culture. Claims that community media first took form in North America in the 1970s belies its much longer and broader development (Fuller, 2007). By adopting an expansive definition of community as a general form of association – and not simply as people who live in close geographical proximity – we can show how oppositional presses of whatever scale and scope worked as community journalism under widely varying conditions. Separate communities of geographical proximity also merged into a widely distributed diasporic community due to sharing, if not intentionally at least structurally, the same interests. For example, in the United States, the interests of separate communities defined by geographical proximity were bound together through the principle of localism, which defended the general value of popular control as an antidote to the commercial consolidation and centralization of media industries (Stavitsky, 1994). Indeed, a keen awareness existed at the time of what was seen as the corruption of the promise of bourgeois journalism due to commercialization, which has been a key theme in Anglo-American, European and other liberal and radical press criticism (Goldstein, 2007; McChesney and Scott, 2004; Theobald, 2004).

Despite their political opposition, however, the various oppositional presses relied upon the conception of bourgeois journalism used by the dominant. Until comparatively recently, bourgeois journalism itself was never the main target for challenge. Rather, it was the coin of the realm for legitimate public discourse and debate, regardless of the purpose or cause. The establishment and increasing institutionalization of objectivity and of professionalization as necessary features of 'legitimate' journalism were accepted by the dominant and the oppositional, with the former always much better placed to attain it than the latter.

The extent to which this was the case is suggested by efforts at the beginning of the twentieth century to establish radical counterparts to commercial newspapers by mirroring all commercial aspects, except for perspective. For example, as Shore notes, the reigning 'models for the radical press to follow [in the United States] while seeking to develop a large audience sometimes came from the successful mainstream press' (Shore, 1985: 158). As editor J.A. Wayland put it in a January 1903 issue of the *Appeal to Reason*, which grew into the largest-circulation socialist newspaper ever to be published in the United States, 'the day has gone by for small mediums [*sic*] to tackle great undertakings, and we must prepare to propagate Socialism in just the proportions that Capitalism operates' (quoted in

Shore, 1985: 158; see also Shore, 1988). The English suffrage newspaper *Votes for Women* is a second example of an effort to harness 'commercial tactics to a radical political agenda' (DiCenzo, 2000: 116; see also Finnegan, 1999). The need to adopt commercial forms and techniques is also implied – if not explicitly stated – in recent assessments of the anaemia of the alternative press based on its small size, meagre capitalization and resulting assumed ineffectuality (Clark and Van Slyke, 2006; Comedia, 1984).

Challenges to Bourgeois Journalism

Although the existing model of bourgeois journalism was rarely challenged in the eighteenth and nineteenth centuries despite the severe political struggles waged, in the twentieth century its tacit acceptance as the coin of the realm for public discourse came to be overtly challenged amidst the consolidation of what is referred to as modernism. Various accounts of the rise of modernity cite such general developments as industrialization, urbanization, the rise of consumer culture, the arrival of electronic means of communications, the proliferation of new kinds of dislocation at once experiential and real, as well as attempts to 'make ourselves at home in a constantly changing world', marked perhaps most dramatically by the collective insanity of two world wars and the development of nuclear weapons capable of global annihilation (Berman, 1988: 6).

It should come as little surprise, then, that such an extensive reformation of conditions and experience included challenges to existing ways of addressing publics and establishing claims of authority. Recognizing the extent of this effort broadens our understanding of just what kind of challenge alternative journalism came to pose – in this case, from challenging a discrete, single political position to also challenging the very forms that knowledge can take. The development of alternative journalism thus came to refer not only to oppositional political, social, cultural and economic movements, but also to claims that bourgeois journalism and the accepted procedures and forms it relies upon were also increasingly suspect. In the wake of such challenges, less and less often could bourgeois journalism – as individual opinion and consensual empirical account – be considered as neutral, natural and 'common-sense'.

The Modernist Critique of Bourgeois Journalism

Subject to a variety of pressures, the consensus acceptance of bourgeois journalism began to fragment. Alternative journalism came to mean not only challenging the dominant social order politically, but also challenging and remaking the very bases of bourgeois journalism itself. The focus of sustained attack was the premise deriving at least from Locke that people can know only what comes to them through direct sensory experience (Peters, 1989). By contrast, the work of Darwin, Marx and Freud refuted claims of human rationality as well as the truth of direct appearances by focusing on forces beyond the control and direct observation of individual humans (evolution, material conditions and the unconscious, respectively), which they claimed to be the real shapers of human lives and actions.

Such criticisms were part of a more politicized critique not only of empiricism and objectivity, but of professionalization. Hierarchical, commercial bureaucracies were seen increasingly as beholden to the interests of their advertisers and, through them, to the social and political elite, and thus as unresponsive to the full range of concerns of readers (Goldstein, 2007; McChesney and Scott, 2004; Theobald, 2004). By contrast, radical republicanism, socialist workerism, anarchism and various other forms of collective and egalitarian organization were seen as viable and often preferable options for organizing journalistic work (Downing, 2003a; Lasch, 1991: 168–225; Thompson, 1966: 87–101).

Criticisms of bourgeois journalism became more global in the wake of decolonization projects of the 1950s and 1960s, joining a much broader critique of Eurocentrism. By this is meant the argument that the suppositions and assumptions underlying not only capitalism but the dominance of Western countries (until recently) in the affairs of the world were directly implicated in the misery experienced by the majority of the world's peoples. The critique of Eurocentrism became the basis for such varied and mixed positions as a critique of colonialism (that the expansion and fortunes of Western societies were built on the back of subjugated and exploited non-Western populations); of capitalism (that European-derived knowledge provided the means and the rationale for dominating people); of patriarchal society as unchallengeable authority (particularly in the form of professionalization and bureaucracy); of racist society in which large segments of the population are systematically and actively disenfranchised and marginalized; and of mass culture and consumer society as hastening both the mass diversion of attention from issues of immense importance and the exhaustion of resources of the natural world to the point of global catastrophe.

New Forms of Journalism

In the wake of such criticism, not only were the claims of bourgeois journalism called into question, but new narrative forms were formulated and developed. The insufficiency of empiricism and naturalism (claims that one could aspire to neutral descriptions of things as they really are) suggested in turn that deeper realities could be apprehended only through seemingly unnatural means of representation. Artistic experimentation, particularly in painting, prefigured radical experiments in factual writing (Berger, 1993).

For example, the refusal to accept the long-standing distinction between fact and fiction paved the way for the rise by the 1950s of the 'documentary novel' and by the 1960s of the 'new journalism' as a non-fictional and authoritative means of representation that relied upon techniques pioneered in ostensibly fictional prose (Wolfe, 1973). Such challenges were also launched in other parts of the world. For example, the *crónica* of Latin America emerged in the 1960s in the wake of North American new journalism, blending 'very extensive popular cultural traditions, from song to television programs' (Bielsa, 2006: xiii). Receptive, non-professionalized organizations such as the underground presses of the 1960s proved to be fertile ground for the development of alternative modes of factual writing (Bizot, 2006; Glessing, 1970; Leamer, 1972; Peck, 1985; Reed, 1989). Variations continue to be practiced in the service of a variety of new social movements (McKay, 1998; Reed, 2005).

Challenges to European bourgeois journalism also manifested themselves in other parts of the world. For example, professionalized elitism was set aside in the popular correspondents' movement in revolutionary Nicaragua during the 1980s. The movement was enabled by institutional support from oppositional political parties, open access to various outlets and the availability of training, the last of which was crucial to a group who had typically ended schooling at the age of eight or nine (Rodriguez, 2001: 70). Large-scale organization and capitalization were set aside in the dissident media of 1970s Iran. In a context in which institutionalized oppositional politics was made impossible by the royalist dictatorship, so-called 'small media' (not only photocopied leaflets and audiocassette tapes but also their grassroots composition and circulation) helped 'foster an imaginative social solidarity, often as a precursor for actual physical mobilization' (Sreberny-Mohammadi and Mohammadi, 1994: 24). In addition to critiquing professionalism and institutionalization, Eastern European samizdat (defined by Skilling as 'the distribution of uncensored writings on one's own, without the medium of a publishing house and without permission of authorities') also broadened the sense of what constituted forms of political engagement beyond traditional reportage (Skilling, 1989: 3). Means of production included typewriters and carbon copiers, mimeographing, photography and hand-copying. Samizdat in 1970s Poland drew significantly on worker correspondence instead of professional journalism. Forms of representation in pre-1989 Czechoslovak samizdat included 'novels, short stories, poetry, plays, literary criticism, historical and philosophical essays, and, more rarely, political essays or studies' (Skilling, 1989: 11–12). What Sibeko called 'clandestine propaganda' had similar importance in pre-revolution South Africa (Sibeko, 1983).

Other more institutionalized efforts have sought to develop a model different from the commercial media company. Developmental journalism emerged in the wake of Western decolonization as a means of consolidating new nations. Such early efforts constituted a critique of Western-style objectivity by setting aside the professional creed due to its ostensible inability to form a national consensus needed for development in favour of often unabashedly single-sided promotion of government programmes of modernization. Through such projects, forms of bourgeois journalism were critiqued, but the rationales and forms for development journalism often came from Westerners too and were implemented at the expense of robust public discussion and debate (Ebo, 1994; Pye, 1964; Schramm, 1964).

In the face of such problems, non-Western efforts have more recently reformed into what is often called participatory journalism, which more clearly embodies an organizational critique (Shah, 1996). These projects often rely on indigenous oral traditions as well as the availability of portable radio and video to put recorders and cameras in the hands of people so that they may produce their own stories (Rodriguez, 2001: 109–128; White et al., 1994).

Conclusion

The historical trajectory of 'alternative journalism' can be best understood as a continual response and challenge to dominant practices. As the dominant has changed, the alternative that challenges it has changed as well. The twentieth-century proliferation of different ways of writing and of organizing the production and distribution of alternative journalism so apparent today emerged from a deep and fundamental challenge to the very bases of journalism itself.

2

POLITICAL-ECONOMIC PRESSURES THAT SHAPE ALTERNATIVE JOURNALISM

The discussion in the previous chapter argued for the historicity and contextual determination of alternative journalism. The formation of alternative journalism was not due simply to the isolated actions of individuals, although a number of biographies document what can legitimately be considered heroic struggles in the face of severe repression. Yet even these episodes were and are determined by larger-scale developments that produced the conditions for such struggle in the first place. Similarly, it should also be clear from the preceding discussion that the emergence of alternative journalism has been no simple, linear account of progress or decline, but a complex series of instances in changing contexts, each with its own specific limits, pressures and potentials.

Recalling these insights frames the argument in this chapter concerning the political economy of alternative journalism. This chapter also responds to dominant accounts of the development of media institutions, which is typically seen in linear terms – most traditionally as a story of the growth of press freedom (measured in terms of commercial strength), as indebted to as well as assisting a growth in democracy (Curran, 2002). This chapter critiques this and other similarly linear analytic frameworks, which are used to describe alternative journalism as well. Instead of posing a linear trend of steady improvement or steady decline, it argues that alternative journalism is better seen as opposing but also as enabled by the conditions in which it exists. The contradiction is worth underscoring. Recognizing it allows us to adequately take account of incorporation and neutralization as well as of challenge and the ways they make each other possible. This chapter seeks to explain these contradictions and developments in an analytic way. Supplementing a description of how something developed is the equally valuable task of offering an analysis of why it developed the way it did. Towards this end, this chapter will propose a political-economic analysis of alternative journalism. After specifying what is meant here by 'political economy', the chapter describes the key political-economic limits and pressures on alternative journalism. The chapter then explores a range of examples to demonstrate how different means of material support in different contexts engenders different kinds of practice and implications. The chapter concludes by reaffirming the importance of political economy for an understanding of alternative journalism.

Political Economy

The compound term 'political economy' suggests a connection between politics and economics. However, such a proposition contradicts popular conceptions. Where politics is typically seen as the realm of intentions and decisions (politicians formulating and lobbying in favour of certain initiatives, while working to defeat others), the economy is often seen as a realm of impersonal forces as far removed from human intention as gravity.

However, it is precisely this conception of the economy as an autonomous, natural thing beyond human ability to affect or change that critical political economy seeks to dismantle. While not denying the exceptional complexity of the globalized world order today (and the hubris of any single individual – no matter how powerful – asserting an ability to change it single-handedly), what can be called critical political economy nevertheless recognizes the constitution of societies as the result not of natural processes but of cumulated human decisions and actions over the span of hundreds of years. More needs to be said here about the differences between a notion of economy as a natural thing and as a human project, as well as how the study of political economy clarifies these differences, and the relevance of such an analysis for the study of alternative journalism.

At the most basic level, the study of political economy focuses on the production and reproduction of society. Meehan, Mosco and Wasko specify this production and reproduction as dealing with matters of survival ('how societies organise themselves to produce what they need to reproduce themselves') and of control ('how societies maintain order to meet economic, political, social, and cultural goals') (Meehan et al., 1993: 107). Political economy is concerned with describing how social production and reproduction take place, but it is also concerned with analysing and evaluating the moral implications of specific modes of production and reproduction. As stated by Golding and Murdock, political economy 'goes beyond technical issues of efficiency to engage with basic moral questions of justice, equity, and the public good' (Golding and Murdock, 1991: 18–19).

This dual focus on evaluation as well as description, and on the moral as well as the technical, is shared by the two general approaches to political-economic analysis, which nevertheless also have key differences that distinguish them from each other (for an expansive summary, see Mosco, 1996:

22–69). One approach, classical political economy, views the economy as a naturally operating process subject to universal laws outside of human intervention. This conception was first generated in the heady days of the European Enlightenment during the eighteenth century, when the entire world and known universe was conceived of as a wonderfully complex machine whose laws could be discovered by humans, and knowledge of it could be used to improve the human condition.

Classical political economy assumes the existence and moral desirability of capitalism not only as inevitable (due to its ubiquity today), and beyond question. As the argument goes, by rewarding unfettered individual initiative, such a system encourages hard work, risk-taking and innovation, which is desirable because it benefits everyone (for a foundational statement, see Smith, 1776/1994). Importantly, these moral results and the system from which they ostensibly arise are assumed as inevitable because they are seen as a fact of nature. While classical political economy does not ignore often vast differences in life and fortune between different peoples and areas (for example, the early nineteenth-century work of David Ricardo and John Stuart Mill noted the developing problems of inequality and exploitation in then-emerging industrial capitalist societies), it accepts such imbalances as inevitable ('this is just the way it is') while seeking to develop better ways of managing the periodic economic booms and busts (Ricardo, 1817/1971; Mill, 1844/1968).

Critical political economy, the second general approach, shares with the classical variation these general preoccupations. It too seeks to evaluate morally the modes of production and reproduction, and to recognize the immense inequalities produced by capitalism. However, also importantly, critical political economy does not take such inequalities and such a system as natural and thus inevitable. By contrast, it views them as the cumulative and ongoing result of countless intentional policies, human decisions and actions that not only reproduce these inequalities and this system, but that also serve particular interests – in some cases, an individual's interests, but much more frequently impersonal, social interests such as the interests of a particular class. Karl Marx remarked drily in the 1840s how classical political economy simply and naïvely 'takes for granted what it is supposed to explain', while later asserting that 'nature does not produce on one side owners of money or commodities, and on the other men possessing nothing but their own labour power. [... Rather, such a division] is clearly the result of a past historical development, the product of many economic revolutions, of the extinction of a whole series of older forms of social production' (Marx, 1844/1975: 271; Marx, 1887/1996: 179). And this historically produced division benefits only a particular segment of society, again as Marx noted more than 150 years ago in an initial statement that would later be echoed in the words and writings of countless critics. 'It is true that labour produces wonderful things for the rich – but for the worker it produces privation. It produces palaces – but for the worker, hovels' (Marx, 1844/1975: 273).

Political Economy and Alternative Journalism

When applied to the study of alternative journalism, critical political economy enables a greater understanding of the nature and implications of relationships between the role of journalism, how journalism is organized and practised, and whose interests are served. However, such a claim should not be taken to imply that these elements are related by simple, causal links – for example, that a role of journalism to 'challenge authority' automatically leads to all authorities being uniformly challenged.

Similarly, the claim of greater understanding should not be taken to suggest that relationships between these elements compose a seamless, stable and consistent whole. In fact, such relationships are exceptionally complex, due in part to the many different kinds of alternative journalism projects, and also to the duality of popular culture discussed in Chapter 1 (that it consists of a complex, shifting mix of challenge and accommodation). Such a degree of complexity means that roles of journalism, modes of organization and particular interests rarely, if ever, fit together cleanly and harmoniously. Indeed, certain combinations can often be contradictory, if not antagonistic. For example, organizing as a commercial business provides working capital and resources (greater control) but also steers projects into particular directions (less control). Professional journalists may provide more extensive coverage of insufficiently understood situations (with the potential for empowering readers and spurring social change), but the forms which such coverage takes and the conditions in which it is used (objective-style writing that encourages disengagement and the lack of political/organizational means of collective action and challenge) exert pressures in a very different direction (for example, see Gitlin, 1980 and Bradley, 2003).

However, while recognizing these complexities, critical political economy helps organize and thus clarify an understanding of these multiple and often contradictory relationships and effects. From the perspective of critical political economy, the most important limits and pressures on alternative journalism derive from its conception and from its context, and centre on means of support and how these together shape the resulting practice.

One major set of pressures comes from the traditions that guide the expectations and practice of alternative journalism. To the degree that these derive from bourgeois journalism, the resulting expectation is to create as large an organization as possible. As discussed earlier, the claims to authority of bourgeois journalism are based in large part on the premises of Baconian empiricism, which requires among other things the development, codification and adherence to strict standards of evidence-gathering and interpretation. This privileges the value of professionalization. Baconian empiricism also requires that efforts in gathering evidence be extensive, as the greater the amount of data gathered, the more comprehensive and thus authoritative the results are seen to be. This privileges the value of a large organizational size.

Arising in turn from such premises and expectations are key political-economic pressures. The need for professionalization and large organizational size means not only supporting people so that they can devote significant time and energy to their journalism, but also supporting a large organization composed of full-time professionals. It is important to emphasize that this problem is not common-sense or automatic, but instead derives from conceptions of what alternative journalism should be, which, in the case of professionalization and large-scale organization, derives in turn from bourgeois journalism.

A second major set of pressures derives from the context in which alternative journalism is practised. If an alternative journalism organization exists in a capitalist society, the key dilemma is whether or not to rely on advertising. Pressure to fund a large organization of professionals means a significant amount of capital is needed. In capitalist societies, the most ready source is advertising. Yet advertising operates in many instances as a means of depoliticization and marginalization, thus creating a situation in which success in supporting a large organization can literally mean failure in achieving social change. As we saw earlier, advertising served as a key means by which the independent radical-popular presses of the nineteenth century in Britain and in the United States were incorporated, absorbed and effectively isolated as sectarian screeds in comparison to what became the 'popular' as constituted by the commercial-popular presses in consumer society (for more general accounts, see Ewen, 1989 and Williams, 1980a).

What adds even more complexity to a critical political economy of alternative journalism is that the two general sets of limits and pressures sketched above are not separate from but intimately a part of each other. Given their combination, the resulting general political-economic dilemma for any critical project is that it needs resources with which to work, but those crucial resources are present only in the very society that it seeks to change or dissolve.

Dilemmas in Practice

Given the current dominance of commercial-popular journalism, one can suggest some different, basic forms that alternative journalism might take, each of which has characteristic political-economic limits and pressures that shape its practice. While the political-economic framework above identifies key general limits and pressures that have much to do in determining alternative journalism, they are not inviolable, rigid formulas. In keeping with our argument about the historicity of alternative journalism, exploring these limits and pressures requires specifying how they work in practice and in context. Accordingly, what follows are a few selected cases that together illustrate the range of ways in which these limits and pressures are formed and negotiated. This survey is organized analytically rather than chronologically in order to avoid the appearance of a simple linear development from one kind to the next, as all developed coterminously, and the boundaries between them are exceptionally fluid.

Patronage

Perhaps the clearest opposition to commercial support is patronage. Support from a donor or benefactor ideally seeks to remove commercial pressures on content that derive from pandering to audiences through salacious, scandalous and superficial content in order to maximize sales. Forms of this kind of support can be seen in the earliest days of bourgeois journalism and political-party support for publications (itself deriving from even earlier practices of royal and ecclesiastical patronage), with the political presses of England and of the United States two of many examples that predate by decades typically cited non-Western examples (Ames, 1972; Baldasty, 1984; Curran and Seaton, 2003; Koss, 1981–84; Lee, 1976; Smith, 1977).

Although avoiding the pressures of the market, such a means of support ensures that the publication will work in concert with the interests of the patron, whether it is a philanthropist or wealthy benefactor, a foundation, or, in the extreme case, a state. Examples of degrees of state support can be found in capitalist societies, although they exemplify at best a partial move in this direction (and one increasingly under fire). Public-service models of broadcasting exist in a number of parliamentary democracies (most prominently the British Broadcasting Corporation), but without any parallel effort for supporting print. Some European countries, such as Sweden, supplement public-service broadcasting with systems of subsidy for print publications, although the ability of even this step to ensure openness and diversity in perspective is unclear (Weibull, 2003). More radical proposals for even less centralized systems of social support include Williams's plan for socially owned production facilities (Williams, 1967). A more recently evolved form of patronage support is developmental journalism, typically a non-Western project in the service of state industrial modernization (Shah, 1996).

In contrast to capitalist or social-democratic examples that seek to distribute ownership or at least to make direct pressures somewhat diffuse to insulate publications from direct control, more uniform examples of patronage exist in countries that are organized in other than capitalist forms. The most prominent in the twentieth century are the former Union of Soviet Socialist Republics (USSR) and the People's Republic of China (PRC). The Soviet system provides an example of the rationale for such support, as well as of its journey from oppositional to often ruthless dominant, thus exemplifying the pitfalls of such a system – particularly one as generalized as this – when measured against democratic ideals.

In Russia, beginning in the 1860s, a mass-circulation commercial-popular press was allowed to emerge that was modelled upon those already thriving in the West. Its establishment sought to aid modernization by boosting the minor place of journalism in Russian life, in which tsarist rulers had 'dominated newspapers completely as the major publisher and a principal source of information', with newspapers relegated to serving a small intellectual elite (McReynolds, 1991: 18). However, by the lead-up to the October revolution of 1917, this aid to modernization had become part of the tsarist society that Vladimir Lenin sought to dismantle. To aid this process, he envisioned a form of journalism whose purpose was not to inform and entertain readers while selling audiences to advertisers, but to bring together a revolutionary social and political movement.

In the formative years of the revolution, Lenin made this difference clear by arguing that the starting point for creating a revolutionary movement 'should be the founding of an All-Russian political newspaper' (Lenin, 1901/1961: 20). Such a newspaper is 'not only a collective propagandist and a collective agitator, it is also a collective organiser', with the last role being crucial (p. 22). Lenin saw the relationship of a newspaper to the movement as analogous to that of scaffolding to a building. It enabled production by helping people coordinate their work 'and [providing a means] to view the common results achieved by their organised labour' (ibid.).

Lenin elaborated this conception in 1902 in a response to critics of his 1901 essay by re-emphasizing the practical, material role of journalism in producing the movement. Although critics argued that Lenin had it backwards and that the political movement was the condition for and not the result of the newspaper, Lenin insisted that the newspaper was the formative condition for organization and not its outcome. He developed further his movement/building analogy by arguing that, just as a newspaper gives form to the movement, bricklayers' use of a line to help lay bricks straight is not mere 'paper work' but what makes the building possible (Lenin 1902/1961).

With the resulting revolution and the establishment of the Soviet state, the movement that had challenged the tsarist state was now the party in power. With this change in role came a conception of journalism in some ways quite different from that of revolutionary organizer. Given the need to modernize and consolidate the new state, Lenin saw the press less as a tool for revolutionary mobilization and more as a means of re-education, although the distinction between the two roles is not hard and fast (Lenin, 1918/1965).

Whether pre- or post-revolutionary, it is hard to imagine a greater difference in conception than between revolutionary and bourgeois journalism (the latter with its emphasis on detached empiricism) or its cousin commercial-popular journalism (with its emphasis on individualized commentary, news and entertainment). The movement- and later state-supported newspaper as envisioned by Lenin was an alternative to commercial-popular journalism not only in role and form, but also in terms of being the means by which the commercial-popular press and the class which supported it would be overthrown and a new society established and consolidated.

However, the state-supported all-Russian newspaper signalled no broadening of popular democratization, with the Soviet situation an example of a more general case. Whether in service of revolution or consolidation, the conception that justifies supporting journalism with state patronage takes what can be called a vanguard view of the role of leaders *vis-à-vis* the rest of the populace. Boggs describes this vanguard conception as 'deeply embedded in the Western intellectual tradition' from Plato to Machiavelli to Hobbes, and prefigured by the complex of premodern institutions of the church, monarchy and the military (Boggs, 1993: 16–17). Although detached from social movements, vanguards seek to use them as tools for seizing political power. Vanguards are often regarded as central to creating and sustaining social and political movements (although this is disputable, as we shall see), and they are the first to respond to any internal dissension or outside challenge by portraying the movement's goals as universal, thus legitimizing the suppression of conflict or difference in the interests of enforcing orthodoxy (Boggs, 1993).

This was certainly the case with the Soviet system. Whether calling for revolutionary change or consolidation, Lenoe argues, 'throughout their history Bolsheviks saw themselves both as tutors of the masses and as their leaders in the war between the classes', thus seeking always to 'embody the role of military officer, instructing and exhorting their readers to battle with class enemies' (Lenoe, 2004: 12, 13). To carry out this role, the Bolsheviks monopolized the press almost immediately after the 1917 revolution, laying down through decree and seizure a basis of state press ownership that remained largely unchallenged for the duration of the state (Murray, 1994).

Communists in other European countries who sympathized with the Soviet experiment (at least in the beginning) developed a more detailed rationale for party-state support of journalism. One such description makes clear the degree to which state patronage is based on the traditions of bourgeois journalism, yet remade to fit a very different context. For example, the necessity of empiricism and of large-size organization are accepted, but facts gathered by the cadre of reporters should not be simply stated in isolation from each other – as is typical of stories written in an 'objective' style – but instead should be placed 'in a coherent context in which every aspect relates to all others, so that the most trivial news preserves its meaning through its links to the basic truths of communism' (Fogarasi, 1921/1983: 151). Certain limits and pressures from bourgeois journalism can be seen to be present in this non-capitalist example, but remade to legitimize a vanguard conception of ruling elites. Also deriving from traditions of bourgeois journalism is the use of individual reasoning and logical argument, but such journalism in our Soviet communist example calls for commentary as a political weapon directed at a singular target. It is meant to unmask 'the capitalist press […] through proof and clear analyses [… thus] shaking the reader's faith [in the capitalist press] to the core' (p. 152).

However, other characteristics worked against both the professionalization of bourgeois journalism and the vanguardism of orthodox communist politics, pointing a way to a more genuinely democratic-popular journalism. In order to broaden the content to address a range of readers, Fogarasi recommended (as Lenin had done earlier) that 'readers [should be encouraged] to work with the press', with the example offered of *Ordine Nuovo* ('The New Order'), an 'Italian communist newspaper edited by Antonio Gramsci', which transcended 'the untenable distance between communist reader and writers, or at least occasionally revers[ed] the roles' (Fogarasi, 1921/1983: 152; for a roughly contemporary English-communist statement, see *Workers' Life*, 1928/1983). Such a recommendation did not begin with communist worker newspapers, but was part of artisanal and later labour newspapers in Britain and elsewhere early in the nineteenth century (Curran and Seaton, 2003). While Lenin's intention was to incorporate readers more closely into the state project by this method, others sought a more radical levelling of the political movement.

However fashioned, though, patronage support – particularly in the form of a state system – exemplifies a vanguard relationship and intention. The confluence of a state-supported system with a vanguard conception of politics too often amounts to a tautological championing of an orthodoxy instead of becoming an enabling means of critical, open and collective exploration. While basing itself in many ways on the traditions of bourgeois journalism, it remakes selected aspects in order to tailor them to its political imperatives. The vanguard model too easily accommodates itself to 'the practice of an authority above the writer […] telling him [or her] what to write and how to write' (Williams, 1980/1989: 78). As such, it works contrary to a conception of creative, democratic practice, with the 'party line' becoming the litmus test of success and of the extent of dominant power.

Commercial Support

That commercial support might be a viable basis for alternative journalism goes against much received wisdom. A good case has been made for many years that the repressive and regressive nature of the commercial-popular press is due to its need to support itself through advertising, which requires the audience size to be maximized by depolitizising and 'dumbing down' the content. Mass-culture and ideological critiques have long focused implicitly or explicitly on the effects of commercialization on journalism and the implications of this for democracy, ranging from Seldes (1929) and Leavis and Thompson (1937) to Rosenberg and White (1957) and more recent commentators such as Herman and Chomsky (1988), Philo (1999), Curran and Seaton (2003) and Bagdikian (2004), to name only a handful of an immense number that in its full range hails from all parts of the world.

Although some recent studies suggest that commercial support for alternative journalism may be a 'new model', such attempts actually have a long history (Khiabany, 2000). In DiCenzo's estimation, the English publication *Votes for Women* (1907–1918) was 'one of the most important women's political periodicals to emerge from the suffrage movement in Britain' (DiCenzo, 2000: 115; for a similar claim in a different case, see Finnegan, 1999). It was advertising support that helped it boost its size and minimize cost (20 pages for 1d.), while also boosting its frequency from monthly to weekly and its peak circulation to 40,000 (DiCenzo, 2000). Although one cannot quibble with its economic success, critics of the day observed the apparent contradiction between the publication's avowed allegiance to all women and much of its middle-class, bourgeois content, which was similar to that of other contemporary popular newspapers, including often extensive advertisements that promoted 'women's fashions and all the conventional feminine apparatus' (DiCenzo, 2000: 121). However, the paper also included among its major stories coverage of Parliament in addition to 'articles about the importance of the vote, the need for militant tactics, the developments in the movement nationally, and more general pieces related to labour practices and legal issues affecting working and married women' (p. 120).

Another, similarly early example of a radical publication using advertising support is the *Appeal to Reason*, which (as noted) was the largest-circulation socialist publication ever to appear in the United States. Its editor, J.A. Wayland, had tried to support it through combinations of reader contributions, party support, organizing as a co-operative and donations from wealthy benefactors, but found them all wanting (Shore, 1985: 148). Confronted with these choices, Wayland 'came to the conclusion that a [financially] solvent paper could only be produced through "sound" business practices' (Shore, 1988: 2). Supplementing revenue with advertising allowed Wayland to replace the lower-cost option of commenting on capitalist news with original reporting. He professionalized newsgathering by hiring reporters and going full-steam into 'the news business', running only 'exclusive stories brought in by the *Appeal*'s own staff' (Shore, 1985: 164–165). By 1902, circulation reached and passed 200,000, peaking prior to World War I at more than 750,000 (Bekken, 1993).

Today, such efforts appear to be less and less unusual (Clark and Van Slyke, 2006). Key developments in the West that have increased the possibility of such an approach include the extension of consumerism into steadily broader and more diverse swathes of society (although not evenly or consistently), and the emergence if not explosion of the youth market in the 1960s, which required businesses to revamp not only their product mix but their style of promotion in order to secure these new markets (Frank, 1997). In the wake of the 1960s, the waning of large-scale programmes of social change – together with the waxing of issues- and identity-based activism – corresponded to businesses' jettisoning of mass marketing and its replacement by marketing narrowly targeted on specific publics. The result of these and related developments is the consumer landscape we have today, in which even subcultures overtly hostile to capitalism inspire cutting-edge marketing campaigns for commercial products (Harold, 2007).

In such a situation, it is no wonder that advertising support and, with it, traditions of bourgeois journalism as refracted through the commercial-popular press are easily seen as neutral tools to be put to use however one chooses. As Eliasoph suggested in a pioneering study, 'the routines themselves [used in the organisation to produce the news] do not preclude oppositional news when they operate in oppositional organisations. The cultural forms of the day, which most leftists share with everyone else [...] are open' (Eliasoph, 1988: 330; see also Benson, 2003). The shrill ideological critiques of commercialization seem by comparison to be quite old hat and tiresome, something like a depressed friend who is determined to have a bad time at the party no matter what.

However, the degree to which the market appears to be ideologically neutral (and thus accepting of any point of view as long as it sells) tends to lessen when one takes a broader view. The limits and pressures that the market exerts operate less at the level of content (although limits do exist, as can be seen in cases of child pornography or overt speech intended to incite insurrection) than at the level of structure. The imperative of capitalism is not just to sell at a profit, but to maximize sales. Today, with electronic, globally interconnected stock and currency exchanges, investment capital is ever more liquid and able to take advantage of the slightest opportunity. With such sensitivity and with the immense pressures to secure the best return on investment, any business must generate a minimum level of profit in order for it to attract financing from managers of ever more mobile capital who are searching restlessly for the best return. In such a climate, an alternative newspaper may indeed be able to turn some kind of profit, but rarely if ever at the level and pace of growth required by financiers, who will quickly put their money behind more lucrative ventures.

These structural pressures of financing shape commercial-alternative journalism in profound ways. Lacking the ability to corral large enough readerships, it cannot compete directly with the commercial-popular press and thus pursues instead smaller and more specialized readerships, whose attention it can sell to similarly specialized businesses. As a result, it comprises relatively small, 'shoe-string' organizations. At the same time, these are professionally organized in order to embody a degree of authority and to compete at least in professional reputation with the commercial-popular while minimizing costly amateurs' errors (which could single-handedly sink the publication).

The formation in the United States of commercial-alternative chain ownership further emphasizes the ways in which the structural pressures of commercialization steer alternative journalism into similar, yet clearly marginalized projects (Murphy, 2005; Project for Excellence in Journalism, 2007a; Siklos, 2005). The effect on practice is as profound as that on structure and size. Without the resources to support a large organization, the resulting emphasis is often on in-house commentary and issue analysis, with the original reporting often done by contributing editors or freelancers rather than by travelling or bureau-based staff reporters.

Though commercial-alternative journalism can and does exist in capitalist societies, it never competes on a level playing field; the need to compete compromises, marginalizes and depoliticizes its oppositional stance. A contemporary example is found in the form of the popular women's magazines of the 1970s and *Ms.* magazine in particular (given the compelling examples of suffragette publications that began this section, it seems appropriate to return to issues of gender).

As Bradley (2003) suggests in a wide-ranging study, a number of conditions made possible the establishment in the United States of a popular feminist commercial magazine. Among them were the radicalism of the 1960s and the rise of second-wave feminism, the selective acceptance and institutionalization of youth culture and the trend toward niche marketing that required niche publications as corresponding means of advertising. *Ms.* defined its readers as of a 'high-enough demographic profile not only to respond to radically different content without offense but also to draw advertisers' interested in reaching this narrowly defined and generally affluent readership (Bradley, 2003: 171). What is more, in order to be taken seriously as professional journalism, it drew its staff and management from 'New York [... which was home to the] nation's largest pool of professional women writers and editors' (ibid.).

Its content mix, which 'merged old forms with new content' (Bradley, 2003: 176), exemplifies the duality of popular culture as both challenge and accommodation that Williams identified. While relying on 'familiar traditions of women's popular commercial magazines' such as the ideal that 'women at home should be mistresses of many arts', it also introduced content that had never been addressed so publicly, such as abortion, the 'glass ceiling' in the workplace and women's rights (ibid.). However, in Bradley's estimation, even controversial issues tended to be 'presented in ways that were consonant with the strains of American liberalism that believed that fairness was accomplished primarily by overcoming prejudicial thinking' (ibid.: 177).

Yet, for Bradley, it was the structural pressures as much as ideological resistance that ultimately depoliticized the magazine. While a number of major companies placed advertising in *Ms.*, others objected to the editorial stance and would not advertise, while companies that wanted to advertise were dropped because *Ms.* management considered their products detrimental to women. The return on investment gained from advertising in *Ms.* simply ceased to be compelling. *Ms.* believed that social change 'could be accelerated when sufficient numbers of women were reached by the broad distribution that mass media allowed. But from the beginning, getting advertiser support made that goal a challenge that finally could not be overcome' (Bradley, 2003: 189).

Whilst commercial support might extend to radical points of view, what is just as clear is larger political-economic structures contain this opposition. Specific examples that enjoy a great amount of ideological leeway do exist, but this is not surprising given the contradictory nature of popular culture and the political-economic containment of opposition by virtue of the commercialization of alternative journalism in capitalist societies.

Personal Journalism

Patronage and commercial relationships seek to make possible large-scale, professionalized organizations. Far from this goal being an obvious or natural one, the justification for the goal in the first place lies within the traditions of bourgeois journalism: its equation of professionalism and empirical comprehensiveness with authority. However, as has been argued, both kinds of relationship are as limiting as they are enabling.

Detecting the roots of such pressures in the traditions of bourgeois journalism suggests how one might avoid them – that is, to refuse the traditions of exclusionary professionalism and empirical comprehensiveness as routes to authority in the first place. One way of doing this is to practise alternative journalism as a personal project. Such a form refuses the imperative of bourgeois journalism toward large organizational size and its extensive information-gathering capability as a means of establishing authority.

One such example is samizdat, which constitutes a crucial, but personal response to often severely repressive regimes. As noted in the previous chapter, samizdat refers to 'the distribution of uncensored writings on one's own, without the medium of a publishing house and without permission of the authorities' (Skilling, 1989: 3). More generally, they are 'ubiquitous informal acts of protest or self-expression by individuals', produced using only personal resources (p. 219). Such conditions lend samizdat a particular kind of form and organization. They refuse the bourgeois-journalism values of comprehensive empiricism, large-scale organization and professionaliza-tion in favour of the personal, the imaginative or the prescriptive, with their authority resting in part on the individual's writing skill and logical argu-ment, but also on the degree of brazenness of the act itself. Taking the Russian experience as an example, varieties of such work include smuggling literary works outside the country in order to be published; producing and circulating underground 'letters, appeals, declarations [... that] began to "fulfil the function not only of a book but of a newspaper"'; and creating 'varied social programmes and expositions of independent social and polit-ical thought' (pp. 6–7). Samizdat can be seen as part of a more general 'sec-ond system of communications' which includes such varied sources and modes as 'foreign radio and television, the spreading of rumours and gossip, as well as foreign news (sometimes transmitted in written form), and sin-cere and frank conversations among close friends and relations' (p. 169).

Although the context of repression is typically quite different in capitalist, liberal-democratic countries, personal projects of alternative journalism are often undertaken in them as well. Due to the different context, the political-economic limits and pressures steer such projects into somewhat different forms. Instead of escaping detection by the secret police, personal projects in capitalist countries seek more often to escape the limits and pressures of commercialization. As with samizdat, a way of avoiding the dilemma of advertising is to organize in such a way as to make it unnecessary in the first place – personal newsletters have that potential.

Whilst early twentieth-century examples include George Seldes's newsletter *In Fact* and recent examples include *CounterPunch*, *Lowdown* and the *Washington Spectator*, the best example from the United States is *I.F. Stone's Weekly* (1952–1971), founded and produced by 'Jeffersonian-Marxist' Isadore (Izzy) Feinstein Stone (1907–1989). Stone began his writ-ing career as a professional journalist working for commercial papers in Philadelphia and New York as well as a number of smaller ones, editing and freelancing for various magazines, and authoring a number of books of analysis and commentary on current affairs (Cottrell, 1992). He started his own four-page weekly newsletter (later, bi-weekly) while middle-aged and unemployed, with a $3,000 loan from a friend and a subscription list ini-tially of 3,000 (Cottrell, 1992; Navasky, 2003).

What enabled Stone to sustain his project was his decidedly 'homey' production (typewritten masters cheaply reproduced), as well as inexpen-sive second-class mailing rates which allowed him to mail the newsletter at a fraction of the cost of personal letters. Not only did his non-doctrinaire and idiosyncratic leftism moderate objections to his project in the Cold-War-obsessed United States, his professionalism endeared the newsletter to a wide range of subscribers. All these pressures in turn steered his project into a specific direction and method, which was to comment on what others had reported and published (Cottrell, 1992). Stone read volumes of publicly available official government reports and documents, 'all the time prospecting for news nuggets (which would appear as boxed paragraphs in his paper), contradictions in the official line, examples of bureaucratic and political mendacity, [and] documentation of incursions on civil rights and liberties' (Navasky, 2003: n.p.). He also spent his time 'reading the dailies, the wire services and such, and then following up where others had not thought to tread. He once told [US journalist and author] David Halberstam that the *Washington Post* was an exciting paper to read "because you never know on what page you would find a page-one story"' (ibid.). Stone's authority was based on exhaustive and exhausting documentation, thus based in traditions of bourgeois journalism and its emphasis on comprehensiveness, but in such a way as to make possible its individual as opposed to collective pursuit (although more people to help would have made it easier!). Not only was his chosen method materially within his reach, his 'use of government sources to document his findings was also a stratagem. Who would have believed this cantankerous-if-whimsical Marxist without all the documentation?' (ibid.). His authority also rested on his professional skill in writing. He '"sweated blood over the writing" of the *Weekly*, Izzy admitted, in an effort "to make it like a soufflé, urbane, erudite, and witty"' (Cottrell, 1992: 178).

Given the great differences in context, samizdat, newsletters and similar personal projects create an oppositional space outside of repression and commercialization. Despite not accepting the institutional imperative of bourgeois journalism for large-scale organization, personal projects nevertheless have the potential of amplifying their prominence through citation and quotation by others. At the same time, because the journalistic method materially available to them is rooted in their personal reach, they cannot avoid their own characteristic limitations. An emphasis on personal expression or reflection runs the risk of aestheticism or solipsism, while an emphasis on document-based commentary and non-sectarian critique focuses attention – as the officially produced documents themselves do, too – on the reigning dominant rather than on emergent challenges. As necessary as this work is, it forms only part of a critical project, in that it highlights what needs to be changed while setting aside the twin necessity of exploring and enabling instances, processes and directions for its change.

Should a personal project of alternative journalism try to move outside the focus on prescriptive and imaginative argument and analysis, or documentary institutional critique, problems rapidly mount and its viability wanes. Among the countless examples of failed projects is the recent website Crisis Pictures, which its founder started 'by accident' (Davis, 2006). The extent of response to his posting on a weblog a series of pictures documenting the carnage in the November 2004 US-led military offensive in Fallujah, Iraq inspired him to expand the effort and include as many pictures as he could. However, due to accepting the institutional imperatives of bourgeois journalism (which requires among other things comprehensiveness), the project soon overwhelmed him. For Crisis Pictures, success quite literally meant failure. Not only had the founder 'never done any [computer] programming or design in [his] life', he 'spent the last six months programming this elaborate content manager to manage thousands of pictures to tell stories in a way that goes beyond "another bad day in the Third World"' (ibid.). Despite this and other attempts to make the one-person project manageable, he reached the point at which 'it's Crisis Pictures or me. I am out of money and out of energy' (ibid.).

The approaches pioneered by samizdat and newsletters inform the practice of webloggers who see themselves as engaging in journalism. Many of them accept the premise of empiricism as a source of authority, but refuse the imperative of comprehensiveness in favour of a non-organizational form of empiricism: witnessing (Couldry, 2000; Peters, 2001). Such a move still operates within the traditions of bourgeois journalism, in that it resuscitates the seventeenth- and eighteenth-century practice of correspondence present in epistolary culture, which helped form bourgeois journalism in the first place (Schneider, 2005). As a personal mode of empiricism, witnessing and its adoption by the commercial-popular press as the convention of what one of this book's authors identifies as the 'native reporter' both accepts and stands outside traditions of bourgeois journalism, with complex results (Atton, 2002b).

Pressures for greater organization and thus implicitly the pressure to occupy more fully the imperatives of bourgeois journalism (if not the imperative of the vanguard leadership) are increasing with the similarly increasing ubiquity of capitalism, and can be seen in such examples as the 15 October 2007 'Blog Action Day' in which 'bloggers around the web will unite to put a single important issue on everyone's mind – the environment' ('Blog Action Day', 2007). Although the project seeks to make room for individuality and difference in that 'every blogger will post about the environment in their own way and relating to their own topic', the act of organizing itself is an effort to reconcile the personal project with ideological pressures for large-size organization (ibid.).

Collective and Movement Support

While volunteer labour and alliance with a social movement is compatible with patronage-supported projects, the volunteer basis also distinguishes 'movement journalism' from patronage-supported journalism by refusing traditions of professionalization and instead opening the project to anyone who wishes to join and contribute in any way. Projects that consist entirely of voluntarism can be organized less like vanguard parties and more like diffuse artistic movements, conceivably doing away with formal organization altogether. Examples include the artistic movement known as Fluxus, which 'exists not in a traditional way of specific members who define and determine a group, but as a network of ideas around which a varied group of artists have collaborated' (Smith, 2005: 118–119). Smith goes on to emphasize the organizational difference that such a form enables, noting that Fluxus is best seen 'as a community and a philosophy rather than an art historical movement' – or, in the terms of the present discussion, a movement of popular culture rather than an organized and professionalized project (p. 119).

As with patronage and commercial support, volunteer collectives shading into social movements and popular culture have important precursors, among them anarchist and syndicalist labour movements. Constituted by a novel and shifting set of influences, during its heyday in the late nineteenth and early twentieth centuries, the Industrial Workers of the World (IWW) carried forward the premises of anarchism and syndicalism – and their fluidity and mobility – in a number of ways (Brissenden, 1919; Brooks, 1913; Dubofsky, 1990; Salerno, 1989). It helped pioneer a flexible, deterritorialized resistance to capitalism that was much less about organizations of local workers confronting local employers, and much more about loosely orienting in the form of a variable, general community of affinity at specific sites to be determined by choice and conditions. Such an 'organization' was actually a dispersed and mobile solidarity that aspired to novel kinds of hybrid association consistent with, for example, Kropotkin's conception of 'communal individuality' (Ritter, 1980: 3; see also Morris, B., 2004). Because of its de-institutionalized nature, calls for specific actions spread through word of mouth, thus becoming much more difficult for foremen, managers and the state to detect, control and punish (Salerno, 1989).

Downing (2003a) argues that a correspondence exists between such efforts and the practice of what has come to be known as 'Indymedia'. The World Trade Organization meeting in Seattle in 1999 not only signalled the arrival of a new social movement but also the remaking and updating of the long-standing volunteer-collective form of support as applied to journalism and its manifestation in popular culture. (Discussions of Indymedia that apply most directly to points raised here about the organization of alternative journalism include Atton, 2004; Coyer, 2005; Kidd, 2003; Meikle, 2002;

Morris, D., 2004; Pickard, 2006; Platon and Deuze, 2003; and van de Donk et al., 2004.)

Like the IWW and many other examples, Independent Media Centres have 'no ambition to be any kind of Leninist directing centre', but instead are a means of open and decentralized publishing, collaboration and discussion as a form of direct action (Downing, 2003a: 251). Although often seen as a global organization, the Indymedia collective is, in its own sense of itself, not a global organization at all, but a confederation of community media organizations. While some of its activists describe Indymedia as 'a worldwide network', they also describe it as 'a community based organisation using media to facilitate political and cultural self-representation' ('What is Indymedia?', 2006). It is a global project that rivals if not exceeds commercial-popular news organizations in scale, reach and potential comprehensiveness, but also one that relies on volunteer work rather than capital from patrons or from advertising, thus evading the limits and pressures of such means of support.

Since 1999, Indymedia has been joined by similar efforts, spilling over into popular culture as forms of variously labelled 'independent journalism', 'community journalism' and 'participatory journalism' as part of broader programmes of challenge and resistance (Howley, 2005; Ostertag, 2006). Such projects seek to enable people to create and distribute their own accounts of their lives and issues, thus enabling work that is often inspired by anarchist-inflected practice and outside the dominant professionalized practice. One such activist saw Indymedia as only one of many forms of 'pure direct action', when 'you are not [simply] talking politics and yelling in the streets; you are doing it, making it real, and sharing it with the community' (Will, 2006).

Even with such diffuse volunteer efforts, capital needs do not disappear. A patronizing and dismissive commercial-popular account of Indymedia notes drily how 'friendly capitalists donated server space and Internet video capacity, on which the whole no-budget anti-corporate media utopia still depends', recalling the criticisms of *Voice of Women* and the *Appeal to Reason* regarding the contradiction of a publication that relies for support on the very capitalism it purports to challenge (Montgomery, 2002). Particular capital needs derive from the political economy of Internet publishing. Curran notes how costs typically incurred with paper-copy publishing and financed by the maker are not vaporized but in effect 'transferred directly to the receiver, who pays for the computer and the connection charge', or borne by society in the form of socially supported Internet-enabled computers in libraries and other 'free' areas (Curran, 2003: 233). More generally, the pressures themselves derive from adherence to traditions of bourgeois journalism. Although open publishing does away with the qualification of professionalism as a requirement for participation, the form of many Indymedia postings – their eyewitness descriptions of events and objective-style accounts – exemplifies the claim on the main website not only that it is a 'democratic media outlet' but also that it is focused on 'radical, accurate, and passionate tellings of truth', a claim that does not so much refuse traditions of bourgeois journalism so much as seek to mix them with Leninist and socialist-anarchist conceptions (Independent Media Centre, 2007).

Conclusion

As this chapter emphasizes, the political economy of alternative journalism can be traced not through a set of static categories, but through an exceedingly complex field of limits and pressures that operate in a wide variety of often contradictory ways. The most recent developments illustrate the protean nature of alternative journalism as it is continually remade by political-economic pressures.

The most important development in the political economy of alternative journalism is its increased amenability to capitalist organization. In some instances, such as the People's Republic of China (PRC), an experiment is currently taking place where an authoritarian, communist regime is permitting and in some cases assisting the formation of commercial media companies. Zhao's analysis charts the change from the 'party principle' of journalism – in which the party prescribes and enforces allowable points of view – to the economic reforms dating from the late 1970s, during which the management of official media organizations (beginning with the *People's Daily*) adopted the form of business enterprises, with the intention of streamlining and making them more efficient. From this point, the PRC's central government has pursued a policy of gradually 'cutting subsidies and encouraging commercial financing' (Zhao, 1998: 53). Such a change not only benefits the state (which now receives revenues from profits and taxes instead of draining them via subsidies); the consumerist content (taken from Western models) coexists nicely with a tight control of the editorial point of view and state control of ownership. Zhao concludes that the apparent Westernization of content and a selected form of commercialization does not preclude authoritarian limits and tight party control.

In other instances, such as in South Korea, experiments are currently under way to combine commercial with social-movement media. Operating in the wake of earlier efforts at commercialized alternative journalism already discussed, the Korean publication *OhmyNews* has developed what it calls 'citizen journalism' as the linchpin of a global social movement of democratization (a conventional, industry-centred discussion of citizen journalism is Nel et al., 2007). While *OhmyNews* opens its pages to a substantial volume of popular contributions (from 'citizen reporters'), and in this way works outside the traditions of bourgeois journalism, it is a for-profit business that funds itself primarily through advertising (Kim and Hamilton, 2006).

And, yet, such a reformulation of bourgeois journalism is also relevant to many established media companies throughout the world, whose readership continues to decline if not haemorrhage (Anderson, 2007).

Whilst efforts such as *OhmyNews* see increasing profits optimistically as a means of enabling greater civic engagement and social change, others who have adopted this business model invert the formulation, seeing instead greater civic engagement cynically as simply a means of increasing profits. Examples include the many efforts at 'citizen journalism' projects in the United States and the BBC programme *Your News*, which purports to be 'the first news programme to be entirely based on emails and views sent in by you' (Project for Excellence in Journalism, 2007b; BBC News, 2007). Some smaller commercial organizations, such as Talking Points Memo, make use of a more engaged volunteer workforce along with a combination of commercial and contributor support. In addition to hosting weblogs on various topics to which users can contribute, it has recruited its readers to help in documentary research regarding such cases as the US Justice Department firings of federal attorneys whose devotion to the Republican Party was suspect (McLeary, 2007).

Such developments simply underscore what should be obvious at this point. The political-economic pressures that have worked on alternative journalism for the past 200 years are continuing to be remade by globalization and digital technology, with the accommodations as well as challenges to traditions of bourgeois journalism remaking alternative journalism.

3

WHO ARE ALTERNATIVE JOURNALISTS?
A SOCIAL DEMOGRAPHIC SURVEY

In Chapter 1, we argued that it is important to avoid essentializing a singular history of alternative journalism and instead multiple histories must be recognized that have been identified, constructed and explored at different times, by different scholars working in specific cultural contexts. We can also apply this approach to an examination of social demographics. It is too easy – and quite misleading – to assume that all alternative media practitioners are cut from the same cloth, that they share the same aims, that they work in similar ways and, crucially for this chapter, that they all come from similar backgrounds. When we explored the political economy of alternative journalism, we argued that it provided two challenges to the dominant modes of media production: capitalization and institutionalization. We also saw in Chapter 2 how alternative media challenge the professionalized ideology of journalism. Taken together, these three challenges might lead us to expect that all alternative journalists practise in environments that are under-funded (and perhaps even have no funding), are unorganized (perhaps even disorganized) and are so far from being professionalized that they are not simply amateurs, but incompetents. If this were the case, how would the challenge to media power – the challenge to 'journalism' itself – be achieved? How could it be sustained? How could it hope to be successful? One way to answer these questions is to explore the backgrounds, motivations and skills of alternative journalists. To do so will be to demonstrate the diversity of alternative journalists and to show how their specific social markers (class, education, gender, race, occupational group) contribute to the nature of the alternative journalism projects with which they are involved.

Unfortunately, there are no systematic and wide-ranging surveys of the demographics of practitioners in alternative journalism on which to draw for these answers. Harcup (2005) provides data for the UK, but this is far from comprehensive (his survey comprises 22 self-selected journalists); Van

Vuuren (2002) examines the social demographics of volunteers working for three Australian community radio stations. The data for this chapter will be drawn from a range of international studies whose concerns are primarily with aims, ideology and organizational methods. It is in such studies that we may find fragments from which we can piece together a picture of those who produce alternative journalism. Inevitably this will not provide us with any detailed knowledge about the practitioners of alternative journalism. For now it is enough to note that, even were there a desire to collect demographic data, the extremely diverse range of publications and projects would make collation and comparison extremely difficult (indeed, comparison might not always be appropriate). Further, the transience and the narrow reach of much alternative journalism, often short-lived and produced within small communities, means that even basic information about specific projects and publications is often hard to come by. For every example of alternative journalism we know about, there might well be dozens, if not hundreds, of which we are ignorant. The absence of systematic collections of alternative publications by libraries and archives exacerbates the situation (Atton, 1996). For example, Harcup (2003) points out that many of the publications listed in Spiers's (1974) bibliography of the British underground and alternative press were 'defunct' by its publication. Spiers himself notes that the publications were often 'short-lived, amorphous ... individually impermanent' (Spiers, 1974: 21). From the many case studies we do have, however, we can appreciate the vast range of practitioners, practices, purposes, forms and audiences that comprise alternative journalism.

It is unrealistic to expect surveys of alternative journalism to capture any general, representative information about its practitioners. However, by studying what material we have, we should be able to observe trends and issues across a range of journalism types. We shall examine alternative media projects using the classic demographic markers of occupational grouping, gender, class, age, ethnicity, education and geographic location. In addition to looking broadly across the range of alternative media and their producers, we shall examine particular types of project, within each of which demographics will be analysed and evaluated. We can think of these projects as points along a continuum, where other characteristics, such as ideology, aims and organizational size and methods, will be seen to play their parts in determining – or offering opportunities for – particular social demographics in alternative journalism. We shall also consider how broader structural variables such as technology, economics and culture intersect with social demographics.

The organization of this chapter needs some explanation. To examine each demographic marker in turn would lead to much repetition. There are many examples where occupational grouping, ethnicity and gender intersect; others where geographic location, class and age are inseparable. Neither is it desirable to examine specific media and their journalists in isolation: to do so would be to miss the intersections between diverse alternative media projects and their differing economic, cultural and social locations. Instead, this overview of social demographics blends these two approaches. It begins with an examination of occupational groupings amongst alternative journalists, which also considers the function of class in these groupings. It goes on to examine the amateur and the professional in alternative journalism, and the effect of the age and cultural background of practitioners on voluntary work (a dominant mode of employment in this sector). This section introduces ideology and lifestyle as determinants of social demographics. A study of the social demographics of fanzines and zines returns us to a discussion of class and introduces gender issues. We then return to ideology and look at the demographics of marginalized social groups such as people with HIV/AIDS and special needs, and children and young people. Finally, we briefly examine the 'shifting demographics' of those who move from alternative media to careers as professional journalists.

Occupational Groupings

It is in the local, alternative community media that we find the greatest concentration of professionals. Dickinson (1997: 86) notes that participation in community media is often a result of 'personal or professional experience in a job or role which involved that community'. Dickinson's study of the alternative press in the north-west of England demonstrates that most of the alternative community press in that region was founded by, for example, professionals, either teachers, social workers or the clergy. It is these people who identify the need for community expression, who set up editorial groups, but they do not seem to use their professional experience (or their middle-class background, another common feature) to control the media. Instead, they seek to make the media available to individuals and groups who are more representative of the local community. In the case of the *Bury Metro News*, founded in 1973 by two teachers, this included 'engineers or paper makers', textile workers, as well as Labour Party and trade union activists (Dickinson, 1997: 89). University education seems to play a significant part: undergraduates (including drop-outs) and graduates dominated the London underground press of the late 1960s and early 1970s (Fountain, 1988; Green, 1998). Publications such as *Oz*, *IT* and *Black Dwarf* were all founded, at least in part, by graduates. As Green (1998: x) notes, the underground press of the British counterculture was urban and middle class: 'it produced, in parallel to the "straight world", the standard features of middle-class culture ... newspapers, arts centres, restaurants, record businesses, bookshops ...' The British counterculture may well have been middle class, but this did not exclude contributors (albeit a minority) from other walks of life. The counter-cultural newspaper *IT*, for example, included a 'former [union] convenor from the Ford car factory in Dagenham, as well as a 17-year-old school leaver' (Fountain, 1988: 54).

It is inevitable that publications that aim to give a voice to members of the local community (particularly in economically deprived areas such as over-spill or 'sink' housing estates) will draw on people with less formal education, who are broadly working class – culturally, economically and socially. In Western Europe and North America, alternative media tends to be urban (whether counter-cultural or community based); elsewhere it is often rural, and resolutely working class. In Nicaragua, the Movement of Popular Correspondents that flourished in the 1980s drew on the inhabitants of impoverished rural areas. They became community journalists in their free time, their main employment being mostly as labourers in tobacco or cotton plantations (Rodriguez, 2001: Ch. 3). Rodriguez also tells of video and tele-vision production by poor, working mothers in Colombia (Ch. 5), by young people in deprived areas of France (p. 42), and writes of the contributions of agricultural workers, miners and hairdressers to Belgian free radio (p. 53).

Alternative Journalism as a Mixed Economy

We must be careful not to essentialize or idealize specific forms of alterna-tive journalism. The notion of giving a 'voice to the voiceless' involves a mixed economy of agency. This is not only at work in community media founded by professional teachers or social workers, who establish structures and opportunities for members of a local community to report on their own conditions, experiences and aspirations (as in the case of the community presses studied by Dickinson). It is also a characteristic, for example, of Nicaragua's popular correspondents, who were trained in newsgathering and reporting by journalism students, and a feature of local radio and tele-vision stations around the world, where typically producers and engineers are professionally trained, providing a structure within which unskilled local people can become broadcasters. This reinforces the argument about hybridity made in Chapter 2: professionals and amateurs working together.

Trained journalists and amateurs often come together more permanently in alternative journalism projects. Though the underground paper *IT* was in part founded by students, it also benefited from the local and national news-paper experience of two professional journalists (Fountain, 1988). The paper of the British Socialist Workers' Party, *Socialist Worker*, was in the main writ-ten by professional journalists, though it frequently encouraged its working-class readership to contribute news and features. Its chronic failure to achieve this (Allen, 1985; Sparks, 1985) seems to be due to the lack of support and training it gave to its potential reporters.

In the United States, we find a further species of mixed economy. The beginnings of the participatory video movement can be located in a bohemian, urban community of artists and students (Boyle, 1997). New York's Downtown Community Television (DCTV) was founded in the 1970s by a video artist (Keiko Tsuno) and a community activist and taxi driver, Jon Alpert. Tsuno bought her first video camera with money saved from her earnings from waiting tables; Alpert is a self-taught film-maker. DCTV's two-person production team remains to the present, but actively involves representatives of various sectors of the local community as programme planners, researchers and interviewees (Howley, 2005).

The professional composition of alternative media projects may provide more than inspiration, skills and structure within which deprofessionalized journalism may be developed. Some projects are set up with the explicit aim of challenging the dominant practices and representations of mainstream media, as well as the dominance of the market. To achieve success, they not only need professionalized organizational structures, but professionalized journalism and access to established networks of distribution (preferably those already used by their mainstream rivals). Alternative media such as these require sound economic planning, capitalization and organization: they represent the desiderata of Comedia (1984), whose vision of alternative media is one that competes with the mainstream using the strategies of the mainstream. It comes as no surprise, therefore, to find alternative media such as these populated by entrepreneurs, accountants, trained graphic artists and professional journalists. As Dickinson points out, such a range of professionalized staff enabled 'technical and logistical structures' for printing and distribution, as well as high-quality investigative journalism, since, as his English examples show, investigative reporters 'moved easily between the mainstream and alternative press worlds' (Dickinson, 1997: 130).

Professionals and Intellectuals

The perceived necessity of having alternative media populated by the professional classes is relevant to more than print media. Some online alternative media projects have been founded by or have chosen to recruit professional journalists. The South Korean online citizens' media project *OhmyNews* comprises an editorial hub staffed by 60 professionals (of whom 35 are reporters), who advise on and edit the contributions of thousands of citizen reporters (Kim and Hamilton, 2006). The international, online magazine *altvoices* was set up in 2006 by journalism students at the University of Cardiff and recruits journalists from across the world. At times, this is intended to lend authority and distinctiveness to a medium that might otherwise be left floundering in a World Wide Web of millions of personal comment pages. At other times, it is a result of their founders' disillusionment with the mainstream media where they began their careers. The online news and comment magazine *openDemocracy* was founded by a journalist from the left-of-centre, British political weekly *New Statesman*, and is mostly written by professional journalists and public intellectuals on the left. *OpenDemocracy*, then, while we might still consider it a type of alternative journalism, is a forum for a dissenting elite, 'a forum of debate for activists, academics, journalists, businesspeople, politicians and international civil servants' (Curran, 2003: 238). In her study of the *Honolulu Weekly*, Gibbs (2003: 593) notes that compared with a staff of eight full-time employees, there were 83 part-time writers, mostly freelancers with no journalism training. Instead, they were hired for their expertise and status as 'local academics, environmentalists, novelists, social rights advocates and community leaders'. Contributors to the British investigative and satirical fortnightly magazine *Private Eye* are mostly professional journalists who 'moonlight' for the publication, using their access to sources to publish stories anonymously that their main employer would not publish, usually because the stories might be subject to legal challenges (Lockyer, 2006).

We also find professional journalists amongst the growing community of bloggers. Here too they are moonlighting from their day jobs, often writing personal accounts of their experiences (for example in war zones), which go beyond their professional obligations to an employer (Allan, 2006; Wall, 2005, 2006). The opportunity to publish accounts of personal experience and individual commentary outside a media organization (even an alternative one), means that blogging has become one of the most demographically diverse forms of alternative journalism (this is not to ignore, however, enduring problems of access to the Internet in some regions of the world, whether for technological, cultural and social, or political and legal reasons). Amateur political commentators, disaffected professionals, soldiers, politicians, academics and students comprise the majority of bloggers. They represent a wide range of backgrounds. During the Gulf War of 2003, blogs were posted from professional journalists moonlighting from their day jobs. These included BBC reporters such as Stuart Hughes. The BBC and the British *Guardian* newspaper established 'warblog' sites during the conflict. Blogs were also employed by NGOs such as Greenpeace as well as by US military officers posted in Iraq such as 'L.T. Smash' and 'Will'. A blog run by 'Salam Pax' claimed to be written by a Baghdad resident; the US journal *New Republic* ran an online diary by Kanan Makiya, a leading Iraqi dissident (Atton, 2004).

Professionals and intellectuals are also to be found in the grassroots protest media of anarchist and radical environmental movements such as *Green Anarchist* and Earth First!'s *Do or Die*, where their writing appears alongside the first-person narratives of direct-action protest. These intellectuals are perhaps better defined as movement intellectuals or organic intellectuals, the latter term coined by the Italian political philosopher Antonio Gramsci (1971) to refer to writers and thinkers whose expertise has been developed through direct experience of particular social or political conditions. O'Connor (2004: 11) argues that the 'sophisticated journalists' who staffed miners' radio stations in Bolivia demonstrate Gramsci's conception of socialist intellectuals in action: their role was to articulate the miners' experiences, defend their trade unions and to facilitate the participation of miners themselves in the radio programmes. A prominent movement intellectual within the contemporary anarchist and anti-globalization movements is Noam Chomsky, whose work appears in a wide range of alternative publications throughout the world.

We also need to distinguish between the contributions of 'established' and 'nonestablished' movement intellectuals (Eyerman and Jamison, 1991, 1995). Established movement intellectuals are those whose primary activity is based in formal educational institutions (ordinarily, universities) and who make a living from their writing and speaking or at least have first gained prominence through such activities as opposed to through activism. Nonestablished intellectuals tend to have developed their expertise outside institutions, or their primary role is to work alongside social movements or marginal groups in society. They include 'counter-experts', whose work goes against the grain of received opinion. The anarchist writer Colin Ward is a useful example: his radical writings on social housing are firmly aimed at the 'common reader'. This category may also include members of professional groups such as lawyers, social workers and representatives of advocacy and pressure groups. As Eyerman and Jamison have shown, this model of intellectual participation in the alternative media of social movements is easily traced back to the 1960s, at least in North America and Europe. However, it is possible to find earlier examples, such as the anarchist movements of the late nineteenth and early twentieth centuries (Quail, 1978) and, even before them, in the American revolutionary press, the English revolutionary press and the English Radical press, where politicians, social reformers, professional writers and journalists, and printers founded and wrote for newspapers aimed at the emerging working class (for a useful bibliography, see Hamilton and Atton, 2001).

In other countries and at other times, the dissident intellectual becomes a radical journalist in response to specific political conditions (Downing et al., 2001). In the former Soviet Union during the 1960s, while the repression of the Stalinist era had been lessened under Khruschchev's regime, political freedom and freedom of expression were still severely controlled. Samizdat began amongst those suffering religious persecution, but soon extended to the secular intelligentsia, in particular to academics and writers whose work was officially banned by the regime. In Poland, opposition to

Soviet rule in the 1970s and 1980s, though first springing from shipyard workers (leading to the formation of the trade union Solidarnosc), resulted in alliances with the Polish intelligentsia and the Roman Catholic church (Jakubowicz, 1991). Papers such as *Robotnik* ('Worker') were written and published by a group that comprised intellectuals and workers (Downing et al., 2001: Ch. 22).

Training and Skills

In some cases, professional training is actively sought by amateur journalists in order to expand their investigative and writing skills. Out of the 22 journalists who took part in Harcup's (2005) survey of alternative journalism in the UK, nine 'had some form of formal training – mostly on courses accredited by the National Council for the Training of Journalists' (p. 364). However, he emphasizes that most of this training took place after their involvement in alternative media; moreover, the majority of his respondents had no formal training at all. Professional training appears to be more common in many of the 'development' media projects examined by Gumucio Dagron (2001). In many of these, we find indigenous members of local communities producing their own videos, programming and hosting their own radio shows, becoming reporters on behalf of their own communities. They will be trained and mentored by professional journalists and broadcasters, who often work for NGOs and development agencies. The demographics of the indigenous journalists will vary according to their locale, the demands of the medium and the community's concerns. For example, a women's video-making collective in the Indian city of Ahmadabad includes those who cannot read or write, but who have learned how to operate a video camera (Gumucio Dagron, 2001: 85–90). Many of the volunteers that comprise the majority of contributors to South Africa's Radio Zibolnele in Cape Town are illiterate and have no formal education, but work with the full-time, professional staff in an organizational culture that emphasizes 'aggressive ongoing training and capacity building interventions' in order to involve the community in broadcasting programmes that are directly relevant to its needs (p. 200). By contrast, the research foundation that established the Village Knowledge Centres of Chennai (India) insists on volunteers being educated to at least high school level and prefers people aged between 20 and 25. These factors are deemed important for a project that is computer-based (including Internet work). However, preference is given to people of low socio-economic status (such as farmers) and to women (p. 320).

This mixed economy, where amateurs and professionals, the untrained and the trained coexist, is not without its tensions. Within organizations that need to employ professionals (whether for training, editing or specialist reporting), hierarchies may emerge between full-time, established staff, part-time staff and volunteers. In the case of social movement media or fanzines, where it is expected that everyone will be a volunteer, or on very low (and occasional) wages, there is little evidence of conflict over employment status (the prominence of collective methods of organization attests to this). Dickinson (1997) distinguishes between two types of individual in his study of the alternative press: the 'radical cultural' (or 'hedonist') and 'radical political' (or 'hard newsman' (*sic*)). The former act as cultural intermediaries by 'grazing' across various structures; they are, that is, open to various forms of organizing and producing, they might move from publishing to organizing concerts, to protests and back again. The latter, by contrast, build permanent structures: they are responsible for ensuring the technical and logistical capacity of an organization. Although the accounts by Rodriguez (2001) suggest that the Latin American experience of this mixed economy is a successful one – where a common ideology of participatory communication binds professional journalists and technical staff with amateur writers and broadcasters – in the UK there is evidence of significant tensions, especially where professional values and status (such as that of the investigative journalist) are highly prized, and competition with mainstream media is sought after (Dickinson, 1997). The issue of status also affects employment opportunities.

Voluntarism in Alternative Journalism

As a whole, alternative media tend to be typified by their volunteer, 'self-exploited' workforce (Atton, 2002a). Voluntarism may be an ideological choice that is arrived at from a deep suspicion of institutionalized organizations, where the accumulation of capital is considered to dominate. To organize and produce voluntarily becomes the ideal, where the democratic aims of alternative media will not be tainted by economics. Inevitably, this approach restricts the types of people who might participate. Apart from the obvious reason that some potential contributors might not be sympathetic to such an ideology, not everyone will be in a stable enough economic situation to be able to afford to dedicate themselves to a project that offers little or no financial reward. Consequently, voluntary alternative media projects (that is, the distinct majority of alternative media projects) across time and location display repeating patterns of social demographics. In the latter part of the twentieth century, whether in the underground press of the 1960s, the fanzines of the 1970s and 1980s or the 'New Protest' social movement media of the 1990s, we find that young people (often students, drop-outs or 'gap year' students) dominate. Co-operatively run cafés, music venues, bookshops and information centres (or 'infoshops': see Atton, 2003c) have been (and continue to be) homes to alternative media projects. Occasionally, activists from previous generations would be involved, but this was rare (McKay, 1996). In its formative years, the British paper *Green Anarchist* included long-standing anarchists as well as younger people: in its case, the ideological tensions between the generations resulted in the 'old guard' being ousted from the editorial group (Atton, 1999).

The safety net of family finances and the absence of the responsibilities of property ownership, a career or a family of their own combine to free many young people to embark on projects out of commitment or enthusiasm, rather than out of ambition or a search for economic security. Voluntarism may also be understood as a lifestyle choice, from which develops a culture that is expressed through alternative journalism. This reflexive, cultural form is perhaps best exemplified in publications founded by and written for 'travellers' and 'homeless' people. In the 1990s, these terms would tend not to refer to Romany/Gypsy travelling people or to people made homeless as a consequence of poverty (whatever its causes: family breakdown, alcoholism or drug addiction, for example). Instead, they signified (mostly) young people who had made a deliberate choice to live their lives outside the dominant culture (McKay, 1996). 'Homeless' signified a deliberate eschewal of property ownership or dependence on landlords for rented accommodation. Instead, throughout Europe, the 1990s, saw a resurgence of the squatting movement, where groups would move into unoccupied premises and consider them as their homes. The precariousness of their situation (legally and culturally) meant that reliable information about squatting became prized: in the absence of advice from mainstream institutions, or the impossibility of paying for legal advice, many publications appeared, which squatters would use as spaces to share information and experiences. Perhaps the most significant of these in the UK was *Squall*, published quarterly from 1992 to 1997 and subsequently online (Atton, 2002a). Comparison with a better-known publication for the homeless, the *Big Issue* series of fortnightly magazines ('helping the homeless to help themselves', as its strapline declares), is instructive. Homeless people – for whom homelessness is not a lifestyle choice – sell the paper on the streets, but trained journalists write and edit it. (Interestingly, some writers from the activist alternative media have gone on to write for the *Big Issue*.) The homeless people whom the paper supports sell the paper on the streets for a small commission; only two pages of any issue are given over to their writing (usually poetry). By contrast, the Canadian homeless people's newspaper, *Street Feat* (published in Halifax, Nova Scotia), blends the approaches of *Squall* and the *Big Issue*. Like the latter, it is organized professionally, with a full-time staff that includes an advertising and fund-raising department. Like *Squall*, it regularly features lengthy articles written by the same homeless people who sell the paper on the streets of Halifax (Howley, 2005).

For many people, though, the pursuit of a lifestyle that is economically impoverished and offers little long-term social stability is not sustainable. Most members of countercultures eventually look for more stable economic and social situations; participants in counter-cultural journalism tend to do likewise. This is one explanation for the movement of activist journalists to papers like the *Big Issue*, where they will be paid for their work. This is a typical trajectory: Harcup (2005) finds it across a wide range of alternative journalism (fanzines, community media, protest and campaigning magazines). More generally, voluntarism can be seen retrospectively as a stepping-stone to a career as a professional journalist, though this rarely seems to be a deliberate reason for becoming an unpaid, alternative journalist in the first instance. The history of rock music journalism, for example, begins with the fanzines and the underground press of the US and the UK, where there is little evidence that its earliest, amateur practitioners saw their early work as a career opportunity (Gudmundsson et al., 2002).

The Problems of Voluntarism

The difficulty of sustaining an alternative media project on little or no wages, with minimal capital, also helps us to understand the relative absence of contributors in their thirties and into middle age. Financial security and the raising of a family are two significant reasons for this. Van Vuuren (2002) argues that young people are also less likely to volunteer for long-term projects in small centres of population, as their 'educational prospects will require them to move to larger centres' (p. 101), whereas in larger urban centres, a wider range of recreational opportunities provide attractive alternatives to community media. Her study of three Australian community radio stations generally finds few volunteers in the 30–39 age group, with the majority of volunteers either unemployed or in part-time work: they 'would therefore have more time on their hands to commit to the station' (ibid.). In the case of one station, for example, volunteers were mostly males aged 50 years or older, with retired people making up 42 per cent. Van Vuuren notes that these figures are in line with national statistics for volunteering, in particular for males, who 'are more inclined to volunteer for recreational and hobby-based organisations' (p. 100). Elsewhere, we find little evidence of older people in alternative journalism, except in the small number of projects aimed at their own age group, particularly in community radio, such as London's Resonance FM's programme *Calling All Pensioners*, which features a blend of information, populist rhetoric and radical politics from an 'activist' pensioner (Atton, 2004). Amongst the 36,000 contributors to South Korea's *OhmyNews*, over 70 per cent are in their twenties and thirties, with less than 10 per cent being over 50; male contributors dominate throughout: over three-quarters are men (Kim and Hamilton, 2006).

Voluntarism is not always a matter of individual choice. It may be a result of lack of success or hyper-specialization, where a publication's remit is so narrow that it lacks a broad enough audience or an adequate advertising base to sustain an economically stable organization. A publication might not be able to pay contributors at all, which will have an impact on the type of content it is able to publish. This is a particular problem for community media, where writers are sought from a specific community, especially from ethnic communities that are economically or socially deprived by comparison to a dominant (usually white and Western) culture. This is even the case where native ethnic groups comprise the majority of a population. Returning to Gibbs's (2003) study of the *Honolulu Weekly*, we find an equal balance between men and women on the staff, though there is a significant imbalance in ethnic origin: approximately two-thirds of the staff were Caucasian on an island (Hawaii) where whites make up 24 per cent of the total population. This is explained in part by the social and cultural advantages enjoyed by whites, resulting in skills and confidence that make them more likely to present themselves as candidates for alternative journalists. Forde et al. (2003) find a similar imbalance within the indigenous (Aboriginal) ethnic press of Australia, where there are few indigenous people working in the sector due to high start-up costs and a lack of 'culturally relevant training' (p. 320). In radio, however, where start-up costs are lower, indigenous journalists are more common. The most senior positions in Radio Margaritas, in the Chiapas region of Mexico, are held by *ladinos* (the 'rich'), with the poorer, indigenous staff discriminated against in terms of salary (Vargas, 1995). Status within an indigenous community may also emerge: in the rural community radio projects of the Philippines, community leaders are trained as broadcasters to represent different sectors of their communities, such as women, young people, agricultural workers and elderly people (Gumucio Dagron, 2001: 122). In less structured projects such as fanzines and zines, we find publications that tend to be organized and edited by much smaller groups, often by one person, where formal training and skills are far less in evidence.

The Demographics of Fanzines and Zines

When we consider fanzines, there appear to be strong reasons for assuming that there will be less middle-class participation and fewer professional contributions. First, this is because the dominant theoretical understanding of the fanzine is that it is subcultural. In other words, it is an expression of a culture that emerges from and is in opposition to a parent culture, typically a working-class culture. Second, the typical production values of the fanzine are far from professional. This is most notable in the 'classic' form of the punk fanzine, which endures as the stereotype of the fanzine: features such as stencilled lettering, primitive cut-and-paste page layouts, photocopied photographs, the use of handwritten copy amongst a variety of typefaces demonstrate a reaction against professionalism and a refusal to conform to the conventions of magazine layout and design; there is a symbolic fit – homology – between the fanzine and the lifestyle and experiences of its producers (Willis, 1978). Fanzines also tend to be produced by a small group of people, often a single editor-writer. There is far less interest in representing the views of a wider community than there is in community media. Together, these factors suggest that the fanzine will tend to be produced by unskilled (in a conventional sense), working-class youth. For the punk fanzines of the late 1970s, this is often the case, but the model does not withstand close scrutiny. For example, while *Sniffin' Glue* was edited and written by a working-class Londoner (Mark Perry), Scotland's first punk fanzine (*Hanging Around*) was put together by middle-class students at the University of Edinburgh. The post-punk fanzine *Stabmental* was produced by pupils of Oundle School, an English public school (Atton, 2006a).

The special pleading for punk as the progenitor of late twentieth-century fanzine production also makes it difficult to consider – and seems to exclude – those people who produced fanzines that dealt with other musical forms, and whose publications were more clearly professional or which had relationships with the mainstream that are not straightforwardly 'oppositional'. The middle-class location of many progressive rock fanzines may result in a homology between musical-cultural and fanzine values, though one that is very different from that found in the 'classic' punk subculture. Professionally printed and desktop-published fanzines like *Facelift* (a fanzine about musicians of the progressive 'Canterbury' scene) and *Proclamation* (covering a single group, Gentle Giant) suggest cultures that wish to be taken seriously, where virtuosity and professionalism are considered virtues and design values reflect the 'weight' of the music. This is not to say that such publications are necessarily intellectual – indeed, despite their middle-class fan base (which is also almost entirely male), progressive rock fanzines generally tend towards a style of writing that is just as affective and exuberant as any other fanzine writing (Atton, 2001).

On rare occasions, we find fanzines established by professional music journalists. One such publication was *Careless Talk Costs Lives*, edited by former *Melody Maker* journalist Everett True with rock photographer Steve Gullick. The title first appeared in 2002 as a rejoinder to the perceived monoglottism of the British mainstream music press. The fanzine sought to re-establish the personality journalist (and True in particular) as the focus of

rock music journalism. Here was a professional, latter-day personality journalist reinventing himself against the corporate grain as a fanzine editor – as
auteur rather than as amateur (Atton, 2006a).

In general, though, the fanzine does not require professional experience
of either journalism or publishing; nor does it require any advanced educational attainment. In principle, age, ethnicity and gender are not significant.
In practice, however, it is young, white males who seem to be responsible
for most music fanzines. Some of the most significant in the history of rock
writing fall into this category, such as Paul Williams's *Crawdaddy!* (founded
in 1966 and not only the first rock fanzine but arguably the first rock magazine) Greg Shaw's *Who Put the Bomp!* (1970), Paul Morley's *Out There* and
Girl Trouble, and Jon Savage's *London's Outrage* (Atton, 2003d). (It is noteworthy that the reason for their status seems to be due to the journalistic
trajectory their editors embarked on and those editors' subsequent
status as professional writers.) There are exceptions: Sarah Champion published her first fanzine, *Alarm*, when she was a 14-year-old schoolgirl. She
went on to produce *Scam* and *Bop City*, two influential publications in the
British post-punk and dance scenes of the late 1980s (Dickinson, 1997).
The prominence of men reflects the gendered nature of much of the popular culture under discussion in fanzines and affects not only rock music, but
also science fiction, horror films and sport. For example, women are not
entirely absent from football fanzines, but they comprise a very small
minority of contributors (Atton, 2006b); by contrast, feminist cultures produce fanzines that are wholly edited and written by women (such as Riot
Grrrl fanzines; Duncombe, 1997: Ch. 7). Where cultural events and arte-
facts are less gendered in their audiences, there appears a more even distribution of gender. This is notable in studies of *Star Trek* fan production, for
example, where we also find significant numbers of gay and lesbian contributors (as writers of 'slash fiction', where Kirk and Spock are portrayed
as a homosexual couple; Jenkins, 1992).

Like fanzines, zines tends to be organized around a small number of
people. The zine (like some fanzines) is most likely to be the product of an
individual. Duncombe (1997) notes that zines tend to be written, edited
and produced by one person, who is usually white, middle class and educated to at least high school level. While he recognizes that there are
instances of publications produced by people of colour and by working-class
writers, the bulk are drawn from the white middle class – moreover, while
there are exceptions, the majority of zine writers will be young, in their
teens or early twenties. From his interviews and case studies, there does
seem to be, however, a fairly even distribution across gender. Similarly, sexual orientation amongst zine producers seems, if anything, to be more
weighted away from heterosexuality than in the general population. This is

no doubt a result of the zine offering one of the few spaces for self-expression through media by members of sexual communities marginalized by the mainstream. A similar argument can be made for the presence of girls and women as zine producers.

Gender, Special Interest Groups and Young People

In other forms of alternative journalism, there is evidence to suggest that gender imbalances in society at large seem to be reproduced in alternative journalism, even where there is an expectation that progressive politics would work against such reproduction. The underground press of London in the late 1960s and early 1970s seems to reflect the norms of the division of labour that pertained at the time: men as editors and writers, women as secretaries, tea-makers and administrative assistants (Fountain, 1988; Green, 1998). The emerging feminist movement saw increasing numbers of women becoming involved in alternative media. In part, this was in response to their marginalization in an otherwise progressive media culture, but also in response to wider societal forces such as unequal pay and limited career opportunities. Significantly, the rise of feminist media sought to counter mainstream representations of the women's movement, where it was depicted as irrational and marginal (Ashley and Olson, 1998). Consequently, the earliest feminist publications of the 1970s (such as *Spare Rib*), in their desire for independence from patriarchy, recruited only women. This absolute separatism emerged in a different form in larger organizations where women had previously been marginalized. At the Italian radio station Radiopop, women operated as a separatist power bloc in the 1970s, collectively producing programmes on women's issues. By the 1980s, separatism had achieved its goal of putting women's programmes on the station's agenda; it was no longer necessary to work collectively and separately. Feminism was now part of the station's daily practice and informed the work of both women and men (Downing et al., 2001: 282–284). Despite the gradual normalization of women's issues as features of both alternative and mainstream journalism, many publications prefer to maintain a separatist agenda, for reasons of privacy and security rather than ideology. This is particularly the case in online publications, where writing and discussion can take place in a forum populated only by women sympathetic to the concerns of the publication (Cresser et al., 2001: 470). There are other cultural and political reasons for restricting access, such as the fear of reprisal. Under the rule of the Taliban, women in Afghanistan were severely repressed. Contributors to the work of the Revolutionary Association for the Women of Afghanistan had to remain unknown to the authorities and used the Internet to anonymously distribute writings and documentaries to an international audience (Waltz, 2005: 128–130).

Amongst the many community media projects in marginalized and impoverished regions of the world, we frequently find deliberate (and successful) attempts to provide women with their own voices. Gumucio Dagron (2001) has identified many of these, such as the 'radio towers' of the Philippines (radio stations that narrowcast through public address systems in rural and urban communities), where women comprise half of the representatives on the Community Media Council and 'are very active as broadcasters' (p. 122). The Nutzij project of Guatemala offers Mayan women 'training and employment … in audio-visual communication, mainly concentrating on video and the Internet' (ibid.: 290). In Egypt, NGOs have co-ordinated participatory video training for women in villages and city slums (ibid.: 314).

Similar forms of advocacy are present in alternative media that deal exclusively with the special interests of particular groups in society. In all these cases, writers, editors and programme makers are drawn from the groups themselves. These include people with special needs. For example, autistics.org is only one of many online publications run by people with a particular medical condition; there are hundreds of publications around the world run by and for gay, lesbian, bisexual and transgendered people (Waltz, 2005: 27–29). These special interest media can be as active in representing the experiences and opinions of a community to its own members as in presenting those experiences and opinions to a wider audience. In her study of AIDS video activism, Alexander Juhasz (1995) emphasizes production processes that involve members of the communities for which (and in which) the video is being produced: 'to look is to see and know *yourself*' (p. 138, original emphasis). Projects of self-education like this demonstrate Rodriguez's theory of citizens' media in action.

The media of special interest groups return us to two issues already raised in this chapter: essentialism and professionalism. First, demographically speaking, it is far too reductive to identify a social group simply by one characteristic (such as a medical condition or sexual orientation). To do so is to ignore how this (supposedly primary) marker intersects with other markers such as gender, age and ethnicity. Unfortunately, we know too little about the specific demographics of participants in special interest media. For now, therefore, we must remember that to be able to identify one social marker of participants is far from being able to propose a single, coherent position for those participants as journalists: why should two gay journalists share similar practices? Second, many special interest groups, however much they seek to represent themselves, will need to rely on professionals for technical training and guidance (if not technical production itself). Even where the project is not aimed at a wider audience than those of the interest group itself, there may be a value in adopting professional practices; not all sectors of an audience might be satisfied with the 'underproduction' that characterizes many activist videos (Harding, 1997). Community media that go beyond activist audiences, such as those established in the UK under the government's Restricted Service Licence scheme, often produce programmes to mainstream industry standards, thus requiring skilled technical staff: 'people don't want to see shaky cameras or home videos' (managing director of TV12, Isle of Wight, cited in Scott, 1999: 13). This is far from the assisted amateurism of the alternative community newspaper, where the trained reporter plays a major role in empowering community members to produce their own reports. In the case of TV12, the professional is dominant.

There are relatively few accounts of children and young people as alternative journalists. Cape Town's Bush Radio has designated Saturday as the day for 'children's voices. No adult voices are heard on Bush Radio on a Saturday. The youngest trainee is eight years old' (Ibrahim, 2000: 201). Rodriguez describes the contribution of two 'kids' to a Fathers' Day broadcast on the Chilean community radio station Radio Estrella del Mar. She emphasizes their self-expression and a freedom from the norms of radio production: 'no one told them what to do; no one suggested a different way to do things' (Rodriguez, 2003: 184). Elsewhere she discusses a video made by three Chicana girls – as part of a participatory media project in San Antonio, Texas – in terms that stress the aestheticization of their experiences in the *barrio* (Rodriguez, 2002). In El Salvador, Radio Izcanal actively seeks young reporters, but here 'young' is understood as people in their early twenties (Gumucio Dagron, 2001: 173). The Rural Media Company, based in Hereford, England, 'focuses on working with marginalised rural audiences, particularly young people, enabling them to become media creators, rather than the subject of occasional reports or passive media consumers' (Waltz, 2005: 31–33). This includes a multimedia online magazine produced by teenagers and young adults, many of whom have low levels of written literacy skills; however, as we have seen in the video projects of India and South Africa, this does not prevent them developing what the project's director terms 'tele-literacy skills' (p. 32).

Conclusion

While alternative journalism is broadly conceptualized as the journalism of amateurs, its organization and practices draw on a far broader range of backgrounds and experiences. The focus of alternative journalism remains on members of communities – whether geographic communities or communities of interest – but these people are often supported, organized or trained by professional journalists, educators and technical staff. Alternative journalism that is aimed at relatively large audiences, and that therefore requires some of the approaches of mainstream media (such as regular funding, standardized methods of organization, communication values that appeal to a general public) will tend to be managed by professionals, with a large number of voluntary, non-professional contributors. Educational background varies throughout alternative journalism: intellectuals might provide their expertise to publications with which they sympathize; in community media, educational achievements are less important than the lived experiences of alternative journalists.

Despite its ideals, at times alternative journalism reproduces prevailing conditions in the wider society: inequalities of representation in gender and ethnicity are often present in larger alternative media projects. Tensions between professionals and amateurs may also arise. These problems can be ameliorated by alternative media that adopts an explicit ideology of equality. 'Separatist' media (ethnic minority media, feminist media) offer a different solution, which is also applied by media that seek to represent the special interests of marginalized or disadvantaged groups. This variety of approaches further underscores the heterogeneous nature of alternative journalism and the mixed economy of its practitioners. As if to reinforce this hybridity, it is important to note the 'shifting demographic' between amateur and professional. We have already seen how the professional popular music journalism of the 1960s and 1970s has its origins in the contributions of alternative journalists. Harcup's survey provides further evidence of this. His respondents were sought through the pages of the *Journalist*, the magazine of the National Union of Journalists in the UK. All his respondents were therefore journalists who had used their skills and experience as alternative journalists to develop professional careers. Not all alternative journalists make this move, of course. The economic precariousness of much alternative media, a lack of opportunities in the profession at a particular time, personal reasons, or simple exhaustion, means that many people will not continue as journalists of any kind.

Part 2

4

MULTIPLE POLICIES, MULTIPLE FORMS, MULTIPLE CHALLENGES

An analysis of current policy developments regarding alternative journalism reveals a great complexity that corresponds to the wide variety of players. They range from the established commercial journalism industry to the alternative-journalism industry, coalitions of media-reform organizations and philanthropic foundations, and diffuse volunteer and personal projects. Given the impossibility of adequately canvassing all policy visions and statements in a single, short chapter, the intention here is to provide a sense of basic policy stances characteristic of each major player, keeping in mind that policy positions overlap, often differing more in degree than in kind. In addition, policies are not formulated in a vacuum, but are structurally determined by other organizations and institutions that intersect with alternative journalism in important ways, and this determination – although not the focus of the chapter – must be acknowledged as well.

In this discussion, policies are considered to be definitions, intentions and goals for, in this case, alternative journalism. In order to take a beneficially broad view of various efforts to envision alternative journalism, one should take into account the many forms that 'policy' can take. For industry groups, a term more appropriate than 'policy' might be 'business strategy' and, for personal projects, 'personal philosophy'. In addition, policies can be expressed often as much through practice as through manifesto or logical argument. This broader range is considered here.

In addition, the terms 'definitions', et cetera, are pluralized here: as previous chapters have discussed, multiple definitions and versions of alternative journalism exist. However, although the immense complexity of policy goals and recommendations needs to be acknowledged, this complexity can be mapped along a dimension suggested earlier in this book. While some policy developments seek to absorb and incorporate alternative journalism into their own projects, others regard alternative journalism as a means of solidifying projects of media-system reform, while still others regard it as irredeemably a part of the dominant and hence needing a complete overhaul – if not reconstitution – into very different forms.

The Absorption and Incorporation of the Alternative

Within the commercial-popular news industry, policy-oriented commentary acknowledges the viability of alternative journalism, especially in the form of 'citizen journalism' as enabled by Internet-based capabilities. But, instead of seeking to battle this threat, the policy response of the commercial-popular news industry has been to plan for how to absorb and incorporate alternative journalism in such a way as to maintain if not strengthen its own commercial viability. For example, the Project for Excellence in Journalism (housed in the Graduate Program in Journalism at Columbia University) sees alternative journalism as, according to a 2007 industry report, 'something that the mainstream media embraced rather than something they saw as a threat' (Project for Excellence in Journalism, 2007b).

Arguments in favour of aggressively incorporating alternative journalism in the form of citizen journalism frequently cite the increasing shift in advertising media-buying to Internet properties. In the United States alone, $16.8 billion was spent in 2006 on online advertising – about 12 per cent of total advertising spending but a 34 per cent increase over 2005, with expectations of reaching $19.5 billion in 2007 (*eMarketer.com*, 2007; Johnson, 2007; Perez, 2007). Although still small in comparison to traditional media spending, the steady and accelerating migration of advertising revenue to online properties is the reason why further extensions of user contribution are being tried as a way to gain and maintain market shares. As a recent industry study puts it, 'analysts believe consumers will come to demand the ability to [not just talk with but] interact with the news producers, or they will migrate elsewhere' (Project for Excellence in Journalism, 2007b). Such an enhanced effort to engage audiences is a response to largely ineffectual earlier projects such as public journalism and civic journalism, which have been criticized both inside and outside the industry as patrician efforts to legitimize professionalism. (Scholarly studies and critiques include Black, 1997; Eksterowicz and Roberts, 2000; Haas and Steiner, 2006; Hardt, 2000; Rosen, 1996.)

The current policy promoted by the industry is to encourage popular participation, but in such a way as to leave unchallenged the partitioning of professional from popular contributions. News remains the province of professionals, whose adherence to accepted practices of reporting ensures the creation of dependable information consistent with the historical claims of bourgeois journalism. Professional journalists solicit and use 'views' as a way of enabling new forms of participation, of broadening a news organization into a hybrid news/social-networking organization: the result builds a more durable brand loyalty with audiences. Despite the many differences between 'hard news' and 'user-contributed content', what allows them to coexist is their potential usefulness in aggregating audiences to sell to advertisers and to form new markets for new kinds of products.

Such a policy objective can be seen in the deliberations of the International Press Institute (IPI), the largest industry consortium in the world, whose members consist of commercial communications companies. Established in 1950, its members are 'editors, media executives and leading journalists working for some of the world's most respected media outlets' in more than 120 countries (International Press Institute, 2007a, 2007b). Each year since its establishment, it holds what it calls a world congress and general assembly. A session at its 2006 congress titled 'The Rise of the Internet Journalist' put these issues and this policy objective in high relief.

Only one of the four presenters during the session did not come from a traditional news organization: Krishna Bharat, principal scientist for Google Inc., India, who had helped develop Google's online news aggregation service, Google News. It is notable that he was the only presenter of the four who saw no definitional problem in opening news organizations more thoroughly to popular participation. In the same way that existing news organizations should not fear Google's news aggregation service (not originating content but simply taking 'on-line traffic coming to Google and direct[ing] it to the many newspapers of the world'), they should not fear incorporating citizen journalism (Bharat, 2006: 28). Bharat suggests the way to do this is to encourage citizen journalists to rely on commercial news organizations. News companies could 'equip them with tools to capture news, and teach them the best practices of the profession' (p. 30). He cites as innovative examples the Korea-based organization *OhmyNews* and the US-based Internet and cable television service, CurrentTV.

Such advice is rapidly becoming orthodox. Media-industry consultants encourage media companies to 'embrace the audience as partners' and 'embrace customers as innovators' (Bowman and Willis, 2003: 59). Suggested ways of maintaining a central role in and creating a revenue stream through this 'empowerment' include providing an open-source style guide and training in journalistic techniques – the intention of which is to standardize and professionalize public contributions to make them better fit existing industry requirements while lessening the labour needed to incorporate them (p. 60).

However, the reaction of the other three panellists – all of whom are or were for a long time professional journalists – emphasized how compelling the traditions of bourgeois journalism and the necessity of protecting professionalism were in maintaining claims of authority. Emily Bent, editor-in-chief of the *Guardian Unlimited*, was much more wary of opening what has been the province of professionals to popular contributions. Instead of embracing popular participation in the gathering and writing of news, she proposed a conception of greater online participation as helping people form communities around content provided by the *Guardian*'s professional journalists. By doing so, she advocated a professional content provider that is also a social-networking site on which people could join in conversations with others about specific topics or viewpoints. Despite the hoped-for greater level of participation, the wall between the 'comment room' and the newsroom in this view remains high indeed (Bent, 2006: 31).

Dan Gillmor, former columnist for the *San Jose Mercury News* and founder and current director of the Centre for Citizen Media, sought to reassure attendees at the outset that his centre's agenda was not 'to replace, God forbid, the current big media' (Gillmor, 2006: 32). While he advocated more collaborative relationships between readers and professional journalists, Gillmor also advocated keeping distinct boundaries between them. Like that of Bent, Gillmor's vision of how commercial-popular journalism should survive – if not flourish – in the face of the threat from citizen journalism is that it should be structurally at the centre of public discourse. For Gillmor, 'rethinking the role of journalism' means simply to become as 'much guides as oracles, as much conveners of the conversations that our communities need to have with themselves as being the ones who totally set the agenda, or try to' (ibid.). Either way, as guides or as oracles, the news organization remains at the centre of public discussion.

In a revealing aside by way of conclusion, Gillmor noted what he considers to be the great unspoken concern of the international news industry: that of uncontrollable competition. He reminds his audience that the competition is not with bloggers in terms of who does better news, but with eBay, Craigslist and other Internet businesses entirely uninterested in news but competing for audiences and advertising revenue. Newspapers in the United States, he felt, were the 'canaries in this coal mine', serving as a warning to the world's media companies (ibid.).

Michael Jermey, editor with the UK's ITV Regional News and the last presenter in the session, concurred with Bent and Gillmor about the necessity of keeping a clear distinction between professional journalism and popular contributions. He readily acknowledged the importance of user-contributed video, which ITV and many other television news organizations incorporate into their coverage, noting in particular mobile-phone video of the aftermath both of the 2004 Indian Ocean tsunami and of the 7 July 2005 bombings in London.

To conceptually anchor a policy of firmly distinguishing the professional from the popular, Jermey distinguished the recording of events as they unfold ('eyewitness testimony, accurate eyewitness testimony, if you like, from cameras') from journalism, which for Jermey is not a recording but a professionalized, interpretive process of 'following up the facts, questioning things, taking it from different perspectives', and one that only professionals are skilled enough and in a position to do (Jermey, 2006: 33). Jermey sees the challenge for the industry as incorporating citizen journalism by selectively 'adopt[ing] some of the new trends' but also by 'bring[ing] them within the traditional media fold' instead of remaking the premises of professional (bourgeois) journalism to fit them (ibid.).

Many news organizations large and small maintain a sharp distinction between the professional and the popular as suggested by Bent, Gillmor and Jermey. One example is the US Cable News Network (CNN) and its 'i-Report' feature. While it consists entirely of popular contributions, these are not 'hard news' (which would threaten professionalism and undercut its claims to truth), but personal commentary and opinion, or recorded images that fit the eyewitness testimony role Jermey advocates. In addition to soliciting dramatic video footage of an event, a recent listing of desired contributions to i-Report include: personal interpretations of US presidential campaign debates; personal testimony regarding the effect of a drought that in late 2007 involved almost half of the continental United States; narratives of personal experiences of exploring underground caves; first-person breast-cancer survival stories; and pictures of pet dogs or cats dressed up for the Hallowe'en holiday (CNN, 2007). Like the commentary from the IPI session, substantial popular contributions are encouraged but ghettoized within a 'comment room' to maintain professionals' traditional claims to authority.

Whether or not news companies in the United States are the first to grapple with the challenges of absorption and incorporation, as Gillmor suggested in his panel presentation, the US news industry is pouring effort and capital into think-tank policy research concerning how best to incorporate alternative journalism, neutralize its challenge to professionalism and assess its economic value. As one of the largest US industry research organizations, the American Press Institute (API) underwrites a number of programmes, all of which focus on how best to incorporate alternative journalism and turn it into a revenue-producing division of existing news companies.

The Media Centre, which is the most aggressive API programme, describes itself as an organization designed 'to help the news industry devise strategies and tactics for digital media' (Media Center, 2007). Two publications outline the conceptual boundaries of its strategizing effort. The April 2005 issue of the Media Center's publication *Synapse* was devoted to 'The future of news'. Despite the confrontational (if not cocky) tone set on the cover, where industry executives were told to 'make way for a generation of [non-professional] storytellers who totally get it', the issue lays out in the second of 'Four Desperate Questions About the News Business' the relationship between ensuring profitability and encouraging a broadening, not of news itself (which challenges professionalization), but of conceptions of how to profit from the news business, which depends on extracting economic value from user-contributed content while clearly distinguishing it from professionalized content:

Old question:	How do we make money?
Really asking:	How do we continue doing what we've always done, [which is] maintain high margins, and control markets?
Should ask:	What are alternatives to the advertising subsidy? What business models can capitalize journalism-based businesses? What is the value proposition for new forms of journalism? (Media Center, 2005: 2)

Ways of realizing this policy vision go beyond encouraging popular contributions to developing 'voluntary ads, each relative to a consumer's wishes and desires, delivered at desired times through all forms of communication', as well as 'personal news networks in which skilled editors, producers and content managers deploy multi-media to inform each other' (ibid.). Here, too, these kinds of participation in no way challenge the professionalized basis of authoritative news.

While major news organizations seek to partition the professional from the popular, smaller organizations are developing more aggressive strategies of absorbing alternative journalism. Such strategies include a sometimes radical degree of convergence in which boundaries between, for example, reporters and advertising sales are breached if not ignored altogether. In the context of traditions of entrepreneurial small business, the high-tech sheen of the Internet and the allure of a personal hobby mushrooming into another billion-dollar property along the lines of MySpace, YouTube, or Facebook, smaller news businesses rarely question the legitimacy of blurring the distinction between reporting and selling. Indeed, a self-styled expert recommended that local citizen journalists also become local citizen advertising salespeople, who could earn an advertising commission while reporting a story (Outing, 2006a). Other citizen-journalism projects are experimenting with syndicating or franchising concepts and contents, and in some cases licensing citizen-journalism software (Outing, 2006b; Willis, 2006).

Present in all such efforts is a clear recognition of the social, political and economic value of extending user participation, suggesting the legitimacy (noted in Chapter 2) of merging business with social change. The benefits of doing so not only includes enabling a conversation with local residents, but also increasing one's share of local advertising revenue, forestalling competition, generating new sources of revenue, and 'reinforc[ing] your leadership position in your community' (Willis, 2006).

Finally, in addition to formulating policies for absorbing, incorporating and thus neutralizing the challenge of alternative journalism through ghettoizing popular contributions, or developing new sources of revenue from news businesses, a third kind of effort envisions a means of commercial support very different from traditional advertising sales. A US-based effort titled 'Journalism That Matters' consists of a series of policy development efforts funded by the Associated Press Managing Editors (APME). In a variety of meetings and events, selected media professionals, academics and media-business and media-reform consultants have discussed how best not simply to incorporate citizen journalism but to remake the basic structure of commercial news industries (Journalism That Matters, 2007a). The intention of the Journalism That Matters project is to 'engag[e] the entire system of journalism – reporters, editors, publishers, camera people, photographers and audience, from newspapers, radio, television, online media, including both mainstream and alternative sources – about the changing nature and definition of news in order to recommit to what is fundamental and to reinvent the means for connecting news with its audience' (Journalism That Matters, 2000).

At its most recent meeting, which took place in August 2007, 'journalists, academics and public advocates critiqued and built upon a 21st-century newsroom prototype – and worked to develop an economic model that supports it' (Journalism That Matters, 2007b). While the model maintains the professional/popular distinction, it seeks to infuse the news business with a civic ethic by creating in effect a privately managed but community-owned business, which would replace the imperative of maximizing profits with serving the community and stable, but modest, economic success. The draft policy plan sought to make a commercial news company 'less dependent upon advertising, [and] more dependent on revenue generated from adding value to news content. The Next Newsroom will be profitable, but margins will be modelled more on the expectations of a community trust or public utility' (Peck, 2007: 4).

Further in, the plan's author elaborated his conception:

> lower margin, community-based funding is the preferred model. Both new revenue sources and traditional revenue sources for newsrooms will be tapped. Content will be packaged, repackaged and resold to help generate revenue. Digital distribution platforms will be the norm, with any print products farmed out to other publishing houses. (Peck, 2007: 5)

Working capital would come from a community stock option plan with every household in the circulation area able to join: members would pay for access to various information services. Lower labour costs would be achieved by the free use of 'citizen-generated content that is hyper-local – names, faces, calendar events', although overseen by a professional staff that would also be engaged in original, traditional 'enterprise' reporting (Peck, 2007: 10). Start-up costs in a town of 200,000 with a college or university (an important source of intern labour) were estimated at $4.9 million for the first year, with projected revenues upon establishment of the organization at $6 million.

No matter the specific strategy, the basic industry policy on alternative journalism is absorption, incorporation and containment of the economic threat. A recent report by Dan Gillmor's Centre for Citizen Media summarizes the task bluntly: that success in securing significant user participation is not to boost democracy so much as to become 'the art of making people feel good about themselves by spending their time and money in a way that benefits you or your organization' (Williams et al., 2007). The industry policy direction can be encapsulated in the paradoxical advice of an industry consultant that 'you have to give up control to gain control' (cited in Bowman and Willis, 2005: 6).

A Challenge to the Dominant

By the mid-1990s, the erstwhile singular 'commercial alternative press' began to fragment under the pressures of commercial niche marketing, a process that can be seen clearly in the United States. While the 'old' alternative press had aged along with its 1960s cohort of readers, a new crop of publications emerged that one commentator of the day called 'alternatives to alternatives' and that had 'little in common with their forebears' (Gremillion, 1995). He explained differences in their coverage and orientation, which suggest differing commercial pressures as well as differing levels of acceptance of the premises of bourgeois journalism and thus policy directions for alternative journalism:

> [The 'new' alternatives] eschew hard news and traditional reporting in favour of satire and socio-cultural commentary; the original alternatives still revel in their roles as gadflies and watchdogs. The new papers only dabble in politics – mostly so-called 'identity politics', or what one might call Who-am-I? Politics – while the grown-ups of the alternative press wear their left-leaning idealism on their sleeves, even as they gear their coverage more and more toward comfortable suburbanites. (Gremillion, 1995)

Such a fragmentation suggests in turn a bifurcation in policies advocated by commercial alternative journalism, due to its no longer being a singular entity (if it ever was one). While the 'new' commercial alternative is less concerned with broad-based structural change and more concerned with enabling and protecting conditions amenable to self-expression, the 'old' commercial alternative press itself is divided further into two positions.

The first policy position is closely aligned with the commercial-popular news industry. It seeks strategies for supporting itself within the existing media system rather than for remaking it. The trade association American Alternative Newsweeklies (AAN), 'a diverse group of 130 alt-weekly news organizations that cover every major metropolitan area in North America', presents its brand identity as delivering unique kinds of content to niche audiences. In a pitch designed to entice niche marketers and their advertising, the AAN promotes the ability of its member news organizations to 'reach a print and online audience of more than 25 million young, educated, active and influential adults in the U.S. and Canada' (American Alternative Newsweeklies, 2007; see also Benson, 2003: 112). The organization promotes the niche-marketing value of its web portal, which delivers not only the 'latest news' but also news with 'a different perspective than what is generally found on wire-service and daily-newspaper websites' (American Alternative Newsweeklies, 2007).

The second policy position advocated by the 'old' alternative is to form an alternative-news system parallel with and to counterbalance the commercial-popular news system. The primary policy and strategic challenge is to gain enough financial support (increasingly from commercial sources) to counterbalance what is portrayed as a politically conservative cabal that has drowned out the diversity of voices with its own blaring monotone.

An example of an 'old' alternative adherent of this view is the Independent Media Institute. As one of the content services overseen by this umbrella organization, AlterNet.org lists as its primary challenge to confront the 'right-wing media machine', noting that 'when compared to the radical conservatives and the religious fundamentalists, the progressive sector lacks media capacity' (AlterNet, 2007). It sees its task as helping 'build the progressive echo chamber that will fight back', hoping to become in essence a mirror image of the despised right-wing media (ibid.).

By contrast to the Journalism That Matters proposal already discussed (Peck, 2007), which seeks an integrative organization with relationships throughout a community (although one professionally managed and driven by nostalgia for a vision of small-town America), AlterNet.org's vision seems much more centralized and sectored, if not vanguard. For example, it seeks to 'provide multimedia content, engage our readers in two-way communications, gather reader-generated content, and respond to breaking news with our various blogs', activities already engaged in by a majority of commercial news organizations if not already surpassed by some (AlterNet, 2007).

Reform of the Dominant

Closely aligned with the policy goal of producing a countervailing media system is often the twin policy of seeking to reform or remake the dominant media system. The range here too is quite wide, including calls for mild as well as substantial changes. Despite the range, the key policy goal is not only to help support individual projects of alternative journalism, but more broadly to support media criticism, particularly that variety which focuses on the regulatory framework within which alternative journalism operates (particularly in its electronic variety).

What links the many and various efforts at media reform is a faith in journalism. When unfettered by commercial interests, it is able to pursue its traditional watchdog role envisioned by bourgeois journalism. For example, the recent emphasis in media-reform efforts in many countries is on remaking the regulatory environment to minimize the effects of ownership concentration. In one sense, then, the policy of media reform is quite traditional, as claims about the dangers of concentration of ownership and the resulting narrowing of the range of views have long been a staple of media criticism. While combined industry/academy efforts to rethink media organization from top to bottom work at the level of a single community and do not recognize larger limits and pressures (Peck, 2007), the policy direction of media-reform efforts that seek to help support alternative journalism focuses on structural determinations.

While a number of organizations engage in media reform and criticism, a prominent umbrella organization in the United States that plays a major role in advocating media reform and that can serve as one example here is Free Press, which describes itself as 'a national nonpartisan organisation working to increase informed public participation in crucial media policy debates, and to generate policies that will produce a more competitive and public interest-oriented media system with a strong nonprofit and noncommercial sector' (Free Press, 2007a). (For a list of 167 US and international organizations involved in various aspects of media reform, see Free Press, 2007e.)

Anchoring its rationale in language that recalls the United Nations Universal Declaration of Human Rights, Free Press focuses its efforts on the institutional and infrastructural areas of 'media ownership; independent and public media; internet freedom; and media reform movement building' (Free Press, 2007b). It regards the key problem of commercial media systems – particularly within the United States – as not solely 'media owners who are especially despicable and who abuse their market power and privileges to enhance their own personal fortunes or to push their narrow political agendas' or 'media corporation employees – be they journalists, writers, actors, executives or whatever – who engage in dubious ethical behaviour', but much more importantly 'the structure of the media system [that] makes socially dubious behaviour – e.g. lousy journalism, violent and mindless entertainment, hypercommercialism – the rational outcome' (Free Press, 2007d). Thus, just as the problem is seen as structural, the resulting policy of media reform must be structurally oriented as well: 'If we wish to change the nature of media content, we need to change the cues so that good journalism and quality material will be the rational product of its operations. To do that requires that we change the government policies that shape and direct the media system' (Free Press, 2007d).

In addition to regulatory reform and adequate antitrust protections, specific ways of meeting these policies include 'carefully' regulating advertising and commercialism and welcoming 'strong democratic trade unions [as] an important and mandatory protection for the public against concentrated commercial media power' (Free Press, 2007c). Such protections are intended to contribute to greater diversity in views, which in turn is seen to 'lead to a more participatory and accountable government and to more sustainable policies and practices regarding national and global development' (Free Press, 2007a).

The activities of organizations such as Free Press are paralleled by closely aligned philanthropic foundations. One example is the Social Science Research Council, which seeks through its 'Media, Technology and Culture' policy initiative to address how 'technologies and structure of the media are transforming public life in the U.S. and around the world' (Social Science Research Council, 2007a). Developments such as 'advances in digital technologies, the concentration of media ownership, the privatisation of communications infrastructures, and the expansion of intellectual property regimes' generate pressing questions such as 'What do these developments mean for a democratic society? What does a rich democratic culture look like under these new conditions of public life and how can we achieve it?' (ibid.). Among its funded initiatives to address such issues is one titled 'Necessary Knowledge for a Democratic Public Sphere', which seeks to 'build a culture of collaboration between researchers, advocates, and activists that can strengthen that knowledge infrastructure' and thus increase understanding of how best to remake the communications infrastructure (Social Science Research Council, 2007b).

Other foundations have greater scale and reach. For example, as part of its 'Knowledge, Creativity & Freedom' initiative, the Ford Foundation identifies 'media, arts and culture' as a key area of interest. To enable a 'free and responsible media that address important civic and social issues', it 'promotes policies and regulations that ensure media and information systems serve the public's diverse constituencies and interests' (Ford Foundation, 2007). In addition to the focus on remaking the structure of communications (which shape alternative journalism), the foundation also 'support[s] high-quality productions that enrich public dialogue on such core issues as building democratic values and pluralism' (ibid.). As part of its perceived global mandate, the foundation maintains offices in ten major cities of the world to administer this policy programme.

Policy objectives of other major philanthropic foundations also place high emphasis on media reform on a global as opposed to national scale and they support similar programmes. The Open Society Institute, established by capitalist-turned-philanthropist George Soros, also supports among its initiatives one defined as 'media, arts and culture' (Open Society Institute, 2007a). Like the Ford Foundation, it places emphasis on assisting what are in effect alternative journalism projects that typically focus on a specific topic, such as the October 2007 crackdown on public assembly and protest in Myanmar (Open Society Institute, 2007b). In addition to funding a wide variety of infrastructure-building and topical projects, the sub-initiative labelled the 'Media Program' provides assistance to 'media outlets that promote democratic values and demonstrate through their editorial approach a high level of professionalism, independence, and openness', as well as financing 'training aimed at current or future media professionals, including instruction in professional skills and in-depth reporting on specialized areas' (Open Society Institute, 2007c). In sum, the policy that guides efforts such as these seeks through combinations of structural reform and financial assistance to build the resources and effectiveness of alternative journalism projects as a way of reforming the dominant through example, criticism and regulatory change.

Subverting the Dominant

Despite their great number and diversity, policy positions centred on absorption and incorporation, the production of a parallel system, or the reform of the existing system all share an organizational if not an institutional basis. By contrast, there exists a policy position that advocates the oppositional aim not only of subverting – if not dissolving – the present practice of alternative journalism (inflected as it often is with the heritage of bourgeois journalism that has worked so well for the dominant in ways described in Chapter 1), but also of developing new conceptions of authoritative representation.

This final position embraces the modernist critique of bourgeois journalism discussed in Chapter 1; it is the most radical and the least institutionalized of all those discussed here. In many of its manifestations, the line between policy proposal, philosophy and personal aesthetic can become impossible to determine. Instead of carefully formulated logical frameworks, views and proposals for subverting or dissolving the dominant persist in scattered, diffuse and popular forms, more often through practice than in the form of a rational policy statement or spirited manifesto. Commentators on these popular forms and their practice seek to weave them perhaps too expertly into plausible positions that, through the alchemy of generalization and paraphrase, also express what can be taken as a policy position (if by that is meant a view of the nature and importance of alternative journalism). While rationalist efforts at reporting are seen to obscure as much as they purport to reveal, modernist efforts do not simply propose to do better journalism. Rather, many also propose modifying or dissolving the authority of journalism itself as a form of authoritative knowledge. As one example, Strangelove (2005) discusses the 'subversion of commercial news' through 'online journalism'. There is no centrally developed policy that can be pointed to and paraphrased, but this absence is precisely the point. There is no validating, coordinating centre of this activity that can formulate – much less enact – an explicit policy in the first place. Instead, the 'policy' of subverting commercial news through online journalism is a diffuse activity of popular culture, much like samizdat discussed in Chapter 2.

This online, popular 'journalism' (the word should be used loosely) goes beyond broadening available viewpoints to express a 'revolt against commercially produced meanings and a general disregard for the notion of private property', whatever the content of specific items (Strangelove, 2005: 162). While such a challenge focuses on matters of structure, as do NGO and philanthropic efforts at media reform, Strangelove argues that the diffuse popular culture of online journalism goes further by ignoring a basic assumption of capitalist society (in this case, the private ownership and control of expression), upon which bourgeois journalism and its claims to authority rest.

What helps substantiate such a claim is a reminder of just how widespread these activities are. Whether combinations of 'event recording, event commentary, [or] criticism of commercial news itself', they constitute a reformulation of what it means to do journalism: in particular, they reject the intervention of commercial organizations (however friendly they may be) in assisting or otherwise enabling popular production (Strangelove, 2005: 165). The degree to which such corporate 'help' is unnecessary is suggested by the 'vast majority of individuals' who are engaged in such activity and who 'do so outside of formal corporate structures, institutional settings, and systems of economic reward' (ibid.).

The range of sites and forms through which these activities are pursued is equally vast. Popular 'news-related discourse takes place in discussion groups [...], on Web sites and Web logs, through peer-to-peer file-exchange programs, instant messaging, and audio/video online broadcasting' (Strangelove, 2005: 172). The forms of discourse are staggering: they range from 'rants to investigative journalism, independent media centres, group authorship, news commentary and analysis, satire, and the outpouring of collective event reporting and commentary that takes place surrounding mass events' (ibid.). While Strangelove's account tends at times to be repetitious and its conclusions (such as that satire is a clearly oppositional practice) have been outpaced since its publication, the point is well taken regarding the depth of challenge to conceptions of professionals as arbiters of quality, as well as to commercial companies as the owners of 'news'. Such a 'policy' can be read from the implications of this practice of popular culture.

A second account discusses a variety of efforts to turn away from bourgeois journalism altogether and to reconstitute what 'authoritative accounts' might be: 'to try to imagine the public and public space in ways other than what the traditional "independence [from the market] versus co-optation [by the market]" binary might afford' (Harold, 2007: xxii). One example deserves to be summarized in some detail, for it illustrates a way of working within the terms of commercial media in order to say something not only critical but also compelling about them. This example would hardly meet the traditional definitional yardstick of 'journalism', but that again is precisely the point. Although it does not fulfil the standards of the traditional form, it nevertheless reveals insights into how, in this case, hypercommercialized journalism works.

In 1976, New York performance artist Joey Skaggs wrote and distributed press releases to local media while also placing a classified advertisement in the *Village Voice* about his new business, a 'Cathouse for Dogs'. The advertisement promised (in salty language) the joys to be had by dogs who were looking for a quick fling. It concluded: 'no weirdoes, please. Dogs only. By appointment' and a phone number. As Harold summarizes, Skaggs then 'set up a storefront and hired actors to play the "doggie pimps" for his phoney cathouse' (Harold, 2007: 75).

While sounding in paraphrase like nothing more than an undergraduate prank, the media attention it attracted exceeded all expectations. In addition to visits by several local television stations who sent camera crews, a national news programme had heard about it and wanted Skaggs's help in producing a segment on its news show. Skaggs provided the network with a generic video clip of dogs mating, and an interview. With this material, network editors produced 'a standard wraparound news piece – interview, footage, interview – and aired it in a larger story about animal abuse' (Harold, 2007: 75). Later, after Skaggs was threatened with lawsuits and the documentary programme that featured the cathouse was nominated for an Emmy Award, Skaggs publicly revealed his hoax, thus ending the project.

What does this hoax have to do with alternative journalism? Its relevance is in how it graphically revealed some central characteristics of journalism in a capitalist society – and in a way slightly less dry than a turgid 3000-word commentary. It displayed keen knowledge of the commercial imperatives that drive news programmes towards the offbeat and sensational isolated event, about the often thin evidence used to support claims made in a news story and about the cumulative construction of credibility in the collective news agenda (that once a story appears, the more it is cited or alluded to, the greater and greater legitimacy it acquires). Finally, the import of the hoax lay in the fact that it did not take the form of a thoroughly reported investigative story or well-reasoned, logically organized journalistic commentary. It thus demonstrated that journalism has no monopoly on truth and that forms of representation other than journalism have as great a potential of revealing our world to us.

5

CONTEMPORARY PRACTICES OF ALTERNATIVE JOURNALISM

The study of alternative media is dominated by an approach that focuses on their political value and, in particular, on the capacity of alternative media to empower citizens. Central to empowerment is the opportunity for 'ordinary' people to tell their own stories without the formal education or professional expertise and status of the mainstream journalist. This approach is relevant not only to politicized alternative media, but to cultural media such as fanzines and zines. However, the study of the working practices of alternative media is absent from most research in the field. To study the practices of alternative journalism, we need to examine the social and political processes such as organizational methods and ideological disputes. We also need to examine the ways in which people work. How do they learn to become journalists or editors? How do they identify and choose their stories? How do they select and represent their sources? Are alternative journalists truly independent, or are their working methods influenced by the practices of mainstream journalists? These questions about media practice require an understanding of its practitioners: their values, motivations, attitudes, ideologies, history, education and relationships. In other words, this is to examine what Pierre Bourdieu terms habitus (Bourdieu, 1993). The habitus of practitioners plays an important part in how they participate in the social arena of media production (Bourdieu's field). While it is possible to conceptualize alternative media production as a field in its own right (Atton, 2002a), it is important to consider that the habitus of alternative journalists might be developed from their experience of mainstream media. (We shall discuss Bourdieu's work in more detail in Chapter 7.)

We have already seen in Chapter 3 that the 'classic' form of alternative media consists of projects that tend to be edited, written and run by non-professionals. Downing (1984) has highlighted a general political perspective of social anarchism that informs and drives such media practices. Downing explicitly places the organization of radical media (his term for politicized alternative media) and their journalistic practices in opposition to a construction of mainstream media that is largely monolithic, centred on profit-making, hierarchical organization and a practice of journalism that, by dint of its routinization and codification as a profession, is implicitly exclusive.

At the same time, and as we show throughout this book, we do not want to perpetuate a binary opposition between alternative and mainstream media. Some features of alternative media practices have not simply broken with mainstream practices, they have often sought to radically redefine them. Though alternative media have found ways of doing journalism that are radical to the extent that they mark dramatic ruptures from existing practices of journalism, their work may draw on existing forms (such as tabloid journalism) and methods (such as investigative journalism). Atton (2002a) has argued that the use of tabloid forms of address (colloquial language, humour, the apparent trivialization of subject matter, the brevity of texts) presents radical opinions in a populist manner that subverts the existing models of tabloid journalism (normally employed to maintain conservative news agendas). These radical forms connect historically with earlier, radical forms of journalism that predate the commercialized and capitalized forms of journalism that are normally considered the originating sites of tabloid journalism (Williams, 1970). Radical journalism developed from social movements thus represents 'social' media that emphasize a communicative democracy based on a 'media commons' rather than on a segregated, elitist and professionalized occupational activity. Hamilton (2003) has taken this argument still further, finding examples of these participatory media as far back as early-modern England.

In this chapter, we shall explore the nature of alternative journalism. We provide an overview of genres and story types such as news, investigative journalism, political commentary, eyewitness reporting and cultural journalism. We also examine broader issues such as ethics, objectivity, representation and sourcing practices, and reliability and credibility. In doing so, we will inevitably need to explore the relationship between alternative and mainstream media practices. Some alternative journalism not only employs populist methods of presentation that resemble the practices of tabloid journalism, it also challenges conventional notions of expertise and authority, particularly in their foregrounding of 'ordinary' people as sources of news. This foregrounding is not without its problems, though: who is to say that these sources might not be used ideologically? However novel their content might appear, alternative media are not as independent of mainstream media ideologies and practices as we might think. Some of the issues that face alternative journalists are not so dissimilar from those facing journalists in the mainstream, while some are specific to alternative media, resulting from those media's intellectual, political and moral standpoints. The latter largely centre on issues of representation and objectivity, particularly developed from the structural and cultural characteristics of radical media, and the radicalizing of journalistic practices through notions such as 'active witnessing'.

Alternative journalists practise across a range of media: newspapers and magazines, as well as local, community-based radio and television stations (Howley, 2005). Broadcast media require technical competence and training, so alternative journalists often need technical and professional support. Dependence on technical expertise leaves fewer opportunities for citizens to participate in production, reducing their contributions to an advisory level, particularly in television (Rushton, 1993). The availability of domestic camcorders and computerized video-editing packages, particularly when used not for conventional broadcasting but for producing videos, DVDs and web-streaming, have minimized the reliance on professional expertise (Harding, 1997). Arguably, the Internet has allowed the greatest expansion in alternative journalism. Notwithstanding enduring barriers to access in many parts of the world, user-driven programmes enable the set-up of websites and discussion groups with minimal technical expertise.

Our discussion of contemporary practices draws on alternative journalism in print, such as community media, fanzines and social movement media. We pay particular attention to online practices such as blogs and the participatory news reporting on sites such as Wikinews and Indymedia. It is to these that we turn first.

Participatory Online News Reporting

The most prevalent function of alternative news is to fill the gaps that its reporters believe have been left by the mainstream media. These gaps are due in part to the increasingly conglomerated nature of commercialized news production, where centralization and bureaucratization result in a standardized and limited repertoire of news across the range of media platforms, such as News Corporation's Fox News and its many print media outlets (Hackett and Carroll, 2006). It is also due to the professionalized nature of journalism, where newsgathering and assessments of newsworthiness are routinized to such an extent that news production relies on repeated formulas. These formulas include story structures (such as the inverted pyramid), sourcing routines that emphasize elite groups in society and news values that privilege events over explanation. Mainstream news is often placed in a context where issues and rationales are presented as largely fixed and motionless (Braudel's (1980) notion of *longue durée*); the emphasis on timeliness reduces news to events within the 24-hour news cycle (Braudel's *histoire événementielle*).

The Internet has made possible two complementary practices that challenge these routines and formulas. First, alternative media sites are able to monitor news output from an immense range of providers, including commercial organizations and other alternative media projects. Second, this monitoring can be undertaken by large numbers of people, who are then able to 'analyse, evaluate, and discuss the information' (Bruns, 2006: n.p.). In contrast to the gatekeeping that is traditionally the preserve of the professional journalist, Bruns (2005) calls this process 'gatewatching'. An alternative news network such as the global Indymedia project gatewatches the output of both mainstream and other alternative media and re-presents selections from that output in ways that encourage comparison and criticism. Indymedia's coverage of the 9/11 attacks in 2001 brought together selections that implicitly critiqued one another while also providing users of the network with material for their own critiques (Atton, 2003e). At the same time, Indymedia provided first-hand accounts from people who had experienced the attacks. Eyewitness reporting is a key feature of Indymedia. It is particularly prominent in the network's news coverage of local and international protests. Most – if not all – Indymedia reporters are activists; the accounts they post to the network, along with video clips and photographs, provide a counter-report from 'the other side of the barricades'; rather than rely on professional journalists to tell their stories, they become 'recorders of their own reality, empowered as participators in the very construction of their own media' (Atton, 2002a: 115).

The participation of large numbers of activists and enthusiasts contributes to a journalism that is open-ended and multiperspectival. Internet-based projects such as Indymedia and the technology news site Slashdot have developed a multiperspectival journalism that brings together breaking news, eyewitness reporting and commentary. It is a journalism that does not depend on the division between producer and consumer; the alternative journalist is both reporter and activist. The news and commentary produced by Indymedia journalists is 'information for action' (Atton, 2002a: 85); these reporters may be thought of as a hybrid, as 'produsers' (Bruns, 2006: n.p.). The multiple reports (often of the same event or issue) are made possible by editorial practices that are very different from the hierarchical practices of mainstream media. Most Indymedia sites operate a practice of open publishing, where all submissions are published. By contrast, Slashdot's editors decide which stories to publish, though there are sites inspired by Slashdot (such as Kuro5hin and Plastic) where registered users can suggest changes to stories and can vote on which stories will be published on the site (Bruns, 2006). This method resembles the open editorial practices of the British radical community press of the 1970s examined by the Minority Press Group (1980).

Despite these differences, the publication of multiple voices promotes a very different notion of the place of news in the formation of public opinion from that of the mainstream media. Heikkila and Kunelius (2002) term this 'deliberative journalism'. Instead of news, commentary and opinion being presented within a limited set of frames – such as the political view-point of a single news provider or the liberal ideology of the journalist as gatekeeper – Heikkila and Kunelius argue that public deliberation should begin with a journalism that 'underscores the variety of ways to frame an issue' (n.p.), rather than presenting an issue already framed in a particular and exclusive way. It is from this multiperspectival approach to news, they argue, that the formation of public opinion should begin.

This view is not shared by all participatory news projects. Wikinews encourages multiple contributors and – like its Wikipedia counterpart – allows any user to edit its content. However, Wikinews also seeks to reduce the multiple perspectives of its contributors into a single, coherent narrative. It places an emphasis on factual reporting and suppresses commentary and opinion. Its ideology of the neutral point of view resembles the objectivity of mainstream journalism, although the synthesis of multiple perspectives, Wikinews argues, leads to a 'more inclusive and unbiased [narrative] than is offered by the mainstream media' (Bruns, 2006: n.p.). Nevertheless, Wikinews resembles mainstream news in its unidirectional flow from writer to reader; because commentary and discussion of the news is forbidden, there are none of the multiple conversations that characterize Indymedia and Slashdot.

A social networking site such as MySpace or the consumer-generated content in Amazon's review sections present a different notion of partici-patory cultural production, one where opinions, experiences and tastes are instances and extensions of everyday life rather than expressions of engage-ment in political life and the public sphere. To what extent are these exam-ples of alternative journalism? All the examples of alternative journalism in this book are deliberate media practices. That is to say, the practitioners demonstrate awareness that what they are doing is media practice. Whether they see themselves as journalists, political activists or subcultural or counter-cultural commentators, they are producing media content within some his-torical context (such as a history of radical media, of protest, of popular music). Contributors to MySpace or amateur reviewers on Amazon are superficially similar to fanzine writers, insofar as they are amateur critics and commentators on popular culture. However, there are two major dif-ferences between these groups. First, fanzine writers work within a frame-work that is entirely independent of the mainstream media. Whether, as with Indymedia, this is through an Internet site or in the pages of a printed publication, the project as a whole may be characterized as alternative. The contributors to MySpace or Amazon are writing in a setting that is not of their making, that is carefully controlled, policed even. Do they consider themselves as journalists at all? Are their contributions simply extensions of bar room conversations? Perhaps these forms of writing are better thought of as background (the stuff of everyday life) rather than foreground (a deliberate act of journalism). Perhaps the cultural commentary found in social networking sites is, as Weigert puts it, part of the 'taken-for-granted reality which provides the unquestioned background of meaning for each person's life' (Weigert, 1981: 36). Perhaps this is too dismissive: after all, the fanzine writer too is supremely concerned with writing about ordinary experience.

Fanzines as Alternative Cultural Journalism

Fanzine writers share much with their professional counterparts, cultural journalists. There is a significant similarity between the fan as amateur writer and the professional writer as fan. This says much about expert culture in popular musical criticism, for example, where knowledge and authority proceed not from formal, educational or professional training but primarily from autodidactic, amateur enthusiasm. Simon Frith (1996: 38, n. 40) argues that 'critics of popular forms (TV, film and to some extent pop) need know nothing about such forms except as consumers; their skill is to be able to write about ordinary experience'. Once again, we see the privileging of the 'ordinary' voice. In the case of fanzines, however (and their online counterparts, ezines), these ordinary voices tend to be self-selected, rather than sought out and encouraged as in the alternative local press.

Fanzine journalism shares with its professionalized counterpart a perspective based on consumption, but this is not to say that the two forms are identical. Fanzines often arise because the objects of their study (which includes football, film, comics and popular television series, as well as popular music) are ignored by mainstream journalism. This might be due to the novelty of the performer or genre (fanzines often draw attention to new and emerging cultural activities) or because they have become unfashionable (Atton, 2001). Fanzines also challenge critical orthodoxy; they may arise because their writers believe that 'their' culture is marginalized or misrepresented by mainstream tastes. Unlike the local alternative press, fanzines offer opportunities to create, maintain and develop taste communities across geographic boundaries. They are less interested in reaching out to broader audiences, preferring to cultivate and consolidate a specialist audience. This consolidation often employs similar methods to mainstream cultural journalism such as interviews and reviews (or match reports, in the case of football fanzines). Fanzine writers, however, tend to write at much greater length than the 'capsule' reviews that are now common in newspapers and specialist, commercial magazines. In some cases, particularly in ezines, a kaleidoscopic approach is obtained by publishing multiple accounts of the same event or product, just as Indymedia does with accounts of protests and demonstrations. The credibility and authority of a music fanzine often enables it to obtain interviews from artists directly, bypassing public-relations professionals.

The fanzine is dominated by comment and opinion. Editorial comment and personal columns are common, as are satire, jokes and cartoons. Newsgathering is a different matter. Fanzines often have erratic publishing schedules; this infrequency militates against the timely reporting of news. The move of many fanzines to the Internet has enabled them to take advantage of increased periodicity and hyperlinking to develop news strands as standard. A study of online British football fanzines (Atton, 2006b) identified three typical approaches to news: stories reproduced verbatim from professional news media; stories summarized from the professional media; and original journalism. The latter was in the minority and usually embedded in interviews. Hard news stories were usually sourced from commercial news providers. Unlike local alternative journalism, there was no evidence of original, investigative reporting. Instead, the fanzines drew mostly on local and national mainstream media, as well as press releases from the football clubs. There was little evidence of agenda-setting. Generally, then, news in football fanzines is dominated by stories from commercial news providers. The dominant model is the editing and republishing of mass media sources.

The lack of original news reporting is not necessarily a weakness. As John Hartley (2000) has pointed out, public communication is becoming increasingly redactional. There is an emphasis on reduction, revision, preparation, editing and publishing; journalism as original writing is less prominent. The specialist audience might be well served by the news digests produced by football fanzines. These digests provide a backdrop against which the primary function of the fanzine is presented: expert, amateur commentary and opinion founded on the accumulation and display of detailed information.

Blogs and Bloggers

In its ideal form, the blog combines the individual approach often found in fanzines with the social responsibility of local alternative journalism. Bloggers present their narratives, news and commentary from the perspective of the individual. Blogs may describe the everyday minutiae of the writer's life, or may function as journalism, and therefore may be understood as comprising a number of practices. These include the publishing of personal diaries by professionals (such as journalists and politicians); amateur investigative journalism, comment and opinion (such as American Matt Drudge's *Drudge Report* and the British blogger, 'Guido Fawkes'); and eyewitness reporting by observers and participants. Amateur blogs have been credited with breaking news in advance of mainstream news organizations: for example, Trent Lott's resignation as the US Senate's majority leader in December 2002 followed his comments expressing 'indulgence towards the racist policies of the Old South' (Burkeman, 2002). These comments, Burkeman notes, were first picked up and commented on by bloggers some days before the mainstream media ran the story. The Gulf War of 2003 saw a variety of bloggers supplementing mainstream media coverage. 'Smash', the pseudonym of an American military officer serving in Iraq, posted chronicles of his experiences (Kurtz, 2003).

This journalism focuses less on the journalist as professional expert; instead it proposes a relationship between writer and reader where episte-mological claims may be made about the status of journalism and its prac-titioners (Matheson, 2004). This has less to do with the novelty of the knowledge being produced (a focus on uncovering 'hidden' stories). Instead, it suggests new ways of thinking about and producing journalism (a focus on what kinds of knowledge are produced and how readers and writers may come together to make sense of them). The blog has become both an alter-native and a mainstream practice. Lowrey (2006) has argued that the incor-poration of blogs into professional journalism 'repairs' the perceived vulnerabilities of professional journalists. Considering bloggers as occupa-tional rivals, professional journalists reassess their professional processes. However, the incorporation of the blogs into news organizations and the use of bloggers as sources are not the only possible strategies: 'the journalism community may try to redefine blogging as journalistic tool, and bloggers as amateur journalists or journalism wannabes (rather than as a unique occu-pation)' (Lowrey, 2006: 493).

We shall now throw these practices into sharper relief against the back-ground of their dominant, mainstream versions. A useful perspective to adopt is that of ethics: how do the norms of alternative journalism help us to understand, for example, the status of alternative journalists and their place in society, their methods and their approach to content? We will begin with what is surely the fundamental issue – as it has become for the pro-fession of journalism as a whole: the ideology of objectivity.

Objectivity Revisited

The professional ideal of objectivity, understood as the separation of 'facts' from 'values', may be considered the key ethical dimension of journalistic practice. Schudson (1978, 2001) locates the emergence of this normative practice in the American press of the 1920s and 1930s. This was due, he argues, to two separate, but linked, social forces. The first was rooted in 'popular disillusionment with state propaganda campaigns' and 'a wariness of "official" channels of information' (Allan, 1999: 24). If 'reality' could no longer be reliably constructed from officialdom, then a more 'rational' method was needed. This was found in the second social force, that of scientific rationalism. Journalism at this time was aligning itself as a profession alongside science, the law and medicine, thus it appeared 'natural' that it should draw for its rigour on the scientific method employed by those professions. The results, as Allan emphasizes, were swift and enduring. Specialized 'beats' emerged, and with them came the expert journalism and the bylined report. Investigative reporting and interviewing flourished; "'impersonal", fact-centred techniques of observation' (Allan, 1999: 25) informed these practices, with the consequent rise of the columnist whose work was clearly separated from 'the news', and who was allowed the freedom to engage in value-driven writing.

Though as Schudson reminds us, the rise of objectivity as an ideology was never a merely technical exercise, not

> just a claim about what kind of knowledge is reliable. It is also a moral philosophy, a declaration of what kind of thinking one should engage in, in making moral decisions. It is, moreover, a political commitment, for it provides a guide to what groups one should acknowledge as relevant audiences for judging one's own thoughts and acts. (Schudson, 1978: 8)

Practitioners of alternative journalism have both recognized the moral and political nature of objectivity and have directed their work to revealing its premises in their work, the better through practice to challenge its central assumptions: that it is possible in the first place to separate facts from values and that it is morally and politically preferable to do so. Such challenges are not the sole province of alternative journalists; neither are they new. The Glasgow University Media Group's (GUMG) work stands as a significant project exploring the concatenation of facts and values in television news reporting that still considers itself objective and impartial (Eldridge, 2000). Journalists in alternative media, however, seek to challenge objectivity and impartiality from both an ethical and a political standpoint in their own journalistic practices. Amongst practitioners in the US and the UK at least, the power to do so in recent decades has come not from the critical media studies of such as GUMG but from American scholars whose prime expertise lies elsewhere. The radical political essays of American dissidents such as Noam Chomsky and Edward Said (especially Chomsky) continue to be cited in alternative media as the major demystifiers of the objectivity of the US corporate media. From these accounts (for example, Chomsky, 1989; Said, 1981), alternative journalists have begun to finish the story, so to speak. Convinced by and sympathetic to such notions as Chomsky's 'worthy and unworthy victims' and the systematic and long-standing pro-Zionist coverage in the American media at the expense of Arab (specifically Palestinian Arab) voices, these journalists have sought to expose the moral claims of their mainstream counterparts. We may consider this stance a supremely ethical one, for it seeks to present through radical journalistic practices moral and political correctives to the 'fact-centred techniques' that have been found to be just as value-laden as the 'pre-objective' journalism they sought to replace. But what ethical issues do these radical practices bring with them? What does being an alternative journalist mean in ethical terms?

Alternative media are characterized by their explicitly partisan character. In the language of ethics, they exhibit clear biases, yet they proclaim their selectivity and their bias, and generally have little interest in 'balanced reporting'. What may we find in such practices that makes them different from, say, the tabloid newspaper that exhibits clear and consistent bias against asylum seekers or the gay and lesbian communities, as many British tabloids continue to do? The dominant moral argument within alternative media has two aspects. First, alternative media projects tend to be set up in order to counter what alternative journalists consider an already biased set of reports. Sceptical of what counts as balance in the mainstream media, they seek to set up their own counterbalance. Hence, the argument runs, the viewpoints already dominant in the mainstream media do not need repeating. What appears as bias and the absence of balance in the alternative media is to be considered not as a set of absolute truths; instead it comprises a set of accounts told from different perspectives. The practice of alternative journalism thus enacts Edgar's (1992: 120) claim that 'journalism cannot be objective, for that presupposes that an inviolable interpretation of the event as action exists prior to the report'. These stories might well use official or semi-official sources in the public domain that have been ignored by mainstream journalism, such as the investigative journalism of *CovertAction Quarterly* in the US and the 'parapolitical' journal *Lobster* in the UK. For example, in 1995 the US journal *CovertAction Quarterly* published an extensive feature on British military tactics to target Republican teenagers in Northern Ireland. *Lobster* was the first to break the story about Colin Wallace and 'Operation Clockwork Orange', the MI5 plot to destabilize the Wilson government.

Second, alternative journalism seeks to invert the 'hierarchy of access' (Glasgow University Media Group, 1976: 245) to the news by explicitly foregrounding the viewpoints of 'ordinary' people (activists, protesters, local residents): citizens whose visibility in the mainstream media tends to be obscured by the presence of elite groups and individuals. Story-telling by those who are normally actors in other people's stories conflates these emblematic types of journalism and challenges the expert culture of both the news journalist and the 'expert' columnist.

The alternative media emphasize a humanistic set of journalistic values that are far removed from either the scientistic attempts at objective reporting or the persistence of the ideological necessity of objectivity. Alternative journalists enact social-responsibility journalism with an important difference. Unlike the social-responsibility journalism attempted in the US, culminating (for the present) in the public journalism movement, alternative journalists do not inhabit the mainstream: where public journalism seeks to effect change from within current practices and organizational regimes, alternative journalism seeks to do so free of the constraints on the development of social responsibility in mainstream journalism (Davis, 2000; Woodstock, 2002).

There is a strong ethical dimension to the organization and production of alternative media. Advertising is largely rejected, for fear that publications will be influenced by external forces (though many publications do take advertising for products and services they approve of, such as those for similar publications and the products of ethically trading companies). The notion of proprietorial influence is quite foreign to alternative media, given that most are run democratically and co-operatively by the media workers themselves. If the loyalties we find in mainstream media tend to be absent, in their place we find loyalties that centre on 'community', whether a community of interest or an 'actually lived', local community. The journalists place themselves firmly within such communities, espousing a loyalty that proceeds both from specific causes or ideologies and from the particular, activist communities in which they are actors. Such loyalties are increasingly established on a transnational scale (as we find in the global Indymedia network). As Harcup has pointed out in his examination of journalism ethics within the mainstream, this is a significant loyalty that can often be overlooked: 'the journalist as citizen, with a sense of loyalty to other citizens' (Harcup, 2002: 103). It is this loyalty, this concern with citizens, and especially with making the voices of those citizens heard, that drives much alternative journalism and has resulted in a particular ethics of representation.

Active Witnessing and Representation

'Active witnessing' (Couldry, 2000: 37) is particularly found in the journalism of new social movements, where subjective testimony and eyewitness reporting dominate and the subjects of news stories are represented by themselves. The journalism thus produced 'situates the activist in both the texts they produce and in the sociopolitical contexts in which they place them (and are themselves placed)' (Atton, 2002a: 113). An illuminating instance of this practice is a video report produced for *Undercurrents* by

'Jen', an activist for the Campaign Against Arms Trade (Atton, 2002a: 113–114). Her piece presents her as advocate for arms control, an activist campaigner, a commentator and an investigative reporter, emphasizing the hybrid nature of much alternative journalism. Here, explicitly partisan accounts are constructed from a personal, ideological commitment that deals with the emotive and the rational through a radicalization of journalistic technique. Bias and selectivity apart, though, what ethical issues does this approach raise? It is clear from Jen's report that she is not a professional journalist, nor does she pretend to professionalism. Her interview with Robin Cook (then Foreign Secretary for the British government) is opportunistic, unplanned, hurried and brief. We have shown Jen's report to many postgraduate journalism students and have found a striking consensus. Whether finding themselves either already sympathetic to the cause being advocated or, if previously ignorant of the issues, finding themselves satisfactorily informed about those issues, almost all the students found Jen's lack of conventional journalistic expertise worrying and at times embarrassing. Is this an example of the threat to professional values that access to technology can bring, where 'anyone with Internet access [or access to a camcorder or a minidisc recorder] can, in theory, set up their own media operation' (Keeble, 2001: 12)? Does this threaten standards to such an extent that it undermines trust in the profession of journalism?

Perhaps these are the wrong questions to ask. Instead, we may identify different, more beneficial ethical dimensions. First, such reports are about mobilizing public opinion. In this respect, they are no different from the campaigning journalism of the mainstream media. The presence of explicit mobilizing information is an enduring characteristic of alternative media, the aim of which is to suggest possibilities for social action to audiences (Bybee, 1982; Lemert and Ashman, 1983). Second, deprofessionalized approaches to doing journalism have been found to encourage audiences to start their own media projects, to become their own reporters (Atton, 2002a: Ch. 5).

But we must not consider this example from *Undercurrents* as typical. The value of acquiring conventional training in journalism has been recognized by many alternative media projects and journalists. The writing styles in US publications such as *CovertAction Quarterly* and *Z Magazine* strongly resemble those found in investigative journalism within the mainstream. In the 1990s, *Undercurrents* offered camcorder training to activists and strove to produce broadcast-quality footage. At the same time, British alternative political newspaper *Squall* was staffed by activists who had or were undergoing journalism training (say, at night classes) and some of their reporters and photographers produced work that has accorded so well with professional standards that it has been published in more mainstream publications (such as Gibby Zobel's work in the *Big Issue* and the *Guardian*). These differences are simply the result of producing journalism for different audiences. Despite *Undercurrents'* desideratum of broadcast-quality footage, it also celebrated 'underproduction': 'turn your weaknesses (few resources, little experience) to an advantage by keeping your feature simple but powerful' (Harding, 1997: 149). The primary audience for such work, it was assumed, would be the activist community itself. *Squall*, on the other hand, was more interested in 'talking to the bridge' and celebrated the diversity of its readership (which included British Members of Parliament). The paper operated its own house style in order to preserve standards. The radical news sheet *SchNEWS*, produced weekly in Bristol, also has a house style of its own. In its employment of pun-filled headlines (such as 'Terror Firmer', 'Chinese Horrorscope', 'Water Disgrace!') and its colloquial and irreverent copy style, *SchNEWS* might be considered the British tabloid of alternative journalism. It takes the ethic of active witnessing and places it in a framework derived from right-wing newspapers whose ideologies could not be further from its own. In so doing, it inverts the hierarchy of access to the media at the same time as it subverts tabloid conventions that are normally used to communicate familiar prejudices such as racism and homophobia.

The representation of, for example, ethnic minorities and of gays and lesbians is rarely an ethical issue for alternative journalists, since they are already operating within a morally 'progressive' environment where discriminatory practices largely do not arise. Where biased representation may arise is, ironically enough, as a result of a politically progressive notion of free speech. Apparently influenced by Noam Chomsky's dictum that 'if you believe in freedom of speech, you believe in freedom of speech for views you don't like' (cited in Achbar, 1994: 184), some alternative media projects have relinquished what has been an abiding ideology of 'no platform for fascists/racists/homophobes' in favour of an 'open platform' approach. This is in part a libertarian impulse, but has also been the result of 'open publishing' software used by Internet-based media such as the Indymedia network. Intended to encourage activist reporting and democratic access to the media, open publishing has predictably been used by racists to post offensive material to Indymedia sites. What began as a technical advance has developed into a political issue. Activist and Indymedia contributor 'ChuckO' (2002) has called for 'aggressive action against racist and anti-semitic posts [which have] damaged Indymedia's reputation with Jewish people and people of color'. The loyalty to communities is once again present, though here it is part of a dilemma: to support free speech but to denounce hate speech. The issue is complicated further by the independence of Indymedia sites. Each of the 70-odd sites that comprise its international network is editorially independent from the rest. As Sara Platon (2002) notes in a response to ChuckO, 'each one of them has its own editorial policy and its own way of dealing with racism or other "unwanted" articles and comments in the main newswire. Some are more pro free speech, and some are more restricted in what they "allow" on the website.' Just as we find a range of hybridized approaches to doing alternative journalism, we also find an array of ethical responses, often apparently in conflict with those prevalent in the mainstream media. Platon argues that 'unlike as in more traditional forms of mass media, disagreements within the Indymedia news network are often out in the public domain'. While alternative journalism has no written code of ethics (nor is it likely to, given its heterogeneous and libertarian nature), its ethical practices are explicit.

We now turn to questions of sourcing to show how alternative journalists construct their stories around the voices of 'ordinary' citizens and how they marginalize elite groups (the dominant voices in mainstream media). We shall then explore the credibility and reliability of alternative journalists. How do audiences judge the credibility and reliability of alternative media? To answer this question, we shall draw on recent research on blogs.

Sourcing

Whereas mainstream media make extensive use of members of elite groups as sources (these are Hall et al.'s (1978) primary definers), alternative media offer access to a much wider range of voices. These often include members of local communities, protesters and activists: 'ordinary' voices compared to the 'privileged' voices of elites. Harcup's study of West Yorkshire's *Leeds Other Paper* (Harcup, 2003) shows how, by comparison with its commercial 'rival', the *Yorkshire Evening Post*, the former systematically used a 'different cast of voices' (p. 360) from its mainstream counterpart. The latter, in common with the commercial press in general, relies on official sources as spokespeople not only for organizations and institutions, but as expert commentators on news events and issues as a whole. This specialist class is a social and political elite who define news values, newsworthiness and the very agenda of the news (Hall et al., 1978). A hierarchy of access to the media is established that routinely marginalizes those without the social and political power to be deemed worthy of accreditation as sources (Glasgow University Media Group, 1976: 245). In mainstream news, these 'ordinary' people are most often used as material for vox pop interviews and their opinions sought for human interest stories (Ross, 2006). By contrast, the local alternative press actively seeks them out as expert sources. This is to do more than merely overturn the routinization of mainstream sourcing practices. To bring the voices of the local community into the centre of journalism is an ethical decision (Atton, 2003b). This decision not only considers the local community as important (after all, the commercial local press makes the same claim), it also places these voices 'from below' at the top of the hierarchy of access, a practice that acknowledges ordinary people as experts in their own lives and experiences.

The radical community press of the 1970s in the UK was concerned with 'the production of revelatory news' (Franklin and Murphy, 1991: 106) that directly affected the lives of working people in their communities. The non-aligned nature of these presses encouraged reporters to investigate all political parties equally, without the restriction of political allegiance. Where political allegiance was observable, it was not at party level, but at grassroots level; many radical papers sought support from local Labour Party and trade union activists, though this did not prevent investigation of the senior members of these organizations.

'Breaking two sorts of silences' is how Franklin and Murphy (1991: 113) sum up the project of the radical local press. The first silence – of elite groups on corruption within their ranks – is broken by investigative and revelatory news reporting. From the breaking of the second silence springs a recognition that such news is not merely there to titillate or to sell papers: it is there as an instance of news that is relevant to the lives of ordinary, unprivileged people. This second silence is about giving voice to those people, about reporting news from their perspective, presenting stories in which they are the main actors, where they are permitted to speak with authority as counters to the mainstream's emphasis on public figures as the only authoritative voices, the predominant sources of 'validating information'. Where the mainstream local media privileged news constructed from the perspective of those in positions of authority, the radical local press of the 1970s and 1980s constructed its news from the perspective of those of low status, producing what have been termed 'parish magazines of the dispossessed' (Harcup, 1994: 3). And in answer to Tony Harcup's question: 'Whose news is it anyway?' (Harcup, 1998: 105), we might answer: 'Their news.' Local people would not only become primary sources and major interviewees in stories, they could also become news-gatherers. Reporters would build up networks of local people: not only political activists, but local residents' groups, parents, workers, the unemployed, the homeless, and encourage them to supply leads for stories.

Other types of community media have little interest in political activism of any kind. A first broad group would include the web-based network of Community Reporters established under the aegis of Steve Thompson at the University of Teesside. These initiatives involve a high proportion of local, non-professional people in their news-gathering, reporting and production – the Newcastle Community News website (www.ncn.org.uk) boasts a youngest writer only eight years of age. There is little interest here in courting controversy. Instead we find the promotion of more neutral, 'universal' values of local communities: place, tradition, conservatism. History, in the form of recollection and reminiscence, is encouraged: much of the reporting in these websites is to do with the preservation of tradition, with community journalism as the practice of a demotic local history. Other initiatives resemble more closely the alternative community newspapers of the 1970s. Grimethorpe's Electronic Village Hall and London's Tower Hamlets Community Network e-base seek to make Internet technology accessible to local communities in order to assist in the regeneration of economically deprived areas. These can directly benefit local economies by enabling small businesses' access to e-commerce. They also offer access to Internet resources to enable campaigning on social issues such as housing through networking with similar organizations, holding discussions online, communicating with local officials, and publicizing causes and issues. As Christopher Mele (1999: 292) has found in the case of a North Carolina residents' group, the technology enables members of a community to 'operate as agents outside the local and exclusive pathways of information, social discourse and social action that were either controlled or influenced by the institution of the housing authority or other local elite groups'.

There are two journalistic consequences of this ethos of inclusivity. First, as Harcup (2006a) shows, many stories in the local alternative press are unique to that medium (though the commercial press might subsequently report them). Stories tend to arise because of the highly varied pool of experts available to the alternative press. These experts might be factory or shop workers, pensioners, working mothers, minor government officials or schoolchildren. This variety of sources may not only provide leads for stories, it can often bypass the event-driven routines of mainstream news practices: '[w]hereas mainstream media tended to notice health and safety stories only when there was a disaster ... [*Leeds Other Paper*] exposed potential health risks before even the workers or their trade unions were aware of them' (Harcup, 2006a: 133). This 'investigative journalism from the grassroots' (p. 132) results from going beyond the typical 'beats' of the local press (such as the emergency services, the courts and local council meetings) to privilege issues above events. The second consequence of this socially inclusive approach to reporting is that 'ordinary' sources often become writers: 'such journalism not only finds common cause with its community through advocacy; its explicit connections with the public sphere of that community serve as its rationale for seeking amongst that community for its news sources' (Atton, 2003a: 270).

A study of the British activist newspaper *SchNEWS* shows this in action in social movement media (Atton and Wickenden, 2005). As in community media, *SchNEWS* employs ordinary people to provide expert knowledge about their own experiences. Their words are used to illustrate issues and perspectives with which *SchNEWS* is sympathetic and which it wishes to promote. For example, a story about the harassment of local residents by violent gangs uses extensive quotes from residents to argue for the power of local community problem-solving 'without the help of apathetic police, archaic laws or an out-of-touch government'. *SchNEWS*'s use of ordinary people as sources for its news stories is very different from the mainstream media's use of vox pop interviews. The typical vox pop gathers brief opinion; *SchNEWS* presents local people as capable of action, as they are able to identify problems and provide solutions. In this example, *SchNEWS* reports that it is local residents, not government officials, who are taking action. The paper does not ignore elite sources, but it does not often quote them directly. Instead, it presents their arguments in order to show their inadequacies and failings. Elite sources tend to be treated with suspicion. In a report of a wildcat postal strike in the UK, *SchNEWS* quotes striking postal workers at length. Their words not only describe and justify their actions; they also provide information and commentary about the economic situation of the postal company. In mainstream journalism, we would expect economic analysis from managers of the company or from independent experts. By contrast, *SchNEWS* uses the voices of ordinary people to set the terms of reference by which its readers are encouraged to understand issues and events.

The representation of ordinary people in alternative journalism sets them apart not as heroes or victims, but as voices that have as equal a right to be heard as do the voices of elite groups. Story-telling by those who are normally actors in other people's stories challenges the expert culture of both the news journalist and the 'expert' columnist. When reporting on other communities, *SchNEWS* does not take the approach of what David Spurr (1993) has called the 'colonizing journalist', but employs members of those communities to speak for themselves. (We shall explore the theoretical value of 'thinking colonially' about alternative journalism in Chapter 7).

However, there is also evidence to suggest that these stories are used by *SchNEWS* to promote its own ideology. In its coverage of the harassment of a local community, the only residents quoted are those who are disillusioned with local government officials and the police. They have placed their faith in local community action that fits well with the paper's aim to provide 'weekly snapshots of the phenomenal rise of positive direct action' (*SchNEWS* editorial, cited in Atton, 2002a: 85). Similarly, the paper displays its broadly anarchist philosophy in its report on striking postal workers. It portrays the postal workers' union as a hierarchical institution that has been 'fumbling' and 'frightened'. It is the rank and file membership, not their leaders, who have 'crushed' the management. In these ways, *SchNEWS* fits the 'ordinary' discourse of its sources to its own politicized discourse.

Do the sources used by *SchNEWS* share the paper's ideology? What does it mean for the paper to claim 'solidarity' with its ordinary sources? The hierarchy of access to the media is inverted by *SchNEWS*: it provides greater access to its pages for ordinary people and less access for elite groups. But do its ordinary sources have any more control over how their words are used than they do when interviewed for vox pops in the mainstream media? To what extent does *SchNEWS* employ these sources for its own ideological ends, which might not be shared by the sources themselves? The conventional hierarchy of access might be inverted, yet perhaps in its place there is a further hierarchy, where the ideology of the media producers dominates the expression of their 'ordinary' sources.

Alternative media such as *SchNEWS* present their ideas in a populist manner that resembles tabloid journalism. We have already noted how this style might be used to produce a communicative democracy that offers a more inclusive ideal of who might be a journalist. The notion of communicative democracy challenges the dominant criteria by which audiences judge the credibility and reliability of journalists and their sources, criteria based on formal education and professional status. Research into mainstream news media has found that the interaction of the media and audience (or the lack of it) has a significant impact on the audience's understanding of the news – and its trust of that news (Hargreaves and Thomas, 2002). Ideally, communicative democracy brings together media producers and audiences in a far closer relationship; it can be argued that this more intimate interaction of the working methods of the journalist with the needs of the audience is able to replace expert-based notions of credibility and reliability.

Credibility and Reliability

There has been little detailed research into audiences of alternative media, as Downing (2003b) has shown. One of the few studies is by Matheson and Allan (2007), who studied bloggers during the war in Iraq. The bloggers included professional journalists as well as military personnel and Iraqi citizens. They presented first-hand accounts of their experiences and thus are less mediated than the experiences of the people used by *SchNEWS*. These accounts raise questions about credibility and reliability, and how audiences judge them.

Matheson and Allan found that even blogs written by professional reporters tended to eschew the established standards of objectivity and impartiality, preferring a style of address that has more in common with eyewitness reporting. That is to say, the professional journalists wrote from direct, personal experience and emphasized their independence from organizational or administrative constraints. From their interviews with professional journalists who maintained blogs during the last Gulf War, Matheson and Allan found that it was these aspects that the reporters believed resonated with their readers. It was the direct, 'authentic' account of personal experience that 'counted' in journalists' blogs, particularly when their newspaper reports were limited by their situation as embedded journalists.

Matheson and Allan argue that the readers trusted the bloggers because their methods were transparently subjective. Journalists did not appear to present their eyewitness reports as 'fact'; they did not use their professional authority to present a definitive version of events. Readers did not consider the blogs as absolute truth. Instead, they understood the war blogs as a set of accounts told from different perspectives. Moreover, readers were able to participate in the construction of these accounts. Allan cites freelance journalist Christopher Allbritton, who argued that his readers 'trusted me to bring them an unfettered view of what I was seeing and hearing' (Allan, 2006: 109). Allan argues that Allbritton's readers 'shap[ed] his reporting' by asking questions and suggesting leads, 'each one of them effectively serving as an editor' (ibid.). These practices challenge both the journalistic ideal of objectivity (the separation of 'facts' from 'values') and the status of journalist as the recognized expert in representing the world to readers. We can understand the work of bloggers and its reception by readers as recognition of the moral and political nature of objectivity. The blogs examined by Matheson and Allan challenge the central assumptions of objectivity: that it is possible to separate facts from values and that it is morally and politically preferable to do so.

We have already seen how the radical populism of some alternative media has its roots in earlier, pre-commercial and pre-professional radical media. These earlier publications were 'pre-objective', that is to say, they were produced before objectivity became an established norm in professional journalism. The Glasgow University Media Group (1976 and 1980; see also Eldridge, 2000) has demonstrated how journalism that considers itself objective can be just as value-laden as the earlier forms it sought to replace. Contemporary alternative media tend to arise in order to provide a counter to what alternative journalists consider an already biased set of reports. Sceptical of what counts as balance in the mainstream media, they seek to set up their own counterbalance. Their radical journalistic practices offer moral and political correctives to the supposedly fact-centred techniques of the mainstream media.

Audiences play an important role in these practices. Readers of blogs encounter multiple interpretations of a single event. They are, however, unwittingly, experiencing the limits of objectivity that Edgar (1992) has argued is found in all forms of journalism. For Matheson and Allan, writers and readers of blogs share a personal experience that is emblematic of a 'new' journalism. This journalism is focused less on the journalist as professional; instead, it proposes a relationship between writer and reader that reimagines the status of journalism and its practitioners.

The non-professional status of alternative journalists tends to restrict the range of their reporting. This form of journalism appears most appropriate when used to report on local community issues or to present personal narratives from within a major event (such as a conflict). In reporting hard news, alternative journalists have less access to elite sources and institutions. The reliance on comment and opinion has left them open to charges of bias and subjectivity, but subjectivity can inspire trust, as we have seen. Alternative media offer new ways of thinking about and producing journalism, focus on what kinds of knowledge are produced, and suggest how readers and writers may come together to make sense of them.

6

ALTERNATIVE JOURNALISM IN THE WORLD:
A COMPARATIVE SURVEY

To attempt international comparisons across the range of alternative journalism projects raises two major problems. First, there is the problem of history: when do we begin our survey? Do we cover the past 20 years, 100 years or even longer? Even a survey covering mere decades will, in a chapter of this length, be no more than general. Second, there is the problem of points of comparison. As we have already seen in Chapter 3, on social demographics, published studies of alternative journalism projects vary greatly in their emphases; some focus on organization, others on ideology. Some examine broad social and political aims, others specific practices and products. Very rarely do two studies examine different projects from the same perspective. This makes comparison difficult, even within a single country or region.

For example, a comparison of alternative journalism in Germany in the 1980s could include both John Downing's (1988) study of West German anti-nuclear media and Mathes and Pfetsch's (1991) study of the 'spill-over' effects from the alternative to the mainstream press. Downing is less interested in the media themselves, whether as organizations or as content creators. Instead, he argues that they constitute – along with 'bookstores, bars, coffee-shops, restaurants, food-stores' – fora in which an alternative public sphere of discussion and debate may arise. He emphasizes social-movement media that encourage 'activity, movement and exchange ... an autonomous sphere in which experiences, critiques and alternatives could be freely developed' (1988: 168).

Mathes and Pfetsch (1991) found a significant 'inter-media' effect: the established West German liberal press tended to adopt both the issue from the alternative press as well as its frame of reference. Key to this process was *Die Tageszeitung* (or *taz*), a large-circulation and nationally distributed alternative daily newspaper, founded in 1978. By the mid-1980s, *taz*'s reach went far beyond any alternative public sphere: it was read by prominent intellectuals and numerous mainstream journalists. It explicitly sought to 'initiate a multiplier effect' (Mathes and Pfetsch, 1991: 37) by highlighting counter-issues to the mainstream media and actively moving these issues into wider public fora than those of the activist left. But Mathes and Pfetsch's emphasis on the content of a single paper ignores the diversity of voices and approaches that is emblematic of alternative media practices. In West Germany alone, we find a far richer media than that suggested by Mathes and Pfetsch, as Downing shows. Despite their different emphases, these two studies do tell us much about the place of alternative journalism in society: whether as a locus for social movement activity, as a source of news unregarded by the mainstream media or even as a source of news for mainstream media.

We might also explore projects across continents in order to account for their particular characteristics. This is to take the opposite approach to our first example. Rather than beginning with conceptual or ideological similarity, we would examine each project from the 'inside out', looking for contextual reasons (social, economic, cultural, technological) for a project developing in the way it has done. This approach is especially profitable in countries and regions that have been paid relatively little academic attention. Such is the case in Latin America. Clemencia Rodriguez is the only researcher to work consistently in Latin America (though Robert Huesca and Alan O'Connor have also done work here; for example, Huesca, 1995 and O'Connor, 2004). A study of the Bolivian miners' radio stations that flourished from 1963 to 1983 (but which first appeared in 1952, the year of National Revolution) emphasizes the value of participatory media production in highlighting the rights of workers in a politically marginalized region of a country (O'Connor, 2004). Similarly the Movement of Popular Correspondents that developed in revolutionary Nicaragua in the 1980s and 1990s produced reports by non-professional, voluntary reporters from poor, rural areas that were published in regional and national newspapers alongside the work of professional journalists (Rodriguez, 2001).

In many cases, these projects take place in regions where the writ of the Western norms of journalism does not apply (or at least is challenged), and therefore where the challenges for alternative journalism might be culturally and politically very different. The survey that follows is far from exhaustive. However, it does emphasize the diversity of alternative journalism throughout the world. In particular, it highlights the specific conditions under which alternative journalism is produced, whether at local, national, regional or even international levels. The survey draws attention to the ways in which politics, economics, and social and cultural systems provide specific contexts that contribute to the shaping of a wide range of journalistic practices. It examines alternative journalism in Asia, Eastern Europe, Latin America and Africa, as well as the UK, the US and Canada. It also compares the different uses of the same medium in different countries (radio, television and the Internet) and explores the internationalized nature of much alternative journalism. Perhaps the best-known example of an international alternative news network is Indymedia.

The Indymedia Network

The network of Independent Media Centres became a highly visible feature of the media landscape of the global anti-capitalism movement at the turn of the millennium. The Independent Media Centres (IMC) or Indymedia network came to prominence during the demonstrations in the American city of Seattle against the World Trade Organization summit meeting there in 1999. The Seattle IMC acted as an independent media focus for the broad coalition of social justice groups, trade unions, anarchists, socialist, communists, environmental groups and others – a coalition that has come to be known as the anti-capitalist movement. In Seattle, the Centre had both a physical and a virtual presence. Its virtual presence on the web enabled its small core staff to distribute streaming audio and video footage of the demonstrations, as well as written reports, across the world. Technically this was achieved through the use of open publishing software, where any independent journalist (any activist, for that matter, though the two were often the same) could upload their reports. No prior approval was needed from the core group, neither was that group responsible for editing the content of reports in any way. Hundreds of hours of audio and video footage and hundreds of thousands of eyewitness reports, analyses and commentary became available to activists, supporters, detractors – to 'global citizens' at large.

Since Seattle, the Indymedia network has expanded, comprising 'approximately 5000 individuals and more than 150 groups that span over 50 countries across six continents' (Pickard, 2006: 317). Yet there is a significant bias towards IMCs in the West, particularly in the US, where over a third of local IMCs are located. Beyond the US and Western Europe, coverage is sparse; there are only 18 IMCs in Latin America, only three in Africa and none in India. The network sustains radical, egalitarian organizational and consensual decision-making procedures in order to prevent individuals and groups from wielding too much influence (though, as Pickard has shown, consensus decision-making is not always straightforward; he notes that in 2002 the Argentine IMC blocked the network from accepting a grant from the Ford Foundation). At a local level, each IMC is able to operate independently, creating its own news on its own site; www.indymedia.org acts as a gateway, republishing stories from local IMCs and directing users to those IMCs without controlling their content. The journalistic key to

Indymedia is open publishing: anyone may upload their contributions to a local IMC site without having to deal with either editors or technical staff as gatekeepers. This is not to say that Indymedia is a free-for-all; the network has an ethical dimension that empowers local IMCs to remove contributions judged unsuitable. Indymedia states that 'The Independent Media Center is a collectively run media outlet for the creation of radical, accurate, and passionate tellings of the truth ... while we struggle to maintain the news wire as a completely open forum we do monitor it and remove posts.' The large majority of these posts are removed for 'being comments, not news, duplicate posts, obviously false or libelous posts, or inappropriate content [such as hate speech]'. Indymedia do, however, still make these posts available in a separate page titled 'hidden stories' (Independent Media Centre, 2007). Thus, while there is editorial control, it does not prevent voices from being heard, nor prevent users from accessing that content. Neither does this quasi-editorial function of an IMC extend to the editing of individual pieces of work: if they do not breach the criteria set out above, then pieces will remain on the 'open' pages of the site.

It is not only the scale (in terms of geographical spread, global reach and volume of material) that makes the Indymedia network an interesting moment for the study of social movement media; it is the most thorough working-out on the Internet of the conditions and processes of radical media projects. The Indymedia network powerfully exemplifies the three core principles of Downing et al.'s (2001) model of radical media organization. First, there is an emphasis on self-management, resulting in small-scale, collectively run projects. Second, the project suggests a 'socialist anarchist angle of vision'. Third, the project embodies 'prefigurative politics, the attempt to practice socialist principles in the present, not merely to imagine them for the future' (Downing et al., 2001: 71). This emphasis on socialism need not prevent us from applying these core principles to an organization as politically, culturally and geographically diffuse as the Indymedia network. Downing and his colleagues present a vision of a democratic, non-corporate media network that comprises non-hierarchically run, independent groups and individuals horizontally linked, where such organization and control as do exist are necessarily light. Nevertheless, as Pickard has shown, 'power asymmetries with the network (north/south, reformist/radical)' persist and the network appears dominated by 'white North American men' (Pickard, 2006: 334). The online citizen journalism site *OhmyNews* also employs a philosophy of open publishing, but within a very different organizational and editorial structure. Its specific cultural and political location in South Korea presents a challenge to the '*a priori* ideal type [of journalism] rooted in conditions found only in Western countries' (Kim and Hamilton, 2006: 544).

OhmyNews

OhmyNews was founded in 2000 by South Korean 'journalist-turned-activist' Yeon-Ho Oh and has since become one of the most prominent and highly regarded alternative journalism projects in the world (Kim and Hamilton, 2006: 541). In addition to its Korean-language publication, its site includes an international, English-language edition, a web-streamed television station (OhmyTV) and a weekly, Korean print edition. Its international fame has come from its thousands of non-professional, citizen reporters (around 35,000 in 2004) who are responsible for up to 200 articles every day. Its organization and practices are more complex, however, and demonstrate the importance of two major themes we have encountered earlier in this book: the hybrid nature of alternative journalism, what Kim and Hamilton call 'the unstable and provisional merging of differences' (p. 544), and the need to consider journalistic practice (indeed, all social practice) in specific historical, cultural and social contexts.

We shall first turn to hybridity. The organization of *OhmyNews* is centred on an editorial office that is professionally staffed. Its 35 staff reporters are responsible for researching and writing stories on 'current, serious issues that need in-depth investigation. By contrast, citizen reporters ... write various stories about their surroundings' (Kim and Hamilton, 2006: 545). There is no necessity to train these citizen reporters, since they write from personal experience and need no special, professional skills. All contributions are edited and evaluated by the central editorial office before they are posted. Once they have been uploaded to the site, they are available for anyone to add to or comment on. While this is clearly a form of open publishing, where opportunities for becoming a reporter are far wider than in the mainstream, commercial press, it is quite different from the much lighter editorial hand we have seen in Indymedia. Nevertheless, the range of writing styles and perspectives has a similar impact on the notion of journalism: expertise and objectivity are less important, and the diversity of the approaches of citizen reporters enables a much wider range of forms than the classic inverted pyramid of Western journalism (though its overall format replicates the typical omnibus newspaper with its home, international, sports, culture and business sections). There is further control in how a citizen becomes a reporter: every contributor has to formally register and agree to abide by *OhmyNews*'s code of ethics and regulations. *OhmyNews* thereby brings together practices from mainstream media with those of alternative journalism. Another influence from mainstream media is the organization's reliance on advertising. *OhmyNews* is very attractive to advertisers because a majority of its reporters and its audience come from the '386 generation', a term which not only signifies a technologically cultured generation (386 referring to a microprocessor), but in Korea also has deeper significance.

Here we turn to our second key factor, the contexts of history, culture and society. The 386 generation is a generation in its thirties (the '3'), who attended college or university in the 1980s (the '8') and who were born in the 1960s (the '6'). These numbers are significant: 1987 saw popular resistance against military rule in South Korea, resulting in the rise of politically progressive civil movements. The 386 generation were at the forefront of these changes. The mainstream media had been very closely allied to the military and even after 1987 remained conservative. The high level of public investment in telecommunications infrastructure since 2000 (South Korea leads the world in such investment) made it possible to establish an online news organization that could be cheaply and easily accessed, and which could be developed as a democratic challenge to the conservative, mainstream media, both in the nature of its content and in its range of contributors. Consequently, rather than remaining a marginal project, *OhmyNews* has emerged as a distinct rival to mainstream news organizations as the first of its kind in South Korea: an independent Internet newspaper. In other countries, political upheaval has also resulted in the rise of independent media. The countries of former Yugoslavia provide three very different instances of how nationalism and regionalization have enabled the rise of media that oppose both centralized government and the new national governments that have replaced them.

Independent Media in the Balkans

Fadzan's (2003) study of three independent media in former Yugoslavia demonstrates three distinctive responses to mainstream media. All have their roots in student-run media and all have established themselves as large organizations whose organization, financing and planning resemble those of their mainstream counterparts. They were inspired by a widespread belief that the mainstream media of the region 'fuelled the conflict' in former Yugoslavia through their 'political misrepresentation, abuse of power, media manipulation and propaganda' (Fadzan, 2003: 4). The political-satirical weekly *Feral Tribune* ('feral' is Croatian for 'street light', as well as having a different, but equally relevant, meaning in English) was among the first of the independent media in the region. It began in 1984 as a supplement to a mainstream Croatian newspaper, but in 1993 became independent after the takeover of its parent paper by the nationalist regime. It blends political commentary and investigative reporting with poetry, cartoons and photomontage to 'ridicule and irritate the authorities' (p. 45). Its popularity is matched by the frequency with which the publication and its journalists have been prosecuted.

B52 began as an underground student radio station in Belgrade. The period of national transition and the consequent weakening of centralized political power enabled it, like *Feral Tribune*, to take on a role that combined a critique of government and media power and the development of an alternative public sphere. The political pluralism that emerged in the region enabled independent media to flourish in a variety of ways. B52 is to be considered a serious rival to long-established mainstream media: it now combines radio and television broadcasting, a record label, book publishing and Internet services. By contrast, *Feral Tribune* remains a weekly (though with a presence on the web) and is far more radical in its eclectic and irreverent approach to journalism, appealing particularly to intellectuals. In Sarajevo, another weekly, *Dani* ('days'), resembles a tabloid newspaper in its colloquial and sensational tone, while presenting itself as a provider of serious news. It too, however, has a radical dimension, resembling more the political populism of the radical press of nineteenth-century England (as we saw in Chapter 5 on alternative journalism practices). In their different ways, each of these titles, Fadzan argues, performs the watchdog role of the fourth estate in similar fashion to the ideal type of their Western counterparts. In former Yugoslavia, however, to act aggressively as part of the fourth estate is a far more dangerous undertaking than in the West, where independent media 'deliberately try to destroy the tranquillity of the "national idylls" created by the mainstream media' (Fadzan, 2003: 73). We must be careful not to assume that all alternative journalism is so successful. The experiences of Taiwan and Malaysia show how, despite over 50 years of alternative journalism, the struggle for democratic media is far from complete.

Alternative Journalism in Taiwan and Malaysia

The origins of what Lee (2003) terms 'guerrilla media' in Taiwan lie in the 1950s with the founding of the *Free China Monthly* by indigenous intellectuals. This was prompted by Chiang Kai-shek's defeat on mainland China by the Communists in 1949 and his move to the island of Taiwan to set up his 'quasi-Leninist Nationalist regime' (Lee, 2003: 164). Chiang Kai-shek's political project was the reunification of China and his mainland nationalism brought with it the marginalization and repression of the local majority of islanders. Alternative media were tolerated by the regime for many years, simply because they were deemed insignificant. However, the 1970s saw the rise of dozens of *Dangwai* ('outside the party') magazines, established by local politicians to mobilize grassroots support against the nationalist 'one China' ideology and to mobilize the island's ethnic population for democratic representation. At this point, alternative media became a threat to the regime: their publishers and editors were fined and imprisoned, titles were closed down and banned. Nevertheless, and despite the persistence of martial law, underground media continued. The emergence of an official opposition party in 1990 strengthened the resolve of these media. In the 1990s, illegal cable television and radio stations began broadcasting, following the end of martial law in 1987. Lee argues that much of the content of these broadcasts, especially from the radio stations, was repressive rather than emancipatory. In offering a voice to the indigenous population, the stations highlighted ethnic and class differences within the population; phone-in talk shows became a popular forum for the airing of such differences. Ironically, it was in part due to international pressure – political and commercial – that legislation was passed that ultimately curtailed the emancipatory aims of dissident alternative journalism in Taiwan. As Taiwan's media structure became more liberal, market forces came into play and competition between stations was fierce. The legalization of independent cable televisions across the country saw the rise of conglomerates. The legal requirement for indigenous content was lowered to 20 per cent for local television stations. The alternative journalism that had flourished under repression and which had brought the indigenous population together in a common cause was now becoming commercialized and fragmented. As competition encroached, the function of alternative journalism shifted from providing a forum for rational, democratic discussion to presenting 'essentalised [and] reductive' representations of ethnic groups in opposition to one another (Lee, 2003: 173). As it did so, the alternative media withered; what remained became commercialized, sensational and regressive.

The role of political movements is also significant in the alternative journalism of Malaysia. Ling (2003) highlights two long-established publications, both of which are produced by civil institutions: *Aliran Monthly*, published by a local NGO for social justice and reform, and *Harakah*, the fortnightly publication of the Pan-Islamic Party of Malaysia (PAS), the main opposition party. Lee's case study examines the coverage of the sacking of deputy prime minister Anwar Ibrahim in 1998, amid allegations of corruption and sexual impropriety. The details of the coverage – and the case itself – need not concern us here. What is important is Lee's argument that, despite their prominence as dissenting publications, neither publication is judged to have contributed to democratic reform (their avowed aim). This is for two reasons. First, Ling argues, the failure is due to their unsubstantiated claims about the reasons for Anwar's sacking. Whilst they did provide economic and political contexts that were absent from the state-controlled media, they did not undertake any investigative journalism: they relied solely on comment and opinion. Second, both publications are subject to regulation that severely limits their readership: *Aliran Monthly* is only permitted to publish in English; *Harakah* may only be sold to members of PAS. It is to the Internet that Malaysians seem to be turning for more authoritative alternative journalism, as the legislation governing print media does not apply to online publications. Malaysia's first (and currently only) online newspaper, *Malaysia Now* (malaysiakini.com), was founded in 1999 and has already become 'highly regarded for breaking news stories' (Ling, 2003: 298). However, as Ling observes, only a minority of Malaysians have regular access to the Internet.

By contrast, in Colombia, we find indigenous media flourishing with the support of a hitherto narrowly nationalist government (though that support has been long awaited and is not as full as local media activists would prefer). In Colombia, as in Taiwan, we find struggles against political repression and against the destructive aspects of nationalism; there are long-standing struggles for political and media representation of indigenous peoples that acknowledges their differences and diversity. In Colombia, the development of indigenous radio provides a vivid illustration of the appropriation of mass media technologies by marginalized communities. It is to Colombia that we now move, after which we explore alternative radio projects in other parts of the world.

Alternative Radio Journalism

We have already seen how constitutional reform in South Korea and the countries of former Yugoslavia has encouraged and enabled alternative journalism. Likewise, the constitutional reform of 1991 in Colombia laid the foundation for the establishment of indigenous radio. This reform saw a move away from considering the state as a monolithic nation and instead formally recognized a plurality of cultural and ethnic identities. Though they comprise less than 2 per cent of the total population, there are 80 different ethnic groups in Colombia, 30 languages and 300 dialects (Rodriguez and El Gazi, 2007). These groups are largely scattered in remote and rural communities and have long fought for rights to their ancestral lands and for the maintenance of their cultures, languages and religions. As Rodriguez and El Gazi show, the Colombian government's guarantee of access to radio by indigenous peoples led to the establishment in 2002 of 14 indigenous stations, which reached almost 80 per cent of the indigenous population. All the stations are owned and operated by indigenous peoples, enabling them to produce programmes that challenge the dominant representations of their communities by the mass media as either irrelevant to modern Colombia or as sites for social unrest and violence. Rather than demanding better representation by state-run broadcasters, each indigenous group established a radio station that catered to its specific cultural and social needs (though in some cases this led to the rejection of radio in favour of more appropriate two-way communication technologies such as telephony, or its rejection as a symbol of Westernized, global capitalism). Rodriguez and El Gazi make an important point that is relevant to all forms of alternative journalism: not only is local control of the media important, but the social practices of media technologies need to be grounded in specific cultural and societal needs. Radio practice should reflect the diversity and heterogeneity of the communities that develop it (what Rodriguez and El Gazi call a 'poetics of radio'; p. 449). Media technologies can therefore be used to 'strengthen [a community's] articulations of reality', to communicate within a community and to communicate to the wider world (p. 454). The oral nature of radio opens up the media to those living in largely oral cultures: many of the peoples examined by Rodriguez and El Gazi are using radio to strengthen indigenous languages. Radio is a popular medium amongst young Colombians and is used to hand down 'tradition, language, music and local wisdom and memory' (p. 458) to them in an attractive format. The most politically active indigenous peoples (the Guambiano and the Nasa in the south of the country) have embraced radio as part of their armoury for political mobilization. Rather than have media technologies colonizing indigenous peoples and forcing them to modernize their communication practices, in Colombia we see radio becoming incorporated into existing 'ancestral communication and information modes and systems' (pp. 459–460).

Community radio in Western countries has also benefited from government policy on media technologies. The results, however, are very different, given the differing historical, demographic and political contexts. In the UK, the Restricted Service Licence scheme (RSL) is a government initiative that promotes local community and specialist radio stations outside the existing state-funded and commercial sectors. The licences do have their limitations: they are typically issued on an annual basis, with renewal dependent on proven success. There are also limits on the content of broadcasts – direct political campaigning is outlawed by the RSL system, for example. Moreover, many UK stations operating under RSLs have adopted a community radio format that has more in common with local, commercial broadcasters. With support from local businesses, such stations are able to professionalize their output and to make programmes that accord more closely with formats and styles familiar to us from public service and commercial radio. However, the low entry costs of radio (when compared to those of television, which also requires higher levels of technical expertise) continue to attract new players in the radio game. The RSL scheme has seen the emergence of a more radical broadcaster.

London's Resonance FM began broadcasting in 1998 and has taken advantage of the scheme to produce some of the most challenging programmes on British radio – challenging in terms of content, experiments with form and the use of non-professional programme makers and presenters. Calling itself London's 'first art radio station', its general remit is to present music and sonic art operating from the creative fringes. It presents contemporary, 'serious' music, free improvised music, electronic music, sound poetry, 'avant rock' and a wide range of sonic art projects that exist even beyond these specialist genres. The ambit of its output is largely defined by terms such as 'experimental' or 'avant-garde'. For many programme makers and presenters, the station offers a first opportunity to work in radio. The station not only presents unusual music, it does so in unusual formats: the *Memorex Hour* is a review programme that plays only home recordings from a global range of musicians. *Xollob Park* is surely the first radio show where 'everything runs backwards', as its publicity states. For 30 minutes each week, its presenter plays commercial recordings and sound collages backwards – ranging from ambient soundscapes to hit songs by the Carpenters. The conditions of the station's licence also require it to produce programmes not only for the 'taste communities' that make up its London audience and beyond; it must also provide community radio programming. In the chapter on demographics, we mentioned the station's daily programme for the elderly, *Calling All Pensioners*. Other programmes are aimed at some of London's diasporic communities and are broadcast in the native languages of those diasporas: *Middle East Forum* in Arabic, *Zerbian Radio Slot* in Serbian. To overcome its limited audience reach – due to its specialist output and the narrowness of its analogue transmission range (central London) – Resonance FM supplements its analogue signal with an Internet stream: this enables it to reach the globally fragmented, minority audience for its programmes.

Despite their specific cultural differences, there are broad similarities between Resonance FM's range of programmes and the aims of indigenous radio projects. Both are based on the production and dissemination of material for specific communities (whether geographic or communities of interest, or both) that is located and created within those communities. They are not about producing content or replicating forms that, as is the case with commercial broadcasters, are concerned with 'deliver[ing] to advertisers a measured and defined group of consumers' (Fornatale and Mills, 1980: 61, cited in Crisell, 2002: 131). Arguably, they are not about consumption at all; instead, they are about participation, development and mobilization. The network is often key to these projects: it enables the sharing of ideas and resources (including programmes), and can engender social and political solidarity. The indigenous radio stations of Colombia are forbidden by law to combine as a network but other radio projects, particularly those employing Internet technology, have established global networks.

OneWorld Radio (www.oneworld.net/radio) is part of the global social-justice network OneWorld, which brings together over a thousand organizations (NGOs, community groups, alternative media organizations). Its radio portal offers these organizations, along with individuals, the facility to listen to and exchange radio programmes produced by activists working in the areas of human rights, social change and sustainable development. These programmes are produced and broadcast by a mix of analogue and Internet radio stations. Programmes uploaded to the OneWorld Radio site may be freely broadcast by any member of the network. For reasons of bandwidth and connection time, programmes are limited in their length to a maximum of 10 minutes, yet the resource makes it possible for small, alternative radio stations to broadcast programming cheaply and to offer programmes from across the world to their own more localized audiences. Programmes have included features on the criminal justice system in Russia, disabled women in Japan, sex education in South Africa and a 'mini-drama' about children and public health in a Senegalese village.

Jo Tacchi (2000: 292) has used the term 'radiobility' to refer to the 'technical ability [of the Internet] to be radio, or to be radio-like or "radiogenic"'. This is a useful way to go beyond our historically and culturally limited notions of radio practice. The technologies of peer-to-peer file-sharing (P2P) have been employed to create what has been termed 'peercasting'. The Peercast (www.peercast.org) program is based on the same protocol as the file-sharing program Gnutella. Users produce their own radio programmes and distribute them through a peer-to-peer system using MP3-formatted sound files and an online broadcasting package such as Shoutcast. This is not only cheap (all the software is freely available), but it does not rely on wide bandwidth for a high transmission speed. The distribution of the programmes through a network of online users reduces the need for expensive bandwidth technology, minimizing the need for advertising or other large capital flows. And, as with Gnutella, the peer-to-peer nature of the operation makes it hard to regulate against, since there is no central server to identify and shut down. In radio terms, we might think of these as the pirates of a digital age (Rojas, 2002). And like the pirates before them, there are attempts to regulate the output of Internet radio stations. Whilst a regulatory body such as the US Federal Communications Commission (FCC) is unable to limit the number of radio stations using the Internet on the historico-legal grounds of spectrum scarcity, other bodies are attempting to do so. The Digital Millennium Copyright Act (DMCA) was passed by the US Congress in 1998. One of its provisions was to secure the right for record companies to collect royalties for works played on digital broadcasting systems (this includes Internet radio). An amateur Internet radio station might easily find itself liable for a bill of tens of thousands of dollars, regardless of the size of the enterprise or its turnover. Such a decision favours the large, commercial broadcasters and is likely to push smaller stations off the air or force them underground. Peercasting, in the US at least, might become that underground.

Peercasting enables consumers of cultural products to become broadcasters and critics, even cultural agenda-setters. Though much alternative media has moved to the Internet, alternative print media persist, particularly where access to the Internet is limited or, as in the case of street papers, where the face-to-face transaction of selling papers is an integral part of their aim.

Street Papers

In the chapter on demographics, we saw how homeless people in Canada and the UK participate in media that seek to raise public awareness of the situation of the homeless. In the case of Halifax's *Street Feat*, this participation extended to homeless people who had become journalists of their experiences. 'Street papers' (as they are called) began to flourish in the 1990s and have been published throughout the world. *Street Feat*, however, is one of the few to feature extensive reporting from homeless people themselves. More usually, the homeless are primarily sellers of the paper, earning a commission for each copy they sell on the streets. This practice not only provides income to enable the sellers to move out of poverty, but also contributes to transforming the popular image of the homeless. Swithinbank (1996: 28) recounts the experience of a London commuter, who regularly buys the *Big Issue*: 'Now I know more about [the seller's] life I don't feel so critical'. The financial and attitudinal benefits of street-selling are universal among street papers, but there are variations in other practices across the world. In the US, there are street papers such as Los Angeles's *Big Issue*, 'a tabloid designed to be sold by homeless people to middle-class youth' (Dodge, 1999: 61), the content of which resembles the mainstream tabloid press with its coverage of celebrities and fashion.

By contrast, Los Angeles's other street paper, *Street Scene*, focuses on the young homeless, who are heavily involved in writing for the paper. Others, such as *Real Change* and *Streetwise* include the homeless as part of their audience, providing information about 'free-meal sites, legal services and shelters' (Dodge, 1999: 60). In Eastern Europe, street papers play a key role in advocacy projects. The collapse of communism in Russia led to increased rents, high unemployment and a weakened welfare state; *The Depths* was founded in 1992 in St Petersburg as part of a city-wide project to raise awareness of and provide support to the homeless. The extreme poverty found in the townships of South Africa is ameliorated for many by their involvement in papers such as Johannesburg's *Homeless Talk*; in Germany, dozens of papers have widened their remit to include the 'unemployed, drug addicts or refugees' (Swithinbank, 1996: 28). These projects often rely on funding from government departments or NGOs; most take advertising to sustain them, which often influences the content of the paper and its audience demographic. Only rarely do street papers carry no advertising: the few that do not tend to be the most politicized. The independence of San Francisco's *Street Spirit* from advertising in part enabled it to campaign against prejudice against the homeless by local businesses, the police and local government officials. In general, and in spite of their variety, street papers promote a journalism of social change, whether they provide advice and information for the homeless or raise awareness about poverty through first-person accounts. At their most successful, street papers promote social change and political activism to the general public to a degree largely unseen in alternative journalism. Finally, we turn to perhaps the most ubiquitous form of media, television, to examine how alternative journalism is penetrating this increasingly sophisticated form of broadcasting.

Alternative Television and Local Identity

In an industry dominated by global media corporations, television is perhaps the most difficult medium in which alternative journalism can survive. Recent studies have shown the rise of 'citizen journalism' as part of mainstream newsgathering. Breaking television news frequently relies on camcorder footage, photographs taken on mobile phones and other forms of citizen journalism. Numerous examples appeared in 2005, for instance, including Hurricane Katrina in New Orleans, the fire at the Buncefield Fuel Depot in England and the terrorist bombings in Madrid (Sampedro Blanco, 2005). Broadcasters routinely incorporate blogs into their websites; some solicit advice and recommendations for stories and programmes from audiences. As Mark Deuze has pointed out (drawing on the work of Henry Jenkins, 2006), 'much of this community-oriented and sometimes participatory media-making takes place within the walls of mainstream and distinctly commercial media organizations' (Deuze, 2006: 272). We might simply see this as the latest manifestation of what has been a long-standing practice in the local press (Pilling, 2006); alternatively, we might ask how amateur media practices might affect the epistemology of professional journalism through the 'sheer *awkwardness*, of communication by "fairly ordinary people"' (Corner, 1996: 174, original emphasis).

In most countries, independent alternative television projects must struggle against a combination of media regulation that limits opportunities for non-commercial broadcasting (apart from state-subsidized, public-service broadcasters), the high levels of technical expertise necessary for television production and the high entry costs in terms of equipment. Despite these formidable barriers, alternative television has been developed around the world. Most often – as we have seen in the examples from Colombia and Taiwan – it has its roots in local and regional struggles for ethnic identity and local culture. An emphasis on the cultural values of a local community may lead to television programming that is organized and produced very differently from the mainstream. In Canada, the state-funded Inuit Broadcasting Corporation reflects the cultural values of its audience. Its news programme, *Qagik*, is modelled on Inuit values such as the autonomy of the individual. There is no public right to know, of the type found in Western journalism. Consequently, permission must be given explicitly by those represented in *Qagik*'s stories, particularly where the coverage is of 'traumatic stories (about death, family tragedies and so forth)' (Rodriguez, 2001: 48). Equality of treatment in the community is displayed in camera shots that encompass a representative range of community members; experts and pundits are avoided. The mechanisms of television production are demystified to the audience: '[e]ach program leaves some time to show how the program was produced and how it is broadcast' (ibid.).

The demystification of television has also been at the heart of the US public access television movement since its inception in the late 1960s. Paper Tiger Television, founded in New York in 1981, produces a weekly show that focuses on media criticism, as well as providing workshops for others wishing to make their own television programmes. Paper Tiger has made a virtue of its marginal status: its producers deliberately use hand-made backdrops and graphics; crew and equipment are often in shot; even mistakes are left in at times. The form of the programmes therefore acts as a critique of mainstream practices and demonstrates that there need not be a single grammar of television. This critical form is mirrored in each programme's content: 'Paper Tiger shows use political economy and critical cultural theory to critique media control and to call attention to the disjuncture between people's lived experiences and media representations' (Stein, 2001: 310). This radically democratic form of programming requires access to a distribution network that is able to broadcast its output nationally. The economically impoverished situation of Paper Tiger, however, militates against this. Its weekly show is cablecast to parts of New York; otherwise it has used video and DVD to distribute its programmes further afield.

Unfortunately, public access television in general has suffered from chronic under-funding, relying mostly on grants and philanthropic donations. Public access stations in the US are forbidden by law from seeking advertising as a revenue stream. Consequently, programming (and broadcasting) is often intermittent. In an attempt to extend the reach of Paper Tiger's programming, some of its members set up Deep Dish Television Network in 1986. This was a satellite-based distribution system (not a satellite broadcaster) that commissioned programmes to be offered to the network of public access cable stations around the country. Once again, though, economic scarcity has limited access. Few stations have satellite access and continuing financial problems restricted the network's production schedule to two hours per week. The

network has had some success, however, particularly with political programmes of national and international significance. Its series of programmes
on the first Gulf War (the *Gulf Crisis TV Project*) was aired not only by public access stations, but also by the much larger, national Public Broadcasting
System. Deep Dish used its satellite connection to feed the programmes to
interested stations, which then taped them for later broadcast. As Lucas and
Wallner (1993) show, however, even working with a network that has a reputation for progressive politics required significant expenditure of time and
effort to raise awareness of the programmes and to persuade broadcasters to
transmit them.

In some countries, the problems appear insurmountable. For many years,
Palestinians in the occupied territories had no television stations of their
own and it was impossible for them to have any control (however modest)
over programmes on Israeli TV. Without even a basic infrastructure for
broadcasting, the daily lives and concerns of Palestinian people were represented though the production of video diaries, which were then screened in
the occupied territories. The reach of such projects could be international.
For example, *Palestinian Diaries* (1991) has been broadcast in Sweden, the
Netherlands and the UK. The *Palestinian Diaries* video project was made
possible by professionals from the US and the UK, who trained local people;
the project was co-ordinated and funded by Al Quds Television, a venture
set up by Daoud Kuttab, a political columnist for the Arabic daily newspaper *Al Quds*. Kuttab (1993) tells how the aim of the project was to present
the everyday lives of Palestinians from within; despite the involvement of
professionals, it was crucial that local people made decisions about who and
what to film and in what ways. To produce films that offered intimate por-
traits of Palestinian experience never seen on national or international television required local people to become documentarists; only they could gain
the trust of communities more used to being essentialized as terrorists by
the Israeli (and other) media. Projects like this were rare in the occupied territories but, as Kuttab argues, they at least demonstrate that alternative journalism, even under extremely repressive conditions, is able to represent a
community not only to itself, but also to an international audience. Katz
(2007) reports on more recent developments. The *Voice of Palestine* is the
official broadcaster of the Palestinian Authority which, along with 'dozens
of unlicensed local television and radio stations' (p. 392), transmits both to
the Arab population in the occupied territories and to Israeli-Arabs.
(Unfortunately, Katz tells us little about their practices, their content or
their reach.)

In Australia, Aboriginal television developed as part of the indigenous
people's continuing fight for cultural recognition. The television projects
that arose in the 1980s recognized the complex cultural entity that is the
Aboriginal 'nation' in Australia, which comprises over 100 languages (Batty,

1993). Ernabella Video and Television (EVTV) started broadcasting in 1985 to the Pitjantjatjarra people of northern South Australia, using equipment constructed by a 'local amateur electronics enthusiast'; Batty calls it 'the world's cheapest TV station' (p. 113). The notion of alternative journalism presented on EVTV seems very different from that in other countries: perhaps its most significant programming has been documentaries that trace the mythic ancestral journeys that form part of the Aboriginal 'dreaming'. The abandonment of a nomadic lifestyle by the indigenous people has made these productions vital to the transmission of their cultural heritage to the younger members of their communities. The success of EVTV is due, perhaps paradoxically, to its uncertain legal status. Whilst it has not been prevented from broadcasting, it has no licence; as non-profit access television, it is effectively illegal, because licences are available only to commercial stations.

By comparison, the commercial arm of the Central Australian Aboriginal Media Association was granted a licence to broadcast its Imparja TV station, established along professional lines. The attendant costs forced it to buy in cheap international programming, over 20 times cheaper than producing its own shows. Consequently, its indigenous content – and the relevance to its original audience – diminished in the wake of attracting advertisers eager to buy subsidized slots to reach what soon became a white-dominated audience, drawn to the channel by its non-native content. EVTV's amateur, grassroots approach to alternative television production is multiplied in Catalonia, where since 1980 over 100 local stations have been set up. The stations invariably use home-made transmitters to broadcast material that is locally produced and almost entirely in the Catalan language (Rodriguez, 2001). The stations have their roots in the popular resistance to Franco's outlawing of Catalan culture and language. As we have seen in Colombia, alternative media serve as a creative and oppositional force against a mythical notion of unified nationalism in a country that is culturally very diverse. Like the Australian EVTV, the Catalan stations inhabit an ambiguous legal terrain; there is no explicit regulation of local television in Spain. Though they differ widely in their frequency of broadcasting (daily, weekly, even once a year only to celebrate a special festival), taken together the Catalan stations exhibit some of the 'classic' features of grassroots alternative journalism.

The stations typically broadcast not from professional studios, but from the back rooms of shops and bars, youth clubs, homes for the elderly and even vans. The participants reflect the composition of the neighbourhood or small town that the stations serve: 'citizens and neighbours, men and women of all ages and professions can be found working in the stations, as volunteer staff' (Rodriguez, 2001: 97). There are programmes produced entirely by a single age group, such as children or retired people, about issues particularly relevant to them. More generally, news items will cover local disputes, especially those involving the local council, and considered too local or trivial to be picked up by professional broadcasters. News might also link the global with the local, as in 1992, when Barcelona's TV Clot produced programmes about the impact of the Olympic Games on local people. Many of the stations produce documentaries about the history of their neighbourhoods. In these respects, as with so many alternative journalism projects around the world, the Catalan television stations act as diffusers of local culture, binding communities together at the same time as expressing their differences. Above all, they demonstrate one of the chief functions of alternative journalism: to report on and represent a community through the voices of the members of that community, regardless of class, ethnic background, age, education or employment.

Part 3

7

THEORIZING ALTERNATIVE JOURNALISM

So far we have explored the contexts in which alternative journalism takes place. We have examined its historical antecedents, its practices and the kinds of people who practise it – their backgrounds, skills and motivations – and how various social, political and economic contexts in different parts of the world help to shape the journalists and their journalism. How, though, are we to understand alternative journalism? In this chapter, we look at how theories of journalism, of the media and of society can help us make sense of the diversity of projects we have discussed so far. At the outset, we must note that, despite the increasing amount of research in this field (which has enjoyed significant and sustained attention from academics only relatively recently), most of the theoretical work has focused not on alternative journalism as such, but on alternative media more generally. Studies of alternative media tend to proceed from a critique of the mass media, of mainstream media. It is here that we shall begin, before we examine the key texts that have shaped our theoretical understanding of alternative media. We then explore studies that have addressed alternative journalism itself, before concluding with an appraisal of how Bourdieu's theory of cultural production might aid our understanding of alternative journalism in all its dimensions: the political, the economic, the social and the cultural.

Critical Media Studies

Critical media studies are concerned with the ideological basis of the mass media. In modern democracies, there are expectations that the media will facilitate democracy by providing pluralistic information from which informed choices can be made and debates can take place. This model, however, assumes that those with significant contributions to make to the media can secure access (Cottle, 2003). The extent to which the less powerful and politically marginal can obtain media access is one of the most significant debates concerning democratic processes and it has consequences for the diversity of information and the interpretive frameworks through which we understand society (Manning, 2001). Cottle argues that questions such as 'whose voices and viewpoints structure and inform news discourse go to the heart of democratic views of, and radical concerns about, the news media' (Cottle, 2003: 5). How social groups and interests are symbolically represented when they do secure access is also 'part and parcel of media access' (ibid.) and has implications for how the media perform their democratic function. As Cottle argues, when groups are 'legitimated or symbolically positioned as "other", labelled deviant or literally rendered speechless [it] can ... have far reaching consequences' (p. 6).

The Glasgow University Media Group (GUMG) have explored how media texts (newspaper reports and television bulletins) are constructed and how they represent different social groups. The GUMG examined BBC television news reports to reveal the BBC's bias towards elite groups in society (politicians, business leaders, law and order professionals). It also showed how workers and trade unions were regularly marginalized and demonized (for example, Glasgow University Media Group, 1976, 1980). The GUMG's work challenges the BBC's claim that it is objective and impartial by showing how facts and values are routinely combined to favour one group in society over another (Eldridge, 2000). As we saw in Chapter 5 on contemporary practices, the GUMG argued that this represented a hierarchy of media access where professional journalists uncritically presented the ideologies of elite groups to the public. Journalists thus refract the worlds of politics, society, economics and culture through the narrow, ideological lens of 'primary definers' (Hall et al., 1978).

Herman and Chomsky (1988) attempt to explain these practices by a political-economy approach that argues that structural forces shape the practices of mainstream journalists. In addition to the routine use of elite sources as primary definers, Herman and Chomsky argue that news is 'filtered' by: the concentrated power and ownership of the mass media; a reliance on advertising; a desire to avoid the displeasure ('flak') of powerful interest groups; and a systemic anti-communist or anti-left-wing bias. Many alternative media projects have used the propaganda model as a framework for their critiques of mainstream media (it appears in work by Indymedia, Fairness and Accuracy in Reporting and MediaLens). Analyses derived from Herman and Chomsky's model tend to be highly deterministic. Studies (such as those at www.medialens.org) typically begin with a detailed textual analysis of news reports and editorials, which are used to produce generalized accounts of mass media power. These accounts tell us little about how journalists work with their sources or with their editors and with other journalists, as Schlesinger (1989) has shown. Critical media scholars such as the GUMG and Herman and Chomsky portray the mass media as monolithic and unchanging. In their accounts, the power of the mass media marginalizes 'ordinary' citizens: not only are they denied access to its production, they are marginalized in its reports.

Taken on their own, such arguments as these seem pessimistic, holding out little hope for change or challenge. Superficially, Paschal Preston seems to share this pessimism in his critique of the information society thesis (Preston, 2001), but he is optimistic about the possibilities for change as a result of the endeavours of popular social movements. As we shall see, this foregrounding of social movements, of the popular mobilization for political and social change, is at the heart of much theorizing about alternative media.

In his analysis of new communication technologies, Preston argues that 'the new social and communication order of informational capitalism' (p. 272) is fundamentally unequal and polarized, and that the neoliberal project of a global information society has failed to deliver on its promise of change in the existing social order. Instead, it reproduces existing social inequalities between the information-rich and the information-poor, as well as deep-rooted inequalities in education, employment opportunities, access to health care, the ability to participate in democratic government and access to markets. He finds hope not in technological advances, or in knowledge or information, but in 'political will and social mobilisation' (ibid.). For Preston, new social movements are at the forefront of this struggle for 'a more egalitarian, inclusive and *social* "information society"' (ibid., original emphasis). Based as they are on notions of equality, inclusivity, social justice and radical notions of democracy, new social movements hold out the possibility of transforming the production and consumption capacities of new communication technologies.

Preston's argument not only applies to new media technologies such as the Internet; it can just as easily be applied to long-established media such as print and broadcasting. What is important is not the medium itself but the democratization of the medium's possibilities for communication. This means opening up the means of communication and media production beyond the institutionalized and professionalized elites of the mainstream media. Access and participation are central to this process:

> the means of communication and expression should be placed in the hands of those people who clearly need to exercise greater control over their immediate environment. [...] Once this happens, a process of internal dialogue in the community can take place, providing opportunities for developing alternative strategies. (Nigg and Wade, 1980: 7)

Raymond Williams (1980b) highlighted three aspects of communication that provide the grounds for this transformation. For Williams, public communication could only be rigorously understood by considering the process of 'skills, capitalization and controls' (p. 54). To apply this principle to alternative media, James Hamilton (2000) has argued that we need to talk of deprofessionalization, decapitalization and deinstitutionalization. In other words, alternative media must be available to 'ordinary' people without the necessity for professional training and excessive capital outlay; they must take place in settings other than media institutions or similar systems. Williams called this democratic communication, the origins of which are:

> genuinely multiple ... [where] all the sources have access to the common channels ... [and where those involved are able] to communicate, to achieve ... [a]ctive reception and living response. (Williams, 1963: 304)

Similarly, Enzensberger (1976) proposed a politically emancipatory use of media that is characterized by (1) interactivity of audiences and creators; (2) collective production; and (3) a concern with everyday life and the ordinary needs of people. McQuail, drawing on Enzensberger, proposed a 'democratic-participant' model for alternative media. Its key elements are the use of the media 'for interaction and communication in small-scale settings of community, interest group and subculture', 'horizontal patterns of interaction' and 'participation and interaction' (McQuail, 1994: 132). McQuail's inclusion of subculture suggests that we should not simply think of alternative media practices as taking place within social movements or local communities. The theory of democratic communication need not only apply to explicitly politicized media; it is also relevant to cultural media such as fanzines and zines:

> the medium of zines is not just a message to be received, but a model of participatory cultural production and organization to be acted upon. (Duncombe, 1997: 129)

It is noteworthy, however, that these theories have only been briefly presented by their authors. This reflects a general marginalization of the study of alternative media in the dominant theoretical traditions of media research. This is surprising, since some theoretical accounts appear to have space for them. The classic Marxist analysis of the media contains within it the seeds of such a space, in that alternative media may be considered as offering radical, anti-capitalist relations of production often coupled to projects of ideological disturbance and rupture. For example, the Gramscian notion of counter-hegemony is discernible in a range of radical media projects such as working-class newspapers (Allen, 1985; Sparks, 1985) and radical socialist publications (Downing, 1984). The Frankfurt School appear to have supported an alternative press through Adorno's assertion that the culture industry was best combated by 'a policy of retreatism in relation to the media which, it was argued, were so compromised that they could not be used by oppositional social forces' (cited in Bennett, 1982: 46). Adorno found the mimeograph 'the only fitting ... unobtrusive means of dissemination', to be preferred over the bourgeois-tainted printing press (ibid.).

It is in the study of the media of social movements and the deployment of alternative media for radical political communication that we find the most developed theory. John Downing's (1984) work is generally considered the starting point for such studies.

Radical and Social Movement Media

The subtitle of Downing's (1984) work, 'the political experience of alternative communication', effectively set the agenda for studies in alternative media (though that agenda has now been broadened to include cultural as well as political media, and their combination). Downing argued that the value of alternative media lay in its potential for social and political change. He considered these radical media as the media of social movements, produced by political activists for specific political and social change. This approach signalled an interest in considering media as radical to the extent that they explicitly shape political consciousness through collective endeavour (Enzensberger, 1976). The revised edition of his 1984 work (Downing et al., 2001) draws on a much wider range of media forms than did the first (which was limited to the classic media forms of print and broadcast.), including eighteenth- and nineteenth-century political cartooning in Britain, German labour songs of the nineteenth and early twentieth centuries, and nineteenth-century African-American public festivals. Woodcuts, flyers, photomontage, posters, murals, street theatre and graffiti are also examined for their radical methods and messages. However, a principal argument remains: that the media of these movements are important not only for what they say but for how they are organized. This position echoes Walter Benjamin's (1934/1982) argument that, in order for political propaganda to be effective, it is not enough merely to reproduce the radical or revolutionary content of an argument in a publication. The medium itself requires transformation; the position of the work in relation to the means of production has to be critically realigned. This requires not only the radicalizing of methods of production but a rethinking of what it means to be a media producer.

What Downing terms 'rebellious communication' does not, therefore, simply challenge the political status quo in its news reports and commentaries: it challenges the ways it is produced. If the aim of radical media is to effect social or political change, then it is crucial, Downing says, that they practise what they preach. He conceptualizes this as 'prefigurative politics' (a term popularized by Epstein, 1991), which he understands as 'the attempt to practice socialist principles in the present, not merely to imagine them for the future' (Downing et al., 2001: 71). To achieve this, Downing proposes a set of 'alternatives in principle' that draw on anarchist philosophy. This leads him to emphasize the importance of encouraging contributions from as many interested parties as possible, in order to reflect the 'multiple realities' of social life (oppression, political cultures, economic situations) (Downing, 1984: 17). Radical media thus come to constitute a major feature of an alternative public sphere (Downing, 1988) or, as the diversity of projects suggests, many alternative public spheres (Fenton and Downey, 2003; Fraser, 1992). Thus, the global Internet-based news network Indymedia may be considered as a multiple of local alternative public spheres that together comprise a '"macro" public sphere ... [which] offers geographically dispersed participants opportunities to debate issues and events ... [and] to collaborate on activist initiatives of a global reach' (Haas, 2004: 118).

Citizens' Media

Downing privileges media that are produced by non-professionals, by groups that are primarily constituted to promote progressive, social change. Like Downing, Clemencia Rodriguez (2001) argues that these independent media enable 'ordinary' citizens to become politically empowered. For her, when people create their own media, they are better able to represent themselves and their communities: 'citizens' media' are primarily projects of self-education. She draws on Paulo Freire's (1970) theories of conscientization and critical pedagogy, and Chantal Mouffe's (1992) notion of radical democracy to argue that the strength of alternative media lies not only in their counter-information role but also in the provision of opportunities for ordinary people to tell their own stories, and to reconstruct their culture and identity using their own symbols, signs and language. In this way, they challenge social codes, validate identities and empower themselves and their communities. For Rodriguez, the term 'citizens' is very specific: it refers to those members of society who 'actively participate in actions that reshape their own identities, the identities of others, and their social environment, [through which] they produce power' (Rodriguez, 2001: 19). She deliberately excludes those citizens whose professional work might be seen as already achieving this (such as politicians and journalists); neither does she appear interested in mass publics. Her studies of Latin American media (Rodriguez, 2001, 2003) demonstrate this. For example, Rodriguez notes how the production of a video by striking women workers in a Colombian maternity clinic led to 'shifting power roles ... [that] facilitate[d] a creative collective dynamic that … challenge[d] institutionalized leadership roles' (Rodriguez, 2001: 123–4).

Rodriguez does not consider citizens' media as media in a classic sense, as communication intended to inform and influence people. Instead, she focuses on communication as social interaction. Atton (2002a, 2004) has also emphasized the social processes and relations that might be developed through the production of alternative media, without losing sight of the media content that is produced. Similarly, Carroll and Hackett (2006) have nuanced the articulation between three outcomes of social movement media (which they term 'democratic media activism'). First, democratic media activism functions 'not simply [as] a political instrument but [as] a collective good', to the extent that its content promotes 'democratic conversations' (p. 88). Second, it 'treats communication as simultaneously means and ends of struggle' (p. 96) to enable the building of identity (whether individual or collective). Third, it offers not simply a symbolic challenge (through its content) to mass communication, but a challenge to the political economy of mass communication itself through its alternative, democratic structures.

A study of Australian community broadcasting by Forde et al. (2003) similarly proposes 'that we should consider alternative journalism as a '*process of cultural empowerment* … [where] content production is not *necessarily* the prime purpose [and] what may be as (or more) important are the ways in which community media outlets facilitate the process of community organization' (p. 317, original emphasis). Carroll and Hackett do acknowledge, however, that media activists are 'especially prone to "getting stuck" at the first stage – the building of counter-publics … creat[ing] their own media spaces, an activity with its own inherent satisfactions' (p. 98). Not that this is an unimportant activity. Citizens' media are aimed not at state-promoted citizenship but at media practices that construct citizenship and political identity within everyday life practices (de Certeau, 1984; Lefebvre, 1947/1991). Rather than relying on the mass media to set the boundaries of political involvement (Dahlgren, 2000), citizens use their own, self-managed media to become politically involved on their own terms (Norris, 1999). To become an active participant in the process of media production is a political education in itself. Amateur media practices are always embedded in everyday life practices; they are therefore already located in broader political, economic, social and cultural contexts. For these reasons, we prefer the terms 'alternative media' and 'alternative journalism' to describe these practices (Atton, 2002a, 2003a). As Nick Couldry and James Curran have argued, 'alternative media' functions as a comparative term to indicate that 'whether indirectly or directly, media power is what is at stake' (Couldry and Curran, 2003b: 7).

Alternative Media and Media Power

Couldry (2000) has argued that challenges to media power do not always take place within conventional practices of media production. His studies of protests in England (such as those at Greenham Common against the US air base there or at Brightlingsea, against live exports of veal calves) show how citizens are able to register their presence and challenge, as Vatikiotis puts it, the 'common sense separation between "ordinary people" and events in mediated public places' (Vatikiotis, 2004: 20). It follows that we can examine amateur media practices for examples of how the mass media representations we take for granted may be challenged and disrupted. Couldry argues that alternative media projects result in the 'de-naturalisation' of dominant media spaces (the 'mainstream'). In other words, the dominant practices of mainstream journalism (such as what counts as newsworthy, how stories are framed and how subjects of those stories are represented) are taken for granted. In Gramscian terms, they are hegemonic practices that appear natural; it seems that there is no other way of doing journalism. But, as Couldry points out, far from being a natural process, 'the media themselves are a social process organised in space' (2000: 25) and therefore may be challenged by other kinds of social process. Amateur media producers play an important role here. They show that it is possible to re-imagine journalism and that there are other ways of practising it beyond its dominant forms. Through the practice of more inclusive and democratic forms of media production, alternative journalists demonstrate that the power of the media does not lie solely in the hands of professional journalists. They are able to rebalance the power of the media, however modestly.

Consequently, alternative journalists can construct realities that oppose the conventions and representations of the mainstream media. This develops Pierre Bourdieu's (1991) position, that symbolic power is the power to construct reality. Participatory, amateur media production contests the concentration of institutional and professional media power and challenges the media monopoly on producing symbolic forms. Therefore, to consider alternative media is to recognize the relationship between dominant, professionalized media practices and marginal, amateur practices. The struggle between them is for 'the place of media power' (Couldry, 2000).

Alternative Journalism

The term 'alternative journalism' is broad and not limited to the journalism of political projects, the priorities of which are radical forms of organizing, the development of social movements, and individual or collective consciousness-raising. It is important not to lose sight of the importance of these social relations, but we also need to consider journalistic practices and products, to consider media content as journalism, not merely as accounts of self-reflexivity or self-education (Atton, 2003a). It is not only social relations (through organization) that can be transformed, but also the media forms themselves (discursively, visually, even distributively). We have already shown in Chapter 5 on contemporary practices how the dominant practices of journalism may be transformed and how notions such as professionalism, competence and expertise can be reassessed.

Hackett and Carroll (2006) offer a threefold definition of alternative media that concisely draws together many of the perspectives that we have already observed in our discussion so far. Their three features may also be usefully applied to the practices of alternative journalism. First, they show that alternative media tend to be 'relatively autonomous from corporate capital and the state' (p. 58). While this autonomy can be a weakness (many projects fail due to lack of funding), their independence from the dominant methods of organizing media encourages them to experiment with more inclusive and egalitarian forms of control, such as collective and consensus decision-making. Second, alternative media tend to pursue politically progressive aims. These are manifested in representational strategies that give access to 'voices and issues marginalized in hegemonic media' (ibid.). Finally, these two features make possible the third: the promotion of horizontal communication between members of marginalized groups and across these groups. Hackett and Carroll stress the importance of this process in transforming audiences from consumers of the media (and even as commodities of the media, to be traded by media corporations and advertisers) to participants in the processes of media production. Though Hackett and Carroll draw their definition from an examination of contemporary practices, the principles of alternative journalism can be found in history (as we showed earlier in the book). It is worth reminding ourselves of these, in particular those of the English Radical press, as they provide a valuable starting point for the next stage of our discussion.

Curran and Seaton's (1997) assessment of the English Radical press includes evidence of the redrawing of technical and professional roles and responsibilities, together with social and cultural transformations. The major features of this journalism were:

1 clandestine, underground distribution networks;
2 'pauper management';
3 journalists seeing themselves 'as activists rather than as professionals';
4 an interest in 'expos[ing] the dynamics of power and inequality rather than report[ing] "hard news"' (Curran and Seaton, 1997: 15);
5 developing close relationships with readers – to the extent that many papers were supplied with reports written by readers (such as those by 'worker correspondents' – *Workers' Life*, 1928/1983);

6 close links with radical organizations, highlighting the value of 'combination' and organized action; and
7 the key role of radical media in a working-class public sphere (Eley, 1992).

We have already encountered some of these features: Downing links democratic communication with political activism and radical organization; Rodriguez's notion of citizens' media entails a journalism that is practised and organized by ordinary citizens outside the institutional arrangements of the mainstream media (Curran and Seaton's pauper management their). Couldry's concept of alternative media as interventions to rebalance media power are suggested by Curran and Seaton's fourth feature, that of exposing the dynamics of power and inequality. What is common to Downing, Rodriguez and Couldry is the notion of ordinary people (that is, people for whom journalism is not a professional activity) who become reporters through either eyewitness testimony or the application of their own specialist, amateur knowledge to the issues being reported. The journalism thus produced adopts very different news values from those of the mass media, foregrounding as its subjects those who, in the mass media, tend only to be regarded as observers or marginal commentators on events (such as in the vox pop interview) or who achieve prominence only when they are the actors in a situation that is bounded by values based on, for instance, conflict or the bizarre.

Langer (1998) has shown how a limited set of narratives and character-types within mainstream narratives operate forms of cultural closure that prevent other forms of story-telling and other representations (whether oppositional or contradictory) from being essayed. In the case of ordinary people, dominant story-types deal with overturning expectations – there is an emphasis on how the 'unremarkable' individual may be capable of extraordinary achievements (for example, as the result of adversity or the lack of cultural and material resources). We also encounter ordinary people as subject to the control of external forces ('fate'), for example, stories of human tragedy (such as accidents, deaths and bereavements). In both cases, such stories and their actors tap into mythic representations of heroes and victims, and from this their cultural-symbolic power and their resonances with audiences derive. By contrast, alternative journalism seeks not to set ordinary people apart as either heroes or victims but as a set of voices which have as equal a right to be heard as do the voices of elite groups. Alternative journalism is populated not by the voices of elite groups in society but by

> alternative social actors [such as] the poor, the oppressed, the marginalised and indeed the ordinary manual labourer, woman, youth and child as the main subjects of [their] news and features. (Traber, 1985: 2)

For Traber, the most thoroughgoing version of alternative journalism is that produced by the people whose concerns it represents, from a position of engagement and direct participation. This need not preclude the involvement of professionals, but they will be firmly in the role of advisers; their presence intended to enable the ordinary people to produce their own work, independent of professional journalists and editors. Traber's primary concerns are with the production of news in the less-developed countries, especially in areas of these countries where the mass media (if there are any) do not penetrate. Traber argues that when media production is placed in the hands of ordinary people, the types of news and the style in which it is presented will be more relevant, more useful and more appropriate to the communities in which they are produced and distributed. Alternative news values are bound up not just in what is considered as news, but also in approaches to newsgathering and in who writes such news and how it is presented.

These values present a direct challenge to the 'regime of objectivity' (Hackett and Zhao, 1998: 86) that dominates professionalized journalism, as we saw in the chapter on contemporary practices. This challenge has both a normative and an epistemological aspect. The normative ideal of professionalized journalism emphasizes the factual nature of news. It is based on the empiricist assumption that there exist 'facts' in the world and that it is possible to identify these facts accurately and without bias (the journalistic norm of detachment). The normative ideal of alternative journalism argues the opposite: that reporting is always bound up with values (personal, professional, institutional) and that it is therefore never possible to separate facts from values. This leads to the epistemological challenge: that different forms of knowledge may be produced, which themselves present different and multiple versions of 'reality' from those of the mass media.

In Chapter 5, we introduced the practice of active witnessing, the process through which participants in an event become reporters on the event, as well as on their own place in that event. To this we can add the application of the specialist, local community knowledge that amateur reporters employ in their stories. We can conceptualize these two practices as 'native reporting' (Atton, 2002a).

Alternative Journalism as Native Reporting

Native reporting can usefully define the activities of alternative journalists working within communities of interest to present news that is relevant to those communities' interests, presented in a manner that is meaningful to them and with their collaboration and support. The term was first used by a mainstream journalist, Robert Chesshyre, to describe himself upon his return to Britain following his posting as the *Observer's* Washington correspondent (Chesshyre, 1987): 'coming home, one had to learn again the native idiom' (p. 13). For Chesshyre, this meant relearning a method of reporting about local, everyday 'situations with which readers can personally identify' (p. 31). He observes how such reports drew many letters from readers

> who have something to say and want to join in [...]. They know more than their masters do of what it is like to have a child in a comprehensive school, or to be unemployed, to try to start a business. They are the reliable witnesses. (Chesshyre, 1987: 31–32)

Within the limits of mainstream journalism, Chesshyre was overturning the hierarchy of access to the media in a way that is similar to the public (or civic) journalism movement in the US. As recent contributions to journalism studies have suggested, it is the professional location of public journalism that has so far prevented its advocates and practitioners from making anything but piecemeal interventions in the dominant practices of journalism (Davis, 2000; Glasser, 2000; Woodstock, 2002). Despite its claims, public journalism – working as it does within the market and within long-standing organizational, institutional and professional structures – operates in similar ways to mainstream journalism (of which it is, after all, a part): 'traditional and public journalisms adopt similar narrative strategies to effect essentially the same ends: placing the power of telling society's stories in the hands of journalists' (Woodstock, 2002: 37). Within the model of public journalism, Chesshyre's 'reliable witnesses' still need professional reporters to tell their stories for them.

On the other hand, native reporting evokes those local grassroots journalists by whom Michael Traber sets so much store, whose value lies not simply in their role as message-creators, but as members of a community whose work enables the entire community to come together, to 'analyse [its] historical situation, which transforms consciousness, and leads to the will to change a situation' (Traber, 1985: 3). Traber is placing these grass-roots journalists within the context of colonialism, in particular within its legacy of dualism: 'a dual culture, a dual economy and a dual polity' (ibid.). Local communities under colonialism found themselves unable to participate in the media that ostensibly reported on matters of concern to them; they were alienated from the methods of production as well as from the practices of reporting.

Their experiences and interests were mediated instead by the colonizing journalist, 'placed either above or at the centre of things, yet apart from them' (Spurr, 1993: 16). Spurr argues that the power relations inherent in this relationship between observer and observed are grounded by the routinized narrative practices of journalism. These practices 'obviate the demand for concrete, practical action on the part of its audience' (p. 45). By contrast, native reporters are at the centre of things as participants; their aim is to feed discussion and debate from the perspective of the colonized. Native reporters seek to take back what is 'their' news, just as the grassroots journalism that Traber discusses seeks to empower local people in Latin America, India and Africa. The native reporter is the Other, what Spurr has his colonizing journalist call 'the antithesis of civilised value' (p. 7).

Fursich (2002: 80) argues that 'most reporting is a form of representing the Other'. It follows that one of the most powerful journalistic methods employed to counter 'othering' within alternative media is surely that where social actors, instead of being subjects of the news, become their own correspondents, reporting on their own experiences, struggles and ideas. In this way, alternative journalism provides a platform for those 'others', acknowledged by Cottle as being 'deviant' or 'speechless', to represent themselves directly through their own expression. This highlights a struggle within the politics of representation, a 'politics of struggle and power in the everyday world' (Said, 1982/1985: 147). The native reporter gains self-respect, and moral and political strength, through self-representation, thereby drawing power away from the mainstream back to the disenfranchised and marginalized groups that are the native reporter's immediate community.

Native reporting need not only refer to actual conditions of colonization; it can have wider applications. In her study of AIDS video production, Alexandra Juhasz (1995) conceptualizes the activists who make the films in a way that is reminiscent of notions of the self-representation of the Other:

> Alternative AIDS media ... actively situates itself *within* the object of study ... to look is to see and know *yourself*, not the other – an entirely different route to pleasure and power. (Juhasz, 1995: 138, original emphases)

The notion of the native reporter can be a hybrid one, where source and writer become one. In this case, such reporters become their own primary definers. At other times, where native reporters employ sources other than themselves, they will tend to privilege ordinary voices above those of elite groups. Harcup's (2003) comparative study of alternative and mainstream reporting in northern England found that reporters for the alternative press favoured the views and comments of bystanders, not in abbreviated vox pop formats, but 'by quoting at length from anonymous eyewitnesses on the streets [and] by reporting overheard conversations within the courtroom' in preference to the official voices favoured by the mainstream (Harcup, 2003: 365). Deuze and Dimoudi's (2002) study of online journalists in the Netherlands finds similar community impulses at work; like Preston, they hold out hope that the converged information and communication technologies of the Internet will enable the development of closer dialogue between journalists and their audiences, resulting in sourcing and agenda-setting that are driven by a wider range of more heterogeneous interest groups than is the norm in mainstream journalism.

So far we have presented the theoretical background against which to place alternative journalism. We have explored theories that aim to explain the function and value of alternative journalism, whether as the media of social movements or as the media production of ordinary people in local communities. The concept of native reporting has demonstrated how the practices of alternative journalism are placed in opposition to dominant, professionalized media practices that tend to marginalize or misrepresent the majority of social actors. Our final task in this chapter is to place the practices of alternative journalism in a much wider setting, as practices of cultural production within society.

Alternative Journalism and Field Theory

The work of Pierre Bourdieu offers a fruitful approach to developing a sociology of alternative journalism. Through his theory of cultural production, Bourdieu (1993, 1996) presents a method of understanding culture in society that neither mystifies the creative process (as ineffable) nor reduces its genesis to social context alone (as some Marxian perspectives have done). Instead, he provides a framework upon which may be built a complex understanding of cultural production in social life, one that takes into account structural determinants such as economics and politics (power), interactions between individuals and institutions, and the development of taste, social and cultural value, and esteem.

As Benson notes, the production of a cultural discourse (such as alternative journalism) is 'marked by the struggle for distinction. In order to exist in a field, one must mark one's difference' (Benson, 2003: 122). This difference is achieved by interactions, borrowings and struggles between agents across related fields or sub-fields (for example, across mainstream and alternative journalism) as well as within a single field or sub-field. Bourdieu's concept of the field can help us account for and understand the differential struggles for distinction between the mainstream and the alternative, and within the alternative itself. Further, field theory offers more precise terms than 'alternative' and 'mainstream' with which to examine difference. Before applying field theory to alternative journalism, we will first set out the broad principles of Bourdieu's theory.

The theory comprises three 'structuring structures' (Toynbee, 2001: 8), which together clarify how producers create in social settings. These are: the field of works, the habitus of individual producers and the field of cultural production itself. The field of works comprises the store of 'historically accumulated symbolic resources' (ibid.) on which creators within a partic-ular cultural activity or genre draw to produce their work. The choices they make and what they do with those resources – the ways in which they com-bine and adapt them (or privilege some over others) – is explained by the creator's habitus, the personal social history and context of each producer (such as class, educational background, professional values, training). Cultural production is therefore to be considered as a set of social processes, one that is determined by these structuring structures at the same time as those structures are contested and struggled over.

The field of production contains both the field of works and the constel-lation of producers. But this field is divided and subject to economic and political constraints (a greater field of power within which Bourdieu places the field of production). Bourdieu divides the field of cultural produc-tion into two sub-fields: large-scale (mass) production and small-scale (restricted) production. The former is primarily concerned with the pro-duction of commercial cultural products on a mass scale. Its dependence on outside forces (primarily economic, but also legal and political) renders it 'heteronomous': it is never fully independent, for example, of market forces. By contrast, the latter sub-field is more autonomous. It is not concerned with a mass audience, nor with economic status (Bourdieu gives avant-garde art as an exemplar). Instead, it is distinguished less by economic capital and more by cultural capital (education, expertise, knowledge and so on).

Bourdieu has applied the principles of field theory to develop the notion of a field of journalism (Bourdieu, 1997). In its original formulation, his pro-posal has been criticized as undifferentiated and too monolithic 'to provide a realistic account of a plural and heterogeneous reality' of dominant jour-nalistic practices, let alone alternatives to them (Marliere, 1998: 223). More recent work, however, has shown useful ways forward. Benson (2006) argues that economic capital 'is expressed via circulation, or advertising rev-enues, or audience ratings' (p. 190). Cultural capital can therefore be seen to lie in journalism that is respected more for its professionalism, its erudi-tion and its originality (though the two forms of capital are not exclusive, the polar relationship of the two forms makes it impossible for high levels of both to coexist in the same journalistic organization).

If we try to understand alternative journalism in these terms, its general disinterest in economic capital (as well as its general lack of mass-popular success or recognition) suggests that it is located in the sub-field of small-scale (restricted) production, while mainstream journalism is located in the sub-field of large-scale (mass) production. Bourdieu's terms (small scale and large scale) have an analytical precision that the terms alternative and main-stream lack (Hesmondhalgh, 2006). This is an important point: the impre-cision of a term like alternative has resulted in much dispute, whether polemic (Abel, 1997) or rational (Atton, 2002a; Couldry and Curran,

2003b). Bourdieu's terms are far more explanatory in terms of the social location of cultural production.

It is important to make further distinctions within each sub-field. Bourdieu posits two poles in each sub-field where he places cultural production according to its level of symbolic càpital (defined by Thompson (1991: 14) as 'accumulated prestige or honour'). This is an especially useful distinction to make in the case of alternative journalism. As we have seen, the sub-field of small-scale production is generally uninterested in economic capital. Bourdieu argues that high levels of symbolic capital are to be found in what he calls the 'consecrated avant garde', that is, at the pole of small-scale cultural production that enjoys significant prestige, critical (though not necessarily public) acclaim and some level of institutional recognition (in the form of awards and prizes). At the opposite pole lies small-scale production that is less interested in seeking – and might never achieve – a high level of symbolic capital.

Symbolic capital may have an ideological function. To show this, Hesmondhalgh uses the example of small-scale popular music production ('alternative music'): 'new entrants [into the field] would vigorously attack the consecrated forms of the alternative' (Hesmondhalgh, 2006: 217). In both cases, however, as Hesmondhalgh puts it, 'cultural producers in the restricted sub-field are left pretty much to 'talk to each other' (p. 214). This is not to say that such conversations are irrelevant or self-indulgent in the case of alternative journalism; after all, spaces for conversation within social movements or local communities can be, as we have seen, essential ingredients in the lifeblood of social groups.

We must remember, however, that Bourdieu developed his theory in order to account for cultural production in the professionalized worlds of art and literature. His emphasis on the individual professional creator, therefore, leaves little room for democratized notions of production, such as those found in alternative journalism, where we frequently find amateurs, where professionals and non-professionals might work together, and where collective methods of production are used as frequently as individualized methods of production.

In applying field theory to alternative journalism, we must therefore be sensitive to the possibility of interaction between the individual and the collective, and between the professional and the non-professional, as in the mixed economies of production and distribution that we encountered in the chapter on social demographics. While Bourdieu's framework is valuable in distinguishing the broad differences between large-scale (mass) and small-scale (restricted) production, it is harder to locate, for example, the *Big Issue*, which relies on a mass audience for its success, or a project such as *OhmyNews*, which combines professional and non-professional writers within professionalized, hierarchical, organizational and editorial settings. Both seem to sit astride the two sub-fields.

The place of non-professional producers is left largely unexamined by Bourdieu. He does not seem to consider non-professional cultural production as a field in its own right; non-professionals inhabit the field of power, not the specific field of cultural production (Bourdieu, 1996: 124). Moreover, Bourdieu has little to say about what it means to be a professional; this also makes it difficult to identify the characteristics of the non-professional. We do know that he ascribes to the non-professional a low level of cultural capital (ibid.). This is confirmed empirically by Klinenberg's (2005) study of youth media activists in the US: 'although they occasionally break into minor media outlets, such as public radio and television, they rarely obtain the levels of cultural capital that are necessary to place work in or earn the respect of the most powerful organizational actors in the field' (p. 189). Klinenberg argues that web-based media offer the means to bypass the professionalized and institutionalized large-scale media: the web 'requires less economic, social, and cultural capital' (p. 190).

Perhaps the answer lies within the specific practices of alternative journalism itself. As Toynbee finds in popular music production, there appears a 'greater openness of the field of production to variations in the habitus of producers, plus the range and diversity of the field of works [which lead to] greater instability than in consecrated art and a less clear-cut distinction between heretical and orthodox positions' (Toynbee, 2001: 9). The habitus and position of individual and collective producers in alternative journalism might be modified as a result, for example, of exposure to professional training, particularly where they hope to speak to audiences wider than those already sympathetic. This means adopting techniques, genres and styles that are dominant in the professionalized, large-scale sub-field of journalism, and that have proven efficacy in attracting larger audiences. Klinenberg is pessimistic about the possibility of this strategy succeeding. For him, when activists adopt professional journalistic techniques, they are hoping to 'gain legitimacy inside the journalistic field' (Klinenberg, 2005: 189). But what if we consider these activists to be within the journalistic field already, rather than in a putative activist field?

Duval (2005) identifies small-scale journalistic production with the 'paradigm [of the] "alternative" press' (p. 141), the sub-field that is 'least dependent on the economic field, but also the least "professionalized"' (p. 146). Duval, however, is studying not alternative journalism but the 'subspace' of economic journalism in France: his examples of an alternative press working in this space includes the left-wing weekly *Charlie Hebdo*, the satirical newspaper *Le Canard Enchaîné* and *Le Monde Diplomatique*. As we find with Bourdieu, Duval has little to say about what he means by 'professionalized'; neither do any of his examples include ideologies and practices that we might think of as 'deprofessionalized'. What is significant is that Duval shows the sub-field of small-scale production to be far from undifferentiated.

Moreover, he shows that it is possible to think of alternative journalism as occupying many different positions within the sub-field: some of these positions might be closer to the large-scale sub-field in terms, say, of their cultural or economic capital (in the UK, for example, this could include the *Big Issue* and *Private Eye*). Other positions might be closer to related fields such as the activist field suggested by Klinenberg.

What is important here is to posit alternative journalism not only as occupying the sub-field of small-scale production, but to consider it as able to occupy liminal positions: whether at the juncture of the two sub-fields of journalism or between an activist (or other) field and the journalistic field. Liminal positions are implied by Bourdieu's field theory (after all, field theory should not be understood as a congeries of discrete spaces), but field theory itself has so far had little to say about them. The low levels of cultural and economic capital Bourdieu assigns to non-professionals might explain the failure of amateur and activist journalists to make any significant impact on large-scale journalistic production. Yet cultural capital might well be achieved at the juncture of the fields of journalism and activism in ways that Bourdieu does not specify.

Evidence of the liminal position that some alternative journalism might occupy comes from Hesmondhalgh's general account of cultural production. He finds some common ground between sub-fields, arguing that: 'there is now a huge amount of cultural production taking place on the boundaries between [the two] sub-fields [...]; or, perhaps better still, that restricted production has become introduced *into* the field of mass production (Hesmondhalgh, 2006: 222, original emphasis). In the context of alternative journalism, examples of these activities at the boundaries include the professionalization and normalization of blogs in large-scale journalism and, though perhaps less obviously, the fanzine-like production taking place on large-scale, international social networking sites such as MySpace.

Gudmundsson et al. (2002)'s assessment of professional rock journalism as 'semi-autonomous' seems to recognize both its liminal nature and its movement into large-scale production from its roots in the amateur, underground press and fanzines, accruing cultural capital as it moves. We might also acknowledge movement in the opposite direction, though this is not to argue that large-scale cultural production will move in its entirety into the restricted field. There are isolated examples of cultural producers making this transition, such as Everett True's movement from professional journalist writing for the UK commercial weekly *Melody Maker* to fanzine writer (Atton, 2006a). In this case, though, we need to bear in mind that such a movement has been achieved thanks to – and not in spite of – the high levels of economic, cultural and symbolic capital accrued by True in his professional work.

Conclusion

We have seen how alternative media have been characterized by their potential for participation. Rather than media production being the province of elite, centralized organizations and institutions, alternative journalism offers the possibilities for individuals and groups to create their own media 'from the periphery'. Studies such as those by Downing and Rodriguez show how radical and citizens' media may be used to develop identity and solidarity within social movements and local communities. To think about alternative journalism in this way is to consider it as far more than mere cultural aberration or marginal practice. At a theoretical level, such thinking encourages critiques of media production in general, challenging what Nick Couldry (2002: n.p.) has termed 'the myth of the mediated centre'.

At an epistemological level, to consider the practices of alternative media producers as alternative journalism is to critique the ethics, norms and routines of professionalized journalism. Alternative journalism will tend, through its very practices, to examine notions of truth, reality, objectivity, expertise, authority and credibility. Hamilton argues for a '"multidimensional" [view that] is meant to emphasize ... a conception of media participation as varied, hybrid and, in many cases, not identifiable at all from within an evaluative framework that allows only producers and consumers' (Hamilton, 2003: 297). We need to consider alternative journalism practices as socially and culturally situated work, as well as processes of political empowerment. These practices might be drawn from mainstream practices, from history and from ideology; they might also challenge those practices or effect new forms of communication. The field theory of Bourdieu offers a sophisticated and nuanced methodology for exploring alternative journalism in relation to professionalized ideologies and practices, as well as to the activism that is so often its wellspring.

Alternative journalism may be understood as a radical challenge to the professionalized and institutionalized practices of the mainstream media. Alternative media privilege journalism that is closely wedded to notions of social responsibility, replacing an ideology of 'objectivity' with overt advocacy and oppositional practices. Its practices 'emphasise first person, eyewitness accounts by participants; reworking of the populist approaches of tabloid newspapers to recover a "radical popular" style of reporting; collective and anti-hierarchical forms of organization ... an inclusive, radical form of civic journalism' (Atton, 2003a: 267). In short, alternative journalism practices present ways of re-imagining journalism.

8

FUTURE DIRECTIONS

This chapter does not set out to predict the future. Instead, it takes its cue from the histories, contexts, and contemporary and comparative practices we have explored throughout this book. There seems to us to be no reason why persistent questions about organization (internal and across networks), economics, participation and access should cease to be relevant. However, the specific claim – about which historical reflection provides possibly the least guidance – is the accelerating importance of the Internet in alternative media production and reception. Indeed, much of what follows focuses on the Internet as the most conspicuous current site for alternative journalism. Despite its popularity and value, we question the continuing value and efficacy of a media technology that has nevertheless been responsible in large part for the massive increase and visibility of alternative forms of journalism. More broadly, we ask to what extent such practices are sustainable in a media-centric world, especially when some of their aims are so grounded in actual political change. Do the number and diversity of alternative journalism projects encourage and sustain 'active' citizenship, or do they merely represent another facet of a media-centric world in which lived experience is diminished? Do such journalisms have a coherent future, or is their very pluralism a threat to their effectiveness?

Organization

We begin with issues centred on organization. We saw in Chapter 3 how voluntary labour, low levels of funding and demographic constraints often prevent alternative journalism projects from achieving stability and longevity. These limitations are particularly relevant to an alternative journalism that promotes democratic dialogue and 'active' citizenship (as in Downing's radical media and Rodriguez's citizens' media). Political projects such as these depend on continuity and consistency to develop the most appropriate strategies and skills for their journalisms. We might also argue that an emphasis on collective and non-hierarchical, consensus decision-making (as a kind of prefigurative politics) can only delay the development of alternative journalism, requiring its practitioners to sustain projects for even longer, if only to establish stable norms and conventions of practice.

One can push questions further about the future of how alternative journalism is organized. Sceptics might argue that the persistence of these organizational conditions, together with the general tendency within alternative media projects towards radical independence, can only lead to alternative journalists remaining isolated and thus marginalized. Their desire for independence might lead to separatism across the practices of alternative journalism. Such a development would take Comedia's argument concerning the ghettoization of alternative journalism even further, asserting that alternative journalists will become increasingly isolated from each other, their audiences fragmented, and wider publics largely ignorant of what from the 'outside' might well appear incoherent and directionless. Williams's claim, noted in Chapter 1, that radical-popular journalism due to marginalization had become seen as specialized, idiosyncratic, 'sectarian and strange' (Williams, 1970: 22) makes this point clear. Such potential consequences would be especially damaging to alternative journalism that is wedded to the activities of social movements. After all, what is the use of radical projects of representation, reporting and commentary if they advance neither the internal goals of a movement nor its wider, increasingly global, goals?

This leads to a related issue that emerges from our discussion of 'the place of media power' (in Nick Couldry's apt phrase). If alternative journalism is above all concerned with contesting and rebalancing – if not democratizing – media power, then it must do so by engaging with broader projects of social transformation: '[b]ridges need to be built not only within the media field but also beyond it' (Hackett and Carroll (2006: 208). Hackett and Carroll argue that the principles of democracy and justice found within social movements for political and social change must be at the centre of thinking about and re-imagining media production, not the other way around. We saw in Chapter 4 how proposals and position papers could form the basis for a philosophy and practice of alternative journalism that is sensitive to specific, local and regional conditions, but at the same time coheres in a global project that links with, and is also sensitive to, the developing agendas of transnational social movements. It appears unlikely, however, that we would ever see such a policy enacted in anything but the most general terms: the terrain of alternative journalism is itself far too contested, its practitioners often too transient, to produce any enduring and articulated response.

Popularization and Challenge

However, the improbability of a unified policy defining alternative journalism is likely to be its most valuable characteristic. Despite the problems noted above, we do not wish to paint a pessimistic picture. As a counterbalance, two more optimistic possibilities for the future present themselves. They both lie, somewhat paradoxically, in what we have already identified as problems: fragmentation and separatism within alternative journalism, and the challenge of transforming alternative journalism from a marginal practice to a meaningful form of public communication. First, one of the strengths of alternative journalism – and perhaps its abiding ideology – is its resistance to homogenization. This resistance derives from critiques of the political economy and the ideological practices of professional journalism. However divergent the specific practices of alternative journalism might be, they share a common principle of reflexivity, through which (ideally at least) they are able to respond to the dominant forms of journalism. As well as being reflexive in relation to the field of media power, practices of alternative journalism must also be 'responsive to the concerns and needs of [the] broad swathe of democratic movements' (Hackett and Carroll, 2006: 208). Rather than consider alternative journalism as irredeemably weakened by diversity and difference, we should consider its norms to be beneficially fluid and mobile, a result of continual reflexivity.

The second more optimistic possibility emerges from the liminal position of alternative journalism in relation to the journalistic field, as we argued in Chapter 7. Both the history and the contemporary practices of alternative journalism show how variously it has formed the wellspring of dominant practices of journalism, borrowing from – while at the same time transforming – those practices. Practices that we think of as experiments in alternative media, such as the blog, now enjoy immense popularity – even if not read by large audiences, almost everyone is aware of them.

The popularization and acceptance of hitherto experimental forms of journalism can be seen as a form of absorption and depoliticization, but they must also be seen as forms of what is, for the time being, a successful challenge. Greater acceptance and use of such forms by general audiences move alternative journalism beyond the typical audiences for alternative media who can be considered 'subaltern counterpublics' (Fraser, 1992: 123). Broad swathes of the public have become media-literate in their use of what otherwise might have remained radical forms of communication. In short, the radical has both changed and been changed by the mainstream in a struggle over the practice of journalism and its relationship to democratic participation. Such a struggle has taken place at a time of an identified democratic deficit in the mass media's relations with the public (Hackett and Carroll, 2006: Ch. 1).

For example, in Chapter 5 we saw how bloggers (whether professional or amateur) were seen by audiences as recovering some of the trust lost by professional journalists; that trust was recovered not by an appeal to objectivity and 'professionalism', but by a credibility that came from audiences being able to find common ground between their own everyday experiences, hopes and fears, and the personalization of the bloggers' reports through methods that equally emphasized the everyday. Livingstone et al.'s (2005) review of the research literature on adult literacy finds that online news sources are becoming increasingly popular, particularly at times of international conflict. They do note, however, that whilst these sources are used to supplement existing print and broadcast media, the sources tend to be dominated by established news providers. What Livingstone, Van Couvering and Thumin call the 'literacy task' therefore begins with comparing and contrasting different sources; when the range of sources narrows to a small number of institutionalized 'big brands', the task becomes one of 'locating and evaluating alternative news sources' (p. 39). There is little evidence about how – and even whether – news consumers are doing this. Anecdotal evidence exists about the use of blogging sites; detailed empirical work is still to emerge.

A key factor in enabling both these literacy tasks is the ability of audiences to find alternative sources: uneven awareness of and access to alternative news sources are likely to lead to a further fragmentation of audiences than we are already seeing within alternative media and in the wider, multi-channel world (though the deregulated and largely deprofessionalized world of alternative media has perhaps always been 'multi-channel'). In the case of alternative journalism wedded to social justice movements, such a continued fragmentation would only worsen the impact and reach of alternative journalism. Signposting, an activity increasingly the province of online content aggregators (Chalaby, 2000), is an integral part of enabling media literacy, but would be reliant on alternative journalism projects working together in a formalized manner that is currently only evident within subdivisions of alternative media practices (as in some ethnic minority media). Even within the alternative media of special interests such as gay and lesbian journalism or environmental activism, there appears to be far too antagonistic a range of ideologies, aims and practices for any systematic signposting or aggregation to have emerged.

There is limited signposting and aggregation of alternative news sources from mainstream media organizations, but these tend to be either event-based and transient (used to enhance a specific news story) or more like consumer guides ('this week's top ten blogs', whose selection is often obscure). This is in part explained by the difficulty – even (perhaps especially) for the professional journalist – in locating anything like a representative sample of the hundreds of thousands of alternative news sources. It is also explained by a particular orientation of the profession (especially in its institutionalized form) towards alternative journalism.

Additional forms of challenge to commercial-popular journalism are likely to persist and change. Throughout this book, we have observed that already alternative journalism in all its forms is never isolated from external pressures and norms. We have discussed how these pressures (prompting critiques of the mass media) and norms (dominant ideologies and practices) might be deployed productively and reflexively to develop a praxis of alternative journalism. However, the relationship between alternative and mainstream journalism is not a one-way street. Neither are borrowings, transformations and interminglings always to the benefit of alternative journalism. If the blog has done something to offset the democratic deficit in the media by demonstrating how mainstream journalism might otherwise be practised, we should remember that, as Lowrey (2006) has argued, the blog has also been used by professional journalists to regain the trust of a disaffected public. On an individual level, this might result in reflexive practice within the profession; at an institutional level, it might lead to the redefinition of blogging 'as a journalistic tool', with non-professional bloggers (alternative journalists) as 'journalism wannabes' (Lowrey, 2006: 493). We encountered this argument in Chapter 5, but now we shall explore some of its consequences for the prospects of alternative journalism.

User-created Content and Participation

The rise of user-created content and citizen journalism presents a current challenge to professional news organizations, and one that is likely to persist. The challenge has been dealt with by the incorporation of this content (and implicitly its techniques) into the routines of professional journalism. Incorporation is particularly frequent in breaking television news, where news organizations find it impossible to obtain images from anything but amateur sources. However, such a strategy has little to do with the principles of alternative journalism that we have explored in this book. Indeed, the use of 'consumer content' is closer to the routines of vox pops than it is to that of the deprofessionalized, politically engaged and reflexive alternative reporter. It is only the content that is being incorporated, not the philosophy or point of view of the citizen (except in the most banal way). On one hand, to the degree that what is presented in such bulletins is not citizen journalism as practised by *OhmyNews* or Indymedia, there might be no problem here at all. However, given that media literacy seems to be largely derived from the knowledge of media practices (however critical an audience might be of those practices), then what *passes for* citizen journalism (that is, crudely speaking, an amateur video of events deemed newsworthy by professional journalists) might well *become* citizen journalism, discursively speaking.

One should keep an eye on blogging to see how this process will play out. The blog has become incorporated into the everyday practices of professional journalism. In the UK, *PM*, one of BBC Radio 4's major news and review programmes, maintains a blog which acts as a forum for its listeners' discussion of the programme's stories, is used to promote the programme and, significantly, invites listeners to discuss ideas for features with the production team (these are broadcast weekly in a special edition of the programme called *iPM*). It is difficult to assess how successful this last proposal will be, but it suggests a method of programming that is modelled, at least in principle, on the US model of public journalism. We might, of course, see this as a cynical attempt to recuperate radical forms of representation for the purposes of marketing, to take emerging forms of alternative journalism and rework them in order to add a contemporary sheen to dominant practices, thus demonstrating that established news organizations are sensitive to popular cultural change. This is not a new strategy, as Williams and many others have observed. Duncombe (1997) shows how institutions as diverse as art galleries, clothing stores and multinational media corporations have adapted the style and content of fanzines and zines to promote their products: in the 1990s, Time-Warner published *Dirt*, a magazine for its younger employees in the form of a zine.

Given such enormous efforts to incorporate and neutralize reflexive, critical alternative journalism as monitored, narrow 'contributions' for marketing purposes, how might alternative journalism (as a cultural response to the dominant practices of the mass media) respond to incorporation? Despite the uncertainties ahead, what seems less and less to be an option is to resort to a principled but eviscerating separation and isolation. To remain on the outside looking in does not seem to be the productive option that it was once thought. What also must be reassessed are many past and existing countercultural strategies of opposition, such as those employed by the situationists of the 1960s (Debord, 1967/1983), which have been incorporated into the logic of commercialization. Christine Harold's (2007) analysis of the practice of cultural critique of commercialization highlights the difficulties and the opportunities. Harold argues that contemporary strategies of incorporation signal a significant shift in the corporate control of the marketplace, and with this comes a necessity to develop new strategies to combat this control. She suggests that oppositional practices that lie outside the dominant practices of corporate culture are no longer sufficient: 'situationist strategies of collage and pastiche, original though they may have been in their original time and place, are now quite at home in the vernacular of advertising' (p. 67), and that critiques of advertising employing collage and pastiche (such as 'subvertising' practised by groups such as the Canadian organization Adbusters) also do not take into account the incorporation of those techniques into the world of marketing. When the institutions of advertising are already subverting notions of truth and authenticity, and employing pastiche and irony in their campaigns, 'to attempt to expose or dismantle the image rhetoric of consumerism' (p. 69) using the same rhetorical tools can have at best limited implications. When dominant culture and counterculture share the same rhetorical tools, where does resistance lie?

The relevance of anti-consumer media activism to future directions of alternative journalism lies in how the incorporation and mimicking of citizen journalism by corporate media resembles the mimicking of 'subvertising' that Harold identifies in the contemporary marketing campaigns of companies such as Diesel and Sony. However, a further correspondence between the case of anti-consumer media activism and the future of alternative journalism might also exist in recognizing the relevance to the latter of certain strategies Harold proposes for the former. For example, instead of considering two sets of cultural strategies (the 'mainstream' and the 'alternative') in opposition, where the markets are perpetually in dominance and publics are marginalized as a cultural force (only able to offer piecemeal and ultimately ineffectual resistance to those markets), Harold suggests that working with, rather than against, the logic of commercialism offers a '*provocation* to commercialism by taking market values more seriously than many free marketers themselves' (Harold, 2007: xxxii, original emphasis).

The tactic for alternative journalism in the future may indeed be to intensify the logic of commercialism, not simply to repudiate it. Harold cites as examples the Creative Commons project (www.creativecommons.org) and the open source movements in computing and in music (Atton, 2004: Ch. 4; Berry, 2004). These projects, Harold argues, intensify the logic of commercialism by pushing notions of property, ownership and creativity to their limits. They offer models of cultural production based not on individual ownership and private control, but on collective ownership and social authorship (Toynbee, 2001). These and other selected facets of commercialism recognize and rely on the contradictions in commercial forms and control, and seek to make critical use of them.

Future Contexts and Pressures

Up to this point, we have focused on the future challenges and directions of the more immediate concerns of organization, professionalization and participation, and the constitution of alternative journalism in relation to commercial efforts to skin its form in order to incorporate and neutralize it. However, one must keep in mind that such developments and possibilities are themselves made possible by larger-scale developments and pressures.

Thus, we also wish to identify and discuss the likely future directions for these enabling conditions.

While the case of the Internet is something we have already alluded to (in that, while important, it cannot on its own be seen as uniformly aiding alternative journalism), it raises the more general issue of technology and corresponding degrees of access. What is clear from the development and practice of alternative journalism to this point is how the emergence of more widely available technologies of reproduction and distribution – when practised within an alternative journalism that emphasizes the values of openness and broad participation – have aided this direction. Technologies earlier than the digital forms so often cited today include photocopying, cheap offset printing, and even earlier the mechanical printing press; and also include the commercial availability of printing and supplies as well as publicly available postal systems. Indeed, when assessing this development, one can suggest a paradoxical relationship between the level of technological sophistication and the expansion of access – that the greater the technological sophistication, the greater the possibility for expanding access and participation (this is, of course, dependent on contexts of use).

All this is to say that the goal of radical-popular forms of alternative journalism must be to work toward a transparency of different levels of training in composition or use. In other words, all who wish to contribute to or make use of alternative journalism should have the technical means and skill to do so. A present capability we see little change in is the continuing potential broadening of the technological means of composing and distributing materials for global distribution. However, this will live up to the intentions of a radical-popular alternative journalism only if it becomes increasingly neutral with respect to technical training and resources. Current limitations in need of continued work include the much-simplified but still often difficult matters of software coding and the management of computer networks, but even more importantly the widely variant knowledge of touch-typing and, further, of basic literacy in the form of reading. With this in mind, the increasing availability and use of video and audio recording as podcasts and vlogs is a quite promising future trend in regard to present barriers to basic literacy. They are promising because they are reliant on what Williams (1980b: 57) calls the more readily available 'primary physical resources' of 'speaking, listening, gesturing, observing' instead of the difficult-to-learn (and comparatively easy to control) skills of alphabetical composition and reading which require years of intensive training, not to mention computer sophistication. Given the present and growing use of audio and video recording, and the accelerating commercial imperative of developing both consumer-grade recorders and broadened digital bandwidth, such a trend will very likely continue for the foreseeable future.

One must also keep in mind the geopolitical unevenness of commercial developments. As increasingly diasporic and distributed social movements rely more and more heavily on digital efforts enabled by the Internet and the commercial computer industry, access to infrastructure – both in the form of networks and of hardware and software – remains a key problem to work out for the future. Among the key points to note is the gulf between Internet capabilities in the West and, for example, many parts of the African continent. No matter what kind of digital means of alternative journalism are available in the West, those same means will continue to play at best a marginal role in many areas of the world for the foreseeable future, and will probably be limited to intellectuals in urban centres, tied as they are to current patterns of commercial infrastructural development.

Taking into account the matters of technology and infrastructure as well as of citizen journalism discussed above, the current challenge to commercial news companies posed by user-created content and the rise of so-called 'citizen journalism' will continue as a key challenge. We have already noted the efforts that commercial news companies are making to steer user contributions into professionalized forms that simply mimic 'eyewitness' accounts typical of traditional news. Despite these efforts at incorporation, the commercial necessity of user-created content will continue as the major challenge not only to individual media companies but to the very structure and viability of media industries as currently conceived.

The likely scenario for the future goes something like this. Being the commercial companies they are, media organizations compete madly for market shares and audiences, using any and all means at their disposal to best their competition. Greater public participation in the form of user-created content is only the latest effort to find the elusive competitive advantage. Thus, if a news company is increasingly compelled to provide substantial content gathered by 'outsiders' in order to gain a competitive advantage, then why have any 'insiders' at all, except to manage the flow of material from the outside? To the degree that this continues to be the case, the long-standing competitive advantage of professionalization – and how it restricts the legitimate practice of journalism to a handful of organizationally validated professionals – will continue to be modified if not even more openly challenged than it already is. Even more generally speaking, the political economy of the news industry today is in a very real sense doing more to shuffle and in some ways to open up access than any degree of boycott or other overt challenge (Hartley's (2000) notion of redactional journalism suggests as much). At the same time, the danger of the incorporation of what has been an oppositional practice into the logic of commercialization cannot be set aside.

Lastly, and perhaps most broadly, we see the remaining and in some ways deepest challenge and most promising trend as the experimentation in new forms of authoritative representations of crises in our world, forms that work in ways very different from bourgeois journalism. Much of this is being done in artistic spheres, as new ways of conceiving a distributed, fluid collectivity but also of one's place and contribution in it. Current examples hardly resemble journalism, but that may turn out to be its advantage. One such form is the collaborative documentary, which is put to use in a variety of projects from the small and decidedly eclectic to the large and minimally commercial. The Echo Chamber Project not only seeks to make a film critical of the performance of the US press's role in the run-up to the Iraq invasion, but also focuses on 'developing collaborative techniques for producing this film' (Echo Chamber Project, 2007). The self-described 'grassroots political documentary' as developed by the Brave New Foundation coordinates 1,200 volunteer field producers, researchers and organizers for the production and distribution of its various documentaries (Brave New Films, 2006; Brave New Foundation, 2006). As an example, it drafted eight self-described 'middle-aged citizens from different backgrounds', asking them to watch three months of Fox News and to offer their own sense of key recurring techniques that the newscast used (News Hounds, 2006). At the same time, the production company recorded the newscast around the clock and then used the volunteer researchers' observations to develop the key points of analysis embodied in the documentary released as *Outfoxed: Rupert Murdoch's War on Journalism* (Boynton, 2004). Over and above the information gathered and the case made, what is notable here is the formation of new, collaborative forms of composition. Despite the significance of the ongoing project of Independent Media Centres and the indebtedness to collaborative composition pioneered in textual form through wiki software, alternative journalism has yet to engage fully with these forms.

Beyond documentary projects (as well as the ever-expanding number of sites on to which users can download their own video and audio), other efforts experiment with forms of knowledge about the world more distantly related to the claims of bourgeois journalism, but no less engaged in issues of the world. For example, the 'Lives Connected' project documents the human implications of the Hurricane Katrina catastrophe for the US city of New Orleans, both by providing a series of public testimonials and also by providing through its innovative linking scheme a sense of common patterns and experiences among the individual stories which enlarges by many times one's understanding of this disaster as a common, social experience. The project was undertaken by a New-Orleans-based advertising agency, thus also complicating easy distinctions between 'mainstream' and 'alternative', while also stretching the digitally enabled forms of knowledge that may yet be possible (Peter A. Mayer Advertising, 2007).

While perhaps unnervingly strange, these and many other experiments at collaborative (as opposed to professionalized) composition and forms of knowledge outside of bourgeois journalism constitute publics in new ways, thus enabling audiences to become creators in ways not fragmented and isolated (emulating the dominant conceptions of creativity), but in ways that are collective, social, negotiable – and open. They also suggest how future directions of alternative journalism are increasingly aspiring not only to information delivery (as valuable as that is), but also to the development of skills and to open experimentation with forms, technologies and uses. Indeed, the future of alternative journalism may very well be best characterized as a growth of media literacy in the broadened sense, not only of learning about the world but also of learning the skills of composition and use. Foregrounding this twin sense of learning might very well become the surest way of escaping the ghetto of marginalization and isolation commented on by Williams, Comedia and many others: it might also escape the need to adopt commercialized and professionalized forms.

9

ALTERNATIVE JOURNALISM: A CRITICAL BIBLIOGRAPHY

As this is the first scholarly book to deal with alternative journalism, we have throughout the preceding chapters acknowledged the necessity of having to build our understanding from histories, surveys, case studies and theories from a wider range of studies. These include broader theories of alternative and radical media, accounts of community and development media, as well as historical and political-economic essays that set our study of alternative journalism in broader contexts. There are, though, some works that specifically address alternative journalism, though they are small in number: it is with these that we begin this critical bibliography. The remainder of this chapter follows the organization of the rest of the book: from each chapter, we have selected what we consider to be key texts that are valuable in informing the theories, philosophies and practices of alternative journalism. To avoid repetition, where key texts are referred to in more than one chapter, we have located them where they seem to make the most substantial contribution. For example, Gumucio Dagron's (2001) international study of development media is placed in our discussion of sources for international comparative surveys (Chapter 6), though it also appears in the chapter on social demographics (Chapter 3).

It is only in recent years that the academic study of journalism as a whole has emerged as a subject area in its own right, informed by studies of the media, culture and society, but with a special emphasis on journalistic practices and their significance in society. Specialist journals such as *Journalism Studies*, *Journalism: Theory, Practice, Criticism* (both founded in 2000) and *Journalism Practice* (2007) have become important sites for this study. *Journalism: Theory, Practice, Criticism* (2003) has hosted a special issue devoted to alternative journalism. The articles collected there include studies of 'public arena journalism' in Australian community media (Forde et al., 2003); a critical analysis of Indymedia as radical journalism (Platon and Deuze, 2003; a theme also explored in Atton, 2004: Ch. 2); and an exploration of the successes and failures of UNESCO's New World Information and Communication Order, and in particular how Third World journalists might revitalize this project (Sosale, 2003). Howley (2003) contrasts the journalism of street newspapers with the public journalism movement: Howley's (2005) book-length study of community media in North America develops this theme in detail. Hamilton (2003) argues for an historical understanding of alternative journalism that not only goes back as far as the early-modern (roughly, starting in the sixteenth century) but also includes as examples of alternative journalism the practices of wall-writing and personal commonplace books, just as Downing et al. (2001) expand radical media production to include street theatre, posters, murals and graffiti; Mano (2007) argues that popular music might also be considered as a form of journalism. Harcup's (2003) comparative study of two local newspapers in northern England (one mainstream, one alternative) provides a valuable discussion of differing approaches to news sources, values and access. Harcup has made a particular study of local alternative journalism; taken together, his work provides an interlocking series of case studies (Harcup, 1994, 1998, 2006a).

The counter-hegemonic role that Harcup argues is central to alternative journalism is the subject of another comparative study, of eyewitness reporting of anti-globalization protests (Atton, 2002b). Other studies have also fruitfully explored the adaptation of mainstream news values in alternative journalism: from an ethical perspective (Atton, 2003b) and through sourcing practices (Atton and Wickenden, 2005). A special issue of the online journal *Scan* (2006) contains a number of papers that show how traditional notions of news as the province of the professional journalist are being challenged by Internet-based, alternative news providers such as Wikinews (Bruns, 2006) and Indymedia (Salter, 2006). Though the articles collected in the special issue of *Media, Culture and Society* (2003) on alternative media are not all concerned with journalistic practices, Gibbs's (2003) study of a Honolulu alternative newspaper is a useful political-economic study of work relations and processes amongst journalists and managers, and should be read alongside the international case studies in Downing et al. (2001) and Rodriguez (2001). Downing's (2003b) plea for more audience research acknowledges a blind spot that is worthy of attention by anyone interested in advancing the study of alternative journalism. Rauch (2007)'s study of activist audiences (using focus groups and diaries) is a rare foray into this area. Other useful collections of articles on alternative media include special issues of the *Journal of Communication Inquiry* (2000), *Media History* (2001) and *Media International Australia* (2002).

Couldry and Curran's (2003a) collection is also centred on alternative media broadly, rather than alternative journalism. However, it does contain numerous studies of interest to the student of alternative journalism, such as those cited in our comparative survey (Lee, 2003; Ling, 2003).

A relatively recent trend in interdisciplinary historical scholarship seeks to establish a tradition of alternative journalism within which many separate cases can be placed (see Armstrong, 1981; Ostertag, 2006; Streitmatter, 2001; with more expansive and theoretically informed studies including Reed, 2005). However, historical studies of alternative journalism typically take a case-study approach, and can be characterized in two general, interlocking ways. First, they can be divided topically and roughly into those that treat the rise of journalism itself as an alternative response, those that describe journalism of labour and working-class movements, journalism of social-reform movements, and journalism as part of the ferment of the 1960s and beyond. Of course, such divisions are only for analytic convenience, in that lines between labour movements, social-reform movements and the like are impossible to draw in practice.

Second, the overarching framework within which historical case studies are placed most often is the rise of capitalism and the struggle of various social groups and movements against it (see Curran, 2002 for a discussion of these and other such historical-interpretive frameworks). The key question that thus arises centres on the radical possibilities of journalism (a linchpin in capitalist cultural production) for challenging capitalist society, suggesting as well a significant overlap between historical studies and political-economic studies. The handful of studies that directly address relationships between alternative-journalism funding, organizational practices and news (such as Benson, 2003; Eliasoph, 1988; Gibbs, 2003; Kim and Hamilton, 2006) mark out a research direction deserving of much more attention. Raymond (1996) authoritatively establishes the forerunners of journalism in newsbooks, where Shaaber (1929), Sommerville (1996) and Sutherland (1986) describe a wide variety of activity that became part of standard journalistic practice. The practice of alternative journalism presupposes 'journalism' itself not only as an organization but as a form of composition. Davis (1983), Schneider (2005) and Shapiro (2000) are indispensable for understanding the key, deep developments in writing and reading in early-modern England that enabled the emergence of journalism.

Accounts of party and patronage presses in the UK (Koss, 1981–84; Lee, 1976) and the US (Ames, 1972; Baldasty, 1984; Smith, 1977) often provide a detailed understanding of organization, support and practice, although more recent works such as Peacey (2004) delve more deeply into their limitations and determinations. Barnhurst and Nerone (2001) develop a useful argument about forms of news in which party and patronage presses comprise a characteristically artisanal project prior to the industrialization of news production and organization. Historical accounts of the rise of journalism in the former USSR suggest the value of non-Western cases (Lenoe, 2004; McReynolds, 1991; Murray, 1994).

The rise of commercial journalism as a popular challenge to privilege is a key dynamic in historical accounts of alternative journalism, but one whose complexities are still under great debate (see Curran, 2002 for a discussion of its varieties). One view that is grounded in the work of Habermas (1989) – see also the collection edited by Calhoun (1992) – and his account of the public sphere regards commercialization in early-modern Europe initially as a progressive development, although becoming regressive with its consolidation and industrialization. Issues surrounding the possibility of journalism enabling a public sphere underlie studies such as Trinkle (2002) and Fanuzzi (2003).

Complexities concerning the degree to which the commercialization of journalism operated in a politically progressive way expand when addressing non-Western countries. While works such as Adam (1995), Geracimos (1996), González (1993) and Huffman (1997) see the rise of commercial journalism generally as the rise of a popular, vernacular press, a good case can be made that commercialization of journalism can also be seen as part of a broader colonial project. Although studies of media imperialism and, more recently, of globalization address these possibilities, they are often preoccupied with so-called 'entertainment' media rather than journalism. A greater number of historical studies of non-Western countries that address relationships between journalism and capitalism is sorely needed.

Other studies see commercialization and the corresponding consolidation of the state as the primary challenge to alternative journalism. One place in which such a case can be clearly seen is in studies of labour journalism. Hardt (1990) and the collection edited by Hardt and Brennen (1995) establish the need for a labour perspective in journalism history that would address not only institutional union journalism but also more broadly the nature of journalistic labour itself. While landmark studies such as Hollis (1970) and the collection edited by Conlin (1974) begin to address questions of labour journalism descriptively, Curran (1978) and a pair of studies by Shore (1985, 1988) address them overtly. The collection edited by Wiener (1988) ably presents the great political contradictions of press commercialization in the UK during the nineteenth century. Curran and Seaton (2003) is a long-standing, continually refined (into its sixth edition) account of the emergence of the press in the UK that also places working-class presses in a broader context.

Still the most useful analytic treatment – although more suggestive than extensive – is a trio of essays by Williams (1970, 1978a, 1978b). By placing the study of alternative journalism within the larger frameworks of popular culture and the historical sociology of culture, these essays still provide insightful, contextual arguments about the interrelations and confrontations between the alternative (the 'radical-popular') and the mainstream (the 'commercial-popular').

While not directly indebted to Williams, more recent historical work investigates commercialization as both enabling and disabling, but requiring nuanced and contextual evaluation instead of blanket assertion. Historical studies of suffrage journalism such as DiCenzo (2000) and Mercer (2004) argue this point, coinciding with larger studies of the relation between suffrage movements and consumer culture (Finnegan, 1999). Biographies of exceptional individuals such as I.F. Stone (see Cottrell, 1992) help suggest the idiosyncratic confluence of factors that enable radical projects of personal journalism. Studies such as Bradley (2003), which addresses more contemporary examples, and Zhao (1998), which examines the case of the People's Republic of China, take a less sanguine view of such potentials.

Historical studies of the underground press of the 1960s in the West such as Bizot (2006), Glessing (1970), Leamer (1972), and Peck (1985) comprise an often nostalgic celebration of popular, vernacular journalism of youth culture, while there are many studies of the rise of so-called 'new journalism' or 'literary journalism', beginning with collections such as Wolfe (1973) and extending to studies such as Hartsock (2000), and Roggenkamp (2005). The remaking of journalistic writing is also beginning to be treated transnationally, with historical studies such as Bielsa (2006) and Kendall (2006) pushing in greatly needed directions.

Historical work on popular, de-institutionalized alternative journalism, notably Skilling (1989) on samizdat in Central and Eastern Europe and Sreberny-Mohammadi and Ali Mohammadi (1994) on the Iranian revolution, lays a very rich basis not only for comparative work outside the UK–US orbit, but also for a better understanding of the varieties and complexities of forms, technologies and practices of alternative journalism. Finally, a pair of studies by Tusan (2003, 2005) demonstrates not only the analytic impossibility but also the necessity of treating the interpenetration of the non-West with the West along with the equal complexity of questions of gender and journalism.

In the introduction to Chapter 3, we observed the absence of any wide-ranging demographic surveys of alternative journalists. Instead, we attempted to survey the demographic landscape by piecing together fragments of observations from many sources. However, we do not want to give the impression that the sources used in Chapter 3 are solely concerned with demographics – apart from, that is, Harcup's (2005) small-scale survey of 22 alternative journalists and Van Vuuren's (2002) study of volunteers working for three Australian community radio stations. Dickinson's (1997) study, for example, is not only rich in demographic detail: it also provides case studies of alternative newspapers, magazines and fanzines in the north-west of England covering over two decades and provides insights into the perennial tensions between professionalism and amateurism, as well as the political and the cultural, and how they might come together in community media as well as in professionalized media. It provides a useful corrective (as does Harcup's work) to accounts of an alternative press centred on London. Fountain's (1988) account of the London underground press does not pretend to be an academic study. Written in large part from first-hand experience, its narratives highlight the personal and political ambitions of the underground's protagonists. Green's (1998) collection of interviews with key players in the London underground culture is less of a narrative, yet has much to offer the reader with time to pick through it. Allen's (1985) and Sparks's (1985) studies of the paper of the British Socialist Workers' Party, *Socialist Worker*, also dwell on ambitions as they recount the failed attempts of the paper to achieve a more inclusive form of journalism in line with its aim of mobilizing its working-class readership. Arguably the formative paper for the study of alternative media in the UK (at least in the sense that much subsequent theoretical and empirical work critiqued and developed its rather superficial arguments) is Comedia's (1984) examination of failure (expanded in Landry et al., 1985, which shares authors with the Comedia paper).

The subculture of zines of all types in the US is comprehensively presented in Duncombe (1997). The closest we have to this for the UK, less scholarly, though highly illustrated, is Sabin and Triggs (2001). Fanzines and zines in the UK are also explored in relation to various aspects, including popular music (Atton 2001, 2006a); football (Atton, 2006b; Haynes, 1995; Jary et al., 1991; and Moorhouse, 1994); and graphic design (Triggs 1995).

As noted in Chapter 4, studies of policy developments of alternative journalism are almost a contradiction in terms, given that their distinctly non-institutional status means that there are few, if any, policies (as distinct from theoretical discussions or manifestos) to study in the first place. As a result, studies of alternative-journalism policy are rare. Studies of public (or civic) journalism such as Black (1997), Eksterowicz and Roberts (2000), Haas and Steiner (2006), Hardt (2000), and Rosen (1996) evaluate the progressive potential of this recent attempted commercial-news policy change, which has since fallen by the wayside due to historical and political-economic imperatives. Distinct from studies of participatory journalism that revolve largely around Indymedia, studies of citizen journalism as a policy development of commercial news companies have only begun to be conducted, with one of the few such studies published by Deuze, et al. (2007).

In addition to the small number of studies that examine the practices of alternative journalism through its news values and sources (as cited earlier in this chapter), there is a growing literature on blogs and bloggers. The dominant themes in research to date are: the relations between the professional and the amateur, as well as the interpenetration of the two, especially in the practices of professional journalists (Allan, 2006; Wall, 2005, 2006), and problems of critical media literacy, particularly those of credibility and reliability (Matheson and Allan, 2007). Harding's (1997) practical guide for the video activist is one of the few texts that explicitly set out to systematize alternative journalism practices. Harcup's (2006b) compelling discussion of ethics in journalism is a very readable introduction to the major issues, and brings together mainstream and alternative journalism practices.

Turning to comparative research, we have already noted the international case studies found in Downing et al. (2001) and Rodriguez (2001). Both sets of studies range widely, offering broad, if not equally detailed international surveys. Their strengths lie in their extended studies: Downing et al. present substantial case studies from the US, Portugal, Italy and the former Soviet Union. Rodriguez focuses on Latin America (Colombia and Nicaragua) and Latino radio in the US, though she also finds space for a study of Catalonian television. In addition to the specific case studies cited in Chapter 6 (such as Kim and Hamilton, 2006; O'Connor, 2004), which are presented there in some detail, it is worth noting Gumucio Dagron's (2001) 50 brief 'case stories' of development media, which attest to the diversity of citizen journalism projects in Africa and the Indian subcontinent. Similarly, Waltz's (2005) textbook is not only a useful teaching aid, but also provides short studies of alternative media projects from countries rarely considered, such as Afghanistan, China, Japan and South Korea. Though these are relatively brief, the last three, when taken together with the work of Kim and Hamilton (2006) and Lee (2003), Lim (2003) and Ling (2003), suggest that south-east Asia is emerging as an especially fruitful site for the study of alternative journalism and democracy.

We have already noted the contribution of Raymond Williams to the understanding of alternative journalism in history. In terms of theory, his work is also valuable. Williams (particularly 1963, 1967, 1970 and 1980b) provides some of the most probing and lucid insights into the notion of democratic communication. Downing's (1984) original formulation of radical media as 'the political experience of alternative communication' remains important, but should be read in conjunction with the more nuanced opening chapters of his revised edition (Downing et al., 2001). Hackett and Carroll (2006) offer a robust model of democratic media activism that brings up to date – and makes explicit – Downing's earlier emphases on media that act not only as alternative forms of news production but also as public engagement with dominant media policies and practices. Rodriguez's conceptualizing of citizens' media is indebted to Downing in its emphasis on social and political change, but highlights the centrality of the ordinary citizen as politicized media producer. Atton's (2002a) critique of Downing builds theory that attempts to account for deprofessionalized media production in new social movements as well as in the popular cultures of fanzines and zines. Couldry's work on media power and its relation to alternative media is found in its most extended form in Couldry (2000). The theoretical essays that form the first section of Couldry and Curran (2003a) are all important contributions to the theoretical debate, not least for their concision and their acuity (Bennett, 2003; Couldry, 2003; Couldry and Curran, 2003b). Vatikiotis (2004) provides an admirably clear overview of the dominant paradigms of alternative media theory. The application of Bourdieu's field theory to alternative media is briefly attempted in Atton (2002a); subsequent studies that apply field theory to journalism make only brief mention of alternative journalism (Duval, 2005; Klinenberg, 2005). Nevertheless, Benson and Neveu's (2005) collection (in which the latter two papers appear) as a whole shows how fruitful a Bourdieusian approach to alternative journalism might become.

REFERENCES

Abel, Richard (1997) 'An Alternative Press. Why?', *Publishing Research Quarterly* 12(4): 78–84.

Achbar, Mark (1994) *Manufacturing Consent: Noam Chomsky and the Media.* Montreal: Black Rose Books.

Adam, Ahmat B. (1995) *The Vernacular Press and the Emergence of Modern Indonesian Consciousness 1855–1913.* Ithaca, NY: Cornell University Press.

Akinfeleye, Ralph A. (1987) 'Press Freedom and Censorship: The Metamorphosis of the Nigerian Press Laws 1903–1984.' In Dokun Bojuwade (ed.), *Journalism and Society.* Ibadan: Evans Brothers, pp. 1–28.

Allan, Stuart (1999) *News Culture.* Buckingham: Open University Press.

Allan, Stuart (2006) *Online News: Journalism and the Internet.* Maidenhead: Open University Press.

Allen, Peter (1985) '*Socialist Worker* – Paper with a Purpose', *Media, Culture and Society* 7: 205–232.

AlterNet (2007) 'The Case for AlterNet.' Available at <http://www.alternet.org/about/> (20 Oct. 2007).

Altschull, J. Herbert (1990) *From Milton to McLuhan: The Ideas behind American Journalism.* New York: Longman.

American Alternative Newsweeklies (2007) 'About A.A.N.' Available at <http://aan.org/alternative/Aan/ViewPage?oid=2086> (20 Oct. 2007).

Ames, William E. (1972) 'Federal Patronage and the Washington D.C. Press', *Journalism Quarterly* 49(1): 22–30.

Anderson, Peter J. (2007) 'Conclusions.' In Peter J. Anderson and Geoff Ward (eds), *The Future of Journalism in the Advanced Democracies.* Aldershot: Ashgate, pp. 259–274.

Armstrong, David (1981) *A Trumpet to Arms: Alternative Media in America.* Boston, Mass.: South End Press.

Ashley, Laura and Olson, Beth (1998) 'Constructing Reality: Print Media's Framing of the Women's Movement, 1966–1986', *Journalism and Mass Communication Quarterly* 75(2): 263–277.

Atton, Chris (1996) *Alternative Literature: A Practical Guide for Librarians.* Aldershot: Gower.

Atton, Chris (1999) '*Green Anarchist*: A Case Study in Radical Media', *Anarchist Studies* 7(1): 25–49.

Atton, Chris (2001) '"Living in the Past"?: Value Discourses in Progressive Rock Fanzines', *Popular Music* 20(1): 29–46.

Atton, Chris (2002a) *Alternative Media*. London: Sage.

Atton, Chris (2002b) 'News Cultures and New Social Movements: Radical Journalism and the Mainstream Media', *Journalism Studies* 3(4): 491–505.

Atton, Chris (2003a) 'What is "Alternative" Journalism?', *Journalism: Theory, Practice, Criticism* 4(3): 267–272.

Atton, Chris (2003b) 'Ethical Issues in Alternative Journalism', *Ethical Space: The International Journal of Communication Ethics* 1(1): 26–31.

Atton, Chris (2003c) 'Infoshops in the Shadow of the State.' In Nick Couldry and James Curran (eds), *Contesting Media Power: Alternative Media in a Networked World*. Lanham, Md.: Rowman and Littlefield, pp. 57–69.

Atton, Chris (2003d) 'Fanzines'. In John Shepherd et al. (eds), *The Continuum Encyclopedia of Popular Music of the World, Volume One: Media, Industry and Society*. London: Continuum, pp. 226–228.

Atton, Chris (2003e) 'Indymedia and "Enduring Freedom": An Exploration of Sources, Perspectives and News in an Alternative Internet Project.' In Naren Chitty, Ramona R. Rush and Mehdi Semati (eds), *Studies in Terrorism: Media Scholarship and the Enigma of Terror*. Penang: Southbound Press, pp. 147–164.

Atton, Chris (2004) *An Alternative Internet: Radical Media, Politics and Creativity*. Edinburgh: Edinburgh University Press; New York: Columbia University Press.

Atton, Chris (2006a) 'Sociologie de la Presse Musicale Alternative en Grande Bretagne', *Copyright Volume!: Autour des Musiques Populaires* 5(1): 7–25.

Atton, Chris (2006b) 'Football Fanzines as Local News.' In Bob Franklin (ed.), *Local Journalism and Local Media: Making the Local News*. London: Routledge, pp. 280–289.

Atton, Chris and Wickenden, Emma (2005) 'Sourcing Routines and Representation in Alternative Journalism: A Case Study Approach', *Journalism Studies* 6(3): 347–359.

Bagdikian, Ben (2004) *The New Media Monopoly*. Boston, Mass.: Beacon Press.

Baldasty, Gerald J. (1984) *The Press and Politics in the Age of Jackson*. Journalism Monographs no. 89. Columbia, SC: Association for Education in Journalism and Mass Communication.

Barnhurst, Kevin and Nerone, John (2001) *The Form of News: A History*. New York: Guilford.

Batty, Philip (1993) 'Singing the Electric: Aboriginal Television in Australia.' In Tony Dowmunt (ed.), *Channels of Resistance: Global Television and Local Empowerment*. London: BFI Publishing in association with Channel Four Television, pp. 106–125.

BBC News (2007) 'Have Your Say I Your News I Have You Got a Good Story?' Available at: http://news.bbc.co.uk/1/hi/talking_point/your_news/ (17 Oct. 2007).

Bekken, Jon (1993) 'The Working Class Press at the Turn of the Century.' In William S. Solomon and Robert McChesney (eds), *Ruthless Criticism: New Perspectives in US Communications History*. Minneapolis: University of Minnesota Press, pp. 55–71.

Benjamin, Walter (1934/1982) 'The Author as Producer.' Edited translation in Francis Frascina and Charles Harrison (eds), *Modern Art and Modernism: A Critical Anthology*. London: Paul Chapman in association with the Open University, 1982, pp. 213–216. Original work published 1934.

Bennett, Tony (1982) 'Theories of the Media, Theories of Society.' In Michael Gurevitch, Tony Bennett, James Curran and Janet Woollacott (eds), *Culture, Society and the Media*. London: Methuen, pp. 30–55.

Bennett, W. Lance (2003) 'New Media Power: The Internet and Global Activism.' In Nick Couldry and James Curran (eds), *Contesting Media Power: Alternative Media in a Networked World*. Lanham, Md.: Rowman and Littlefield, pp. 17–37.

Benson, Rodney (2003) 'Commercialism and Critique: California's Alternative Weeklies.' In Nick Couldry and James Curran (eds), *Contesting Media Power: Alternative Media in a Networked World*. Lanham, Md.: Rowman and Littlefield, pp. 111–127.

Benson, Rodney (2006) 'News Media as a "Journalistic Field": What Bourdieu Adds to New Institutionalism, and Vice Versa', *Political Communication* 23: 187–202.

Benson, Rodney and Neveu, Erik (eds) (2005) *Bourdieu and the Journalistic Field*. Cambridge: Polity Press.

Bent, Emily (2006) 'The Foothills of Everest.' In *Congress Report*, World Congress and 55th General Assembly, International Press Institute. Vienna: International Press Institute, p. 31.

Berger, John (1993) 'The Moment of Cubism.' In *The Sense of Sight; Writings by John Berger*. New York: Vintage International, pp. 159–188.

Berman, Marshall (1988) *All That is Solid Melts Into Air: The Experience of Modernity*. New York: Penguin.

Berry, David M. (2004) 'The Contestation of Code: A Preliminary Investigation into the Discourse of the Free/Libre and Open Source Movements', *Critical Discourse Studies* 1(1): 65–89.

Bharat, Krishna (2006) 'Internet Journalism and Google News.' In *Congress Report*, World Congress and 55th General Assembly, International Press Institute. Vienna: International Press Institute, pp. 28–30.

Bielsa, Esperanca (2006) *The Latin American Urban Crónica: Between Literature and Mass Culture*. Lanham, Md.: Lexington.

Bizot, Jean-François (2006) *Free Press: Underground and Alternative Publications 1965–1975*. New York: Universe.

Black, Jay (ed.) (1997) *Mixed News: The Public/Civic/Communitarian Journalism Debate*. Mahwah, NJ: Lawrence Erlbaum.

'Blog Action Day' (2007) *Blog Action Day*. Available at: http://blogactionday.com/ (15 Oct. 2007).

Boggs, Carl (1993) *Intellectuals and the Crisis of Modernity*. Albany, NY: State University of New York Press.

Bourdieu, Pierre (1991) *Language and Symbolic Power*. Cambridge: Polity Press.

Bourdieu, Pierre (1993) *The Field of Cultural Production: Essays on Art and Literature*. Cambridge: Polity Press.

Bourdieu, Pierre (1996) *The Rules of Art: Genesis and Structure of the Literary Field*. Cambridge: Polity Press.

Bourdieu, Pierre (1997) *Sur la Télévision*. Paris: Liber-Raisons d'Agir.

Bowman, Shayne and Willis, Chris (2003) *We Media: How Audiences are Shaping the Future of News and Information*. Reston, Va.: Media Center, American Press Institute.

Bowman, Shayne and Willis, Chris (2005) 'The Future Is Here, but Do News Media Companies See it?', *Nieman Report* 59(4): 6–10.

Boyle, Deirdre (1997) *Subject to Change: Guerrilla Television Revisited*. New York: Oxford University Press.

Boynton, Robert (2004) 'How to Make a Guerrilla Documentary', *The New York Times Magazine*, 11 July: 20–23.

Bradley, Patricia (2003) *Mass Media and the Shaping of American Feminism: 1963–1975*. Jackson, Miss.: University of Mississippi Press.

Braudel, Fernand (1980) *On History*. London: Weidenfeld and Nicolson.

Brave New Films (2006) 'Meet Brave New Films.' Available at <http://www.bravenew films.org/who.php > (31 Aug. 2006).

Brave New Foundation (2006) 'About the Brave New Foundation.' Available at <http://www.bravenewfoundation.org/about.php > (19 Oct. 2006).

Brissenden, Paul (1919) *The IWW: A Study of American Syndicalism*. New York: Columbia University Press.

Brooks, John Graham (1913) *American Syndicalism: The IWW*. New York: Macmillan.

Bruns, Axel (2005) *Gatewatching: Collaborative Online News Production*. New York: Peter Lang.

Bruns, Axel (2006) 'Wikinews: The Next Generation of Alternative Online News?', *Scan* 3(1). Available at <http://scan.net.au> (10 Aug. 2007).

Burkeman, Oliver (2002) 'Bloggers Catch What *Washington Post* Missed', *Guardian*, 21 December.

Bybee, Carl R. (1982) 'Mobilizing Information and Reader Involvement', *Journalism Quarterly* 59(3): 399–405, 413.

Calhoun, Craig (ed.) (1992) *Habermas and the Public Sphere*. Cambridge, Mass.: MIT Press.

Carroll, William K. and Hackett, Robert A. (2006) 'Democratic Media Activism through the Lens of Social Movement Theory', *Media, Culture and Society* 28(1): 83–104.

Chalaby, Jean K. (2000) 'Journalism Studies in an Era of Transition in Public Communications,' *Journalism: Theory, Practice and Criticism* 1(1) April: 33–39.

Chesshyre, Robert (1987) *The Return of a Native Reporter*. London: Viking.

Chomsky, Noam (1989) *Necessary Illusions: Thought Control in Democratic Societies*. London: Pluto Press.

'ChuckO' (2002) 'The Sad Decline of Indymedia.' Available at < http://info.interactivist. net/article.pl?sid=02/12/09/1843207 > (12 Oct. 2007).

Clark, Jessica and Van Slyke, Tracy (2006) 'Welcome to the Media Revolution: How Today's Media Makers are Shaping Tomorrow's News', *In These Times*, 28 June, <http://www.inthesetimes.com/site/main/article/2687/> (1 Oct. 2007).

Clark, Sandra (1983) *The Elizabethan Pamphleteers: Popular Moralistic Pamphlets 1580–1640*. Rutherford, NJ: Fairleigh Dickinson University Press.

CNN (2007). 'I-Report topics', *CNN.com*. Available at <http://www.cnn.com/ exchange/ireports/topics/> (20 Oct. 2007).

Comedia (1984) 'The Alternative Press: The Development of Underdevelopment', *Media, Culture and Society* 6: 95–102.

Conlin, Joseph (ed.) (1974) *The American Radical Press: 1880–1960*, 2 vols. Westport, Conn.: Greenwood Press.

Corner, John (1994/1996) 'Mediating the Ordinary: The "Access" Idea and Television Form.' In M. Aldridge and N. Hewitt (eds), *Controlling Broadcasting*. Manchester: Manchester University Press, 1994, pp. 20–33. Reprinted in an abridged form in John Corner and Sylvia Harvey (eds), *Television Times: A Reader*. London: Arnold, 1996, pp. 165–174. References are to the latter.

Cottle, Simon (2003) *News, Public Relations and Power*. London: Sage.

Cottrell, Robert C. (1992) *Izzy: A Biography of I.F. Stone*. New Brunswick, NJ: Rutgers University Press.

Couldry, Nick (2000) *The Place of Media Power: Pilgrims and Witnesses of the Media Age*. London and New York: Routledge.

Couldry, Nick (2002) 'Alternative Media and Mediated Community', paper presented at the International Association for Media and Communication Research, Barcelona, 23 July.

Couldry, Nick (2003) 'Beyond the Hall of Mirrors? Some Theoretical Reflections on the Global Contestation of Media Power.' In Nick Couldry and James Curran (eds), *Contesting Media Power: Alternative Media in a Networked World*. Lanham, Md.: Rowman and Littlefield, pp. 39–54.

Couldry, Nick and Curran, James (eds) (2003a) *Contesting Media Power: Alternative Media in a Networked World*. Lanham, Md.: Rowman and Littlefield.

Couldry, Nick and Curran, James (2003b) 'The Paradox of Media Power.' In Nick Couldry and James Curran (eds), *Contesting Media Power: Alternative Media in a Networked World*. Lanham, Md.: Rowman and Littlefield, pp. 3–15.

Coyer, Kate (2005) 'If it Leads it Bleeds: The Participatory Newsmaking of the Independent Media Centre.' In Wilma De Jong, Martin Shaw and Neil Stammers (eds), *Global Activism, Global Media*. London: Pluto Press, pp. 165–178.

Cresser, Frances, Gunn, Lesley and Balme, Helen (2001) 'Women's Experiences of On-line E-zine Publication', *Media, Culture and Society* 23: 457–473.

Crisell, Andrew (2002) 'Radio: Public Service, Commercialism and the Paradox of Choice.' In Adam Briggs and Paul Cobley (eds), *The Media: An Introduction*. Harrow: Longman, pp. 121–134.

Curran, James (1978) 'The Press as an Agency of Social Control: An Historical Perspective.' In George Boyce, James Curran and Pauline Wingate (eds), *Newspaper History from the Seventeenth Century to the Present Day*. London: Constable, pp. 51–75.

Curran, James (2002) 'Media and the Making of British Society', *Media History* 8(2): 135–154.

Curran, James (2003) 'Global Journalism: A Case Study of the Internet.' In Nick Couldry and James Curran (eds), *Contesting Media Power: Alternative Media in a Networked World*. Lanham, Md.: Rowman and Littlefield, pp. 227–241.

Curran, James and Seaton, Jean (1997) *Power without Responsibility: The Press and Broadcasting in Britain*, 5th edn. London: Routledge.

Curran, James and Seaton, Jean (2003) *Power without Responsibility: The Press, Broadcasting and New Media in Britain*, 6th edn. London: Routledge.

Dahlgren, Peter (2000) 'Media, Citizenship and Civic Culture.' In James Curran and Michael Gurevitch (eds), *Mass Media and Society*. London: Arnold, pp. 310–328.

Davis, Lennard (1983) *Factual Fictions: The Origins of the English Novel*. New York: Columbia University Press.

Davis, Steve (2000) 'Public Journalism: The Case Against', *Journalism Studies* 1(4): 686–689.

Davis, Trevor Hugh (2006) 'Coda?', *Crisis Pictures*. Available at: <http://crisispictures. org/AFG/354/ (8 March 2006).

de Certeau, Michel (1984) *The Practice of Everyday Life*. Berkeley, Calif.: University of California Press.

de Lange, William (1998) *A History of Japanese Journalism: Japan's Press Club as the Last Obstacle to a Mature Press*. Richmond: Japan Library.

Debord, Guy (1967/1983) *Society of the Spectacle*. Detroit, Mich.: Black and Red, 1983. Originally published, Paris: Editions Buchet-Chastel, 1967.

Deuze, Mark (2006) 'Ethnic Media, Community Media and Participatory Culture', *Journalism: Theory, Practice and Criticism* 7(3): 262–280.

Deuze, Mark and Dimoudi, Christina (2002) 'Online Journalists in the Netherlands: Towards a Profile of a New Profession', *Journalism: Theory, Practice and Criticism* 3(1): 85–100.

Deuze, Mark, Bruns, Axel and Neuberger, Christoph (2007) 'Preparing for an Age of Participatory News', *Journalism Practice* 1(3): 322–338.

DiCenzo, Maria (2000) 'Militant Distribution: *Votes for Women* and the Public Sphere', *Media History* 6(2): 115–128.

Dickinson, Robert (1997) *Imprinting the Sticks: The Alternative Press Outside London*. Aldershot: Arena.

Dodge, Chris (1999) 'Words on the Street: Homeless People's Newspapers', *American Libraries*, August: 60–62.

Downing, John (1984) *Radical Media: The Political Experience of Alternative Communication*. Boston, Mass.: South End Press.

Downing, John (1988) 'The Alternative Public Realm: The Organization of the 1980s Anti-nuclear Press in West Germany and Britain', *Media, Culture and Society* 10: 163–181.

Downing, John (2003a) 'The Independent Media Center Movement and the Anarchist Socialist Tradition.' In Nick Couldry and James Curran (eds), *Contesting Media Power: Alternative Media in a Networked World*. Lanham, Md.: Rowman and Littlefield, pp. 243–257.

Downing, John (2003b) 'Audiences and Readers of Alternative Media: The Absent Lure of the Virtually Unknown', *Media, Culture and Society* 25(5): 625–645.

Downing, John, Villareal Ford, Tamara, Gil, Geneve and Stein, Laura (2001) *Radical Media: Rebellious Communication and Social Movements*. Thousand Oaks, Calif.: Sage.

Dubofsky, Melvin (1990) 'The Rise and Fall of Revolutionary Syndicalism in the United States.' In Marcel van der Linden and Wayne Thorpe (eds), *Revolutionary Syndicalism: An International Perspective*. Aldershot: Scolar Press, pp. 203–220.

Duncombe, Stephen (1997) *Notes from Underground: Zines and the Politics of Alternative Culture*. London: Verso.

Duval, Julien (2005) 'Economic Journalism in France.' In Rodney Benson and Erik Neveu (eds), *Bourdieu and the Journalistic Field*. Cambridge: Polity Press, pp. 135–155.

Ebo, Bosah (1994) 'The Ethical Dilemma of African Journalists: A Nigerian Perspective', *Journal of Mass Media Ethics* 9(2): 84–93.

Echo Chamber Project (2007) Available at <http://www.echochamberproject.com/> (12 Nov. 2007).

Edgar, Andrew (1992) 'Objectivity, Bias and Truth.' In Andrew Belsey and Ruth Chadwick (eds), *Ethical Issues in Journalism and the Media*. London: Routledge, pp. 112–219.

Eksterowicz, Anthony J. and Roberts, Robert N. (eds) (2000) *Public Journalism and Political Knowledge*. Lanham, Md.: Rowman and Littlefield.

Eldridge, John (2000) 'The Contribution of the Glasgow Media Group to the Study of Television and Print Journalism', *Journalism Studies* 1(1): 113–127.

Eley, Geoff (1992) 'Nations, Publics and Political Cultures: Placing Habermas in the Nineteenth Century.' In Craig Calhoun (ed.), *Habermas and the Public Sphere*. Cambridge, Mass.; London: MIT Press, pp. 289–339.

Eliasoph, Nina (1988) 'Routines and the Making of Oppositional News', *Critical Studies in Mass Communication* 5(4): 313–334.

eMarketer.com (2007) 'Online Ad Spending to Total $19.5 Billion in 2007', 28 February. Available at <http://www.emarketer.com/Article.aspx ?1004635> (10 March 2007).

Enzensberger, Hans Magnus (1976) 'Constituents of a Theory of the Media.' In *Raids and Reconstructions: Essays on Politics, Crime and Culture*. London: Pluto Press, pp. 20–53.

Epstein, Barbara (1991) *Political Protest and Cultural Revolution: Nonviolent Direct Action in the 1970s and 1980s*. Berkeley: University of California Press.

Ewen, Stuart (1989) 'Advertising and the Development of Consumer Society.' In Ian Angus and Sut Jhally (eds), *Cultural Politics in Contemporary America*. New York: Routledge, pp. 82–95.

Eyerman, Ron and Jamison, Andrew (1991) *Social Movements: A Cognitive Approach*. Cambridge: Polity Press.

Eyerman, Ron and Jamison, Andrew (1995) 'Social Movements and Cultural Transformation: Popular Music in the 1960s', *Media, Culture and Society* 17: 449–468.

Fadzan, Smaragd (2003) 'Freedom of Expression and Independent Media in the Balkans.' Bergen: Institute for Media and Information Science, University of Bergen. Unpublished Master's thesis.

Fanuzzi, Robert (2003) *Abolition's Public Sphere*. Minneapolis, Minn.: University of Minnesota Press.

Farrington, Benjamin (1964) *The Philosophy of Francis Bacon: An Essay on its Development from 1603 to 1609, with New Translation of Fundamental Texts*. Liverpool: Liverpool University Press.

Fenton, Natalie and Downey, John (2003) 'Counter Public Spheres and Global Modernity', *Javnost/The Public* 10: 1–17.

Finnegan, Margaret (1999) *Selling Suffrage: Consumer Culture and Votes for Women*. New York: Columbia University Press.

Fletcher, Anthony and MacCulloch, Diarmaid (1997) *Tudor Rebellions*, 4th edn. London: Longman.

Fogarasi, Adalbert (1921/1983) 'The Tasks of the Communist Press.' In Armand Mattelart and Seth Siegelaub (eds), *Communication and Class Struggle, Vol. 2: Liberation, Socialism*. New York: International General, 1983, pp. 149–153. Original work published 1921.

Ford Foundation (2007) 'Media, Arts & Culture.' Available at <http://www.ford-found.org/program/media.cfm> (22 Oct. 2007).

Forde, Susan, Foxwell, Kerrie and Meadows, Michael (2003) 'Through the Lens of the Local: Public Arena Journalism in the Australian Community Broadcasting Sector', *Journalism: Theory, Practice and Criticism* 4(3): 314–335.

Fornatale, Peter and Mills, Joshua E. (1980) *Radio in the Television Age*. Woodstock, NY: Overlook.

Fountain, Nigel (1988) *Underground: The London Alternative Press, 1966–74*. London: Comedia/Routledge.

Frank, Thomas (1997) *The Conquest of Cool: Business Culture, Counterculture, and the Rise of Hip Consumerism*. Chicago, Ill.: University of Chicago Press.

Franklin, Bob and Murphy, David (1991) *What News? The Market, Politics and the Local Press*. London: Routledge.

Fraser, Nancy (1992) 'Rethinking the Public Sphere – A Contribution to the Critique of Actually Existing Democracy.' In Craig Calhoun (ed.), *Habermas and the Public Sphere*. Cambridge, Mass.; London: MIT Press, pp. 109–142.

Free Press (2007a) 'Free Press: About Us.' Available at <http://www.freepress.net/content/about> (22 Oct. 2007).

Free Press (2007b) 'What Issues Does Free Press Work On?' Available at <http://www.freepress.net/content/faqs#question5> (22 Oct. 2007).

Free Press (2007c) 'What Does Free Press Stand For?', Available at <http://www.freepress.net/content/faqs#question6> (22 Oct. 2007).

Free Press (2007d) 'Is the Problem with the Media Bad or Incompetent Owners and Employees?' Available at <http://www.freepress.net/content/faqs#question42> (22 Oct. 2007).

Free Press (2007e) 'Free Press: Reform Organizations.' Available at <http://www.freepress.net/content/orgs> (22 Oct. 2007).

Freire, Paulo (1970) *Pedagogy of the Oppressed*. New York: Continuum.

Frith, Simon (1996) *Performing Rites: Evaluating Popular Music*. Oxford: Oxford University Press.

Fuller, Linda (ed.) (2007) *Community Media: International Perspectives*. New York: Palgrave Macmillan.

Fursich, Elfriede (2002) 'How Can Global Journalists Represent the "Other"? A Critical Assessment of the Cultural Studies Concept for Media Practice', *Journalism: Theory, Practice and Criticism* 3(1): 57–84.

Geracimos, Helen Chapin (1996) *Shaping History: The Role of Newspapers in Hawaii*. Honolulu: University of Hawaii Press.

Gibbs, Patricia L. (2003) 'Alternative Things Considered: A Political Economic Analysis of Labour Processes and Relations at a Honolulu Alternative Newspaper', *Media, Culture and Society* 25(5): 587–605.

Gillmor, Dan (2006) 'Elevating Citizen Journalism.' In *Congress Report*, World Congress and 55th General Assembly, International Press Institute. Vienna: International Press Institute, p. 32.

Gitlin, Todd (1980) *The Whole World is Watching: Mass Media in the Making and Unmaking of the New Left*. Berkeley, Calif.: University of California Press.

Glasgow University Media Group (1976) *Bad News*. London: Routledge and Kegan Paul.

Glasgow University Media Group (1980) *More Bad News*. London: Routledge and Kegan Paul.

Glasser, Theodore L. (2000) 'The Politics of Public Journalism', *Journalism Studies* 1(4): 683–686.

Glessing, Robert (1970) *The Underground Press in America*. Bloomington, Ind.: Indiana University Press.

Golding, Peter and Murdock, Graham (1991) 'Culture, Communication, and Political Economy.' In James Curran and Michael Gurevitch (eds), *Mass Media and Society*. London: Edward Arnold, pp. 15–32.

Goldstein, Tom (ed.) (2007) *Killing the Messenger: 100 Years of Press Criticism*. New York: Columbia University Press.

González, Aníbal (1993) *Journalism and the Development of Spanish American Narrative*. Cambridge: Cambridge University Press.

Gramsci, Antonio (1971) *Selections from the Prison Notebooks*, edited and translated by Quintin Hoare and Geoffrey Nowell Smith. London: Lawrence and Wishart.

Green, Jonathon (1998) *Days in the Life: Voices from the English Underground, 1961–1971*. London: Pimlico.

Gremillion, Jeff (1995) 'Showdown at Generation Gap: Here Come the Young Guns of the Alternative Press', *Columbia Journalism Review*, July/August. Available at <http://backissues.cjrarchives.org/year/95/4/generation.asp> (22 Oct. 2007).

Gudmundsson, Gestur, Lindberg, Ulf, Michelsen, Morten and Weisethaunet, Hans (2002) 'Brit Crit: Turning Points in British Rock Criticism, 1960–1990.' In Steve

Jones (ed.), *Pop Music and the Press*. Philadelphia: Temple University Press, pp. 41–64.

Gumucio Dagron, Alfonso (2001) *Making Waves: Stories of Participatory Communication for Social Change*. New York: Rockefeller Foundation.

Haas, Tanni (2004) 'Alternative Media, Public Journalism and the Pursuit of Democratization', *Journalism Studies* 5(1): 115–121.

Haas, Tanni and Steiner, Linda (2006) 'Public Journalism: A Reply to the Critics', *Journalism: Theory, Practice, Criticism* 7(2): 238–254.

Habermas, Jürgen (1989) *The Structural Transformation of the Public Sphere: An Inquiry into a Category of Bourgeois Society*, translated by Thomas Burger and Frederick Lawrence. Cambridge, Mass.: MIT Press.

Hackett, Robert A. and Carroll, William K. (2006) *Remaking Media: The Struggle to Democratize Public Communication*. New York and London: Routledge.

Hackett, Robert A. and Zhao, Yuezhi (1998) *Sustaining Democracy? Journalism and the Politics of Objectivity*. Toronto: Garamond.

Hall, Stuart, Critcher, Chas, Jefferson, Tony, Clarke, John and Roberts, Brian (1978) *Policing the Crisis: Mugging, the State, and Law and Order*. London: Methuen.

Hamilton, James W. (2000) 'Alternative Media: Conceptual Difficulties, Critical Possibilities', *Journal of Communication Inquiry* 24(4): 357–378.

Hamilton, James W. (2003) 'Remaking Media Participation in Early Modern England,' *Journalism: Theory, Practice, Criticism* 4(3): 293–313.

Hamilton, James and Atton, Chris (2001) 'Theorizing Anglo-American Alternative Media: Toward a Contextual History and Analysis of US and UK Scholarship', *Media History* 7(2): 119–135.

Harcup, Tony (1994) *A Northern Star: Leeds Other Paper and the Alternative Press 1974–1994*. London and Pontefract: Campaign for Press and Broadcasting Freedom.

Harcup, Tony (1998) 'There Is No Alternative: The Demise of the Alternative Local Newspaper.' In Bob Franklin and David Murphy (eds), *Making the Local News: Local Journalism in Context*. London: Routledge, pp. 105–116.

Harcup, Tony (2002) 'Journalists and Ethics: The Quest for a Collective Voice,' *Journalism Studies* 3(1): 101–114.

Harcup, Tony (2003) '"The Unspoken – Said": The Journalism of Alternative Media', *Journalism: Theory, Practice, Criticism* 4(3): 356–376.

Harcup, Tony (2005) '"I'm Doing This to Change the World": Journalism in Alternative and Mainstream Media', *Journalism Studies* 6(3): 361–374.

Harcup, Tony (2006a) 'The Alternative Local Press.' In Bob Franklin (ed.), *Local Journalism and Local Media: Making the Local News*. London: Routledge. pp. 129–139.

Harcup, Tony (2006b) *The Ethical Journalist*. London: Sage.

Harding, Thomas (1997) *The Video Activist Handbook*. London: Pluto Press.

Hardt, Hanno (1990) 'Newsworkers, Technology, and Journalism History', *Critical Studies in Mass Communication* 7(4): 346–365.

Hardt, Hanno (2000) 'Conflicts of Interest: Newsworkers, Media, and Patronage Journalism.' In Howard Tumber (ed.), *Media Power, Professionals and Policies*. New York: Routledge, pp. 209–224.

Hardt, Hanno and Brennen, Bonnie (eds) (1995) *Newsworkers: Toward a History of the Rank and File*. Minneapolis, Minn.: University of Minnesota Press.

Hargreaves, Ian and Thomas, James (2002) *New News, Old News*. London: ITC/BSC.

Harold, Christine (2007) *OurSpace: Resisting the Corporate Control of Culture.* Minneapolis: University of Minnesota Press.

Hartley, John (2000) 'Communicative Democracy in a Redactional Society: The Future of Journalism Studies', *Journalism: Theory, Practice and Criticism* 1(1): 39–48.

Hartsock, John C. (2000) *A History of American Literary Journalism: The Emergence of a Modern Narrative Form.* Amherst, Mass.: University of Massachusetts Press.

Hawkes, David (2001) *Idols of the Marketplace: Idolatry and Commodity Fetishism in English Literature, 1580–1680.* New York: Palgrave Macmillan.

Haynes, Richard (1995) *The Football Imagination: The Rise of Football Fanzine Culture.* Aldershot: Arena.

Heikkila, Heikki and Kunelius, Risto (2002) 'Access, Dialogue, Deliberation: Experimenting with Three Concepts of Journalism Criticism.' In *The International Media and Democracy Project: Theoretical Foundations.* Available at: <http://www.imdp.org/artman/publish/article_27.shtml> (12 Oct. 2007).

Herman, Edward S. and Chomsky, Noam (1988) *Manufacturing Consent: The Political Economy of the Mass Media.* London: Vintage; New York: Pantheon.

Hesmondhalgh, David (2006) 'Bourdieu, the Media and Cultural Production', *Media, Culture and Society* 28(2): 211–231.

Hindle, Steve (2000) *The State and Social Change in Early Modern England, c. 1550–1640.* New York: St Martin's.

Hollis, Patricia (1970) *The Pauper Press.* London: Oxford University Press.

Howley, Kevin (2003) 'A Poverty of Voices: Street Papers as Communicative Democracy', *Journalism: Theory, Practice and Criticism* 4(3): 273–292.

Howley, Kevin (2005) *Community Media: People, Places, and Communication Technologies.* Cambridge: Cambridge University Press.

Huesca, Robert (1995) 'A Procedural View of Participatory Communication: Lessons from Bolivian Tin Miners' Radio', *Media, Culture and Society* 17(1): 101–119.

Huffman, James L. (1997) *Creating a Public: People and Press in Meiji Japan.* Honolulu: University of Hawaii Press.

Ibrahim, Zane (2000) 'Tarzan Doesn't Live Here Any More: Musings on Being Donor-sponsored in Africa', *International Journal of Cultural Studies* 3(2): 199–205.

Independent Media Centre (2007) 'IMC: Independent Media Centre.' Available at: http://www.indymedia.org/en/ (17 Oct. 2007).

International Press Institute (2007a) 'About the I.P.I.' Available at <http://www.freemedia.at/cms/ipi/about_detail.html?ctxid=CH0058&docid=CMS1132668373749> (19 Oct. 2007).

International Press Institute (2007b) 'I.P.I. profile.' Available at <http://www.freemedia.at/cms/ipi/about_detail.html?ctxid=CH0058&docid=CMS1132651076756> (19 Oct. 2007).

Jakubowicz, Karol (1991) 'Musical Chairs? The Three Public Spheres in Poland.' In Peter Dahlgren and Colin Sparks (eds), *Communication and Citizenship: Journalism and the Public Sphere in the New Media Age.* London: Routledge, pp. 155–175.

Jary, David, Horne, John and Bucke, Tom (1991) 'Football "Fanzines" and Football Culture: A Case of Successful "Cultural Contestation"', *Sociological Review* 39(3): 581–597.

Jenkins, Henry (1992) '"Strangers No More, We Sing": Filking and the Construction of the Science Fiction Fan Community.' In Lisa A. Lewis (ed.), *The Adoring Audience: Fan Culture and Popular Media*. London: Routledge, pp. 208–236.

Jenkins, Henry (2006) *Convergence Culture*. New York: New York University Press.

Jermey, Michael (2006) 'Involving Viewers.' In *Congress Report*, World Congress and 55th General Assembly, International Press Institute. Vienna: International Press Institute, p. 33.

Jhally, Sut (1989) 'The Political Economy of Culture.' In Ian Angus and Sut Jhally (eds), *Cultural Politics in Contemporary America*. New York: Routledge, pp. 65–81.

Johnson, Bradley (2007) 'Adwatch', *Advertising Age*, 12 February: 8.

Journal of Communication Inquiry (2000) Special Issue: Alternative Media, 24(4).

Journalism: Theory, Practice and Criticism (2003) Special Issue: What Is 'Alternative' Journalism?, 4(3).

Journalism That Matters (2000) 'Proposal: Reinventing Journalism That Matters: A National Conversation.' Available at <http://www.journalismthatmatters.org/newsecology/OriginalProposal.htm> (20 Oct. 2007).

Journalism That Matters (2007a) 'Background.' Available at <http://www.journalismthatmatters.org/newsecology/Background.htm> (20 Oct. 2007).

Journalism That Matters (2007b) 'Journalism That Matters: The Next Newsroom.' Available at <http://www.mediagiraffe.org/jtm/> (20 Oct. 2007).

Juhasz, Alexandra (1995) *AIDS TV: Identity, Community and Alternative Video*. Durham, NC and London: Duke University Press.

Kaplan, Richard L. (2002) *Politics and the American Press: The Rise of Objectivity, 1865–1920*. New York: Cambridge University Press.

Katz, Yaron (2007) 'The "Other Media": Alternative Communications in Israel', *International Journal of Cultural Studies* 10(3): 383–400.

Keeble, Richard (2001) *Ethics for Journalists*. London: Routledge.

Kendall, Elisabeth (2006) *Literature, Journalism and the Avant-Garde: Intersection in Egypt*. London: Routledge.

Khiabany, Gholam (2000) '*Red Pepper*: A New Model for the Alternative Press?', *Media, Culture, and Society* 22: 447–463.

Kidd, Dorothy (2003) 'Indymedia.org: A New Communication Commons.' In Martha McCaughey and Michael D. Ayers (eds), *Cyberactivism: Online Activism in Theory and Practice*. New York: Routledge, pp. 47–69.

Kim, Eun-Gyoo and Hamilton, James (2006) 'Capitulation to Capital? *OhmyNews* as Alternative Media', *Media, Culture and Society* 28(4): 541–560.

Klinenberg, Eric (2005) 'Channeling into the Journalistic Field: Youth Activism and the Media Justice Movement.' In Rodney Benson and Erik Neveu (eds), *Bourdieu and the Journalistic Field*. Cambridge: Polity Press, pp. 174–192.

Koss, Stephen (1981–84) *The Rise and Fall of the Political Press in Britain*. 2 vols. Chapel Hill, NC: University of North Carolina Press.

Kurtz, Howard (2003) '"Webloggers," Signing on as War Correspondents', *Washington Post,* 23 March.

Kuttab, Daoud (1993) 'Palestinian Diaries: Grass Roots TV Production in the Occupied Territories.' In Tony Dowmunt (ed.), *Channels of Resistance: Global Television and Local Empowerment*. London: BFI Publishing in association with Channel Four Television, pp. 138–145.

Landry, Charles, Morley, Dave, Southwood, Russell and Wright, Patrick (1985) *What a Way to Run a Railroad: An Analysis of Radical Failure*. London: Comedia.

Langer, John (1998) *Tabloid Television: Popular Journalism and the 'Other' News*. London: Routledge.

Lasch, Christopher (1991) *The True and Only Heaven: Progress and its Critics*. New York: W.W. Norton.

Leamer, Laurence (1972) *The Paper Revolutionaries: The Rise of the Underground Press*. New York: Simon and Schuster.

Leavis, F.R. and Thompson, Denys (1937) *Culture and Environment*. London: Chatto and Windus.

Lee, Alan (1976) *The Origins of the Popular Press in England: 1855–1914*. London: Croom Helm.

Lee, Chin-Chuan (2003) 'Liberalization without Full Democracy: Guerrilla Media and Political Movements in Taiwan.' In Nick Couldry and James Curran (eds), *Contesting Media Power: Alternative Media in a Networked World*. Lanham, Md.: Rowman and Littlefield, pp. 163–175.

Lefebvre, Henri (1947/1991) *Critique of Everyday Life. Vol. I: Introduction*, translated by John Moore. London: Verso, 1991. Original work published 1947.

Lemert, James B. and Ashman, Marguerite Gemson (1983) 'Extent of Mobilizing Information in Opinion and News Magazines', *Journalism Quarterly* 60(4): 657–662.

Lenin, Vladimir (1901/1961) 'Where to Begin?' In *V.I. Lenin: Collected Works. Volume 5, May 1901–February 1902*. Moscow: Foreign Languages Publishing House, 1961, pp. 17–24. Original work published 1901.

Lenin, Vladimir (1902/1961) 'What Is To Be Done? Burning Questions of Our Movement.' In *V.I. Lenin: Collected Works. Volume 5, May 1901–February 1902*. Moscow: Foreign Languages Publishing House, 1961, pp. 347–529. Original work published 1902.

Lenin, Vladimir (1918/1965) 'The Character of Our Newspapers.' In *V.I. Lenin: Collected Works. Volume 28, July 1918 – March 1919*. Moscow: Progress Publishers, 1965, pp. 96–98. Original work published 1918.

Lenoe, Matthew (2004) *Closer to the Masses: Stalinist Culture, Social Revolution, and Soviet Newspapers*. Cambridge, Mass.: Harvard University Press.

Lim, Merlyna (2003) 'The Internet, Social Networks, and Reform in Indonesia.' In Nick Couldry and James Curran (eds), *Contesting Media Power: Alternative Media in a Networked World*. Lanham, Md.: Rowman and Littlefield, pp. 273–288.

Ling, Sharon (2003) 'The Alternative Media in Malaysia: Their Potential and Limitations.' In Nick Couldry and James Curran (eds), *Contesting Media Power: Alternative Media in a Networked World*. Lanham, Md.: Rowman and Littlefield, pp. 289–301.

Livingstone, Sonia, Van Couvering, Elizabeth and Thumin, Nancy (2005) *Adult Media Literacy: A Review of the Research Literature*. London: Ofcom.

Loades, David (2000) *England's Maritime Empire: Seapower, Commerce, and Policy, 1490–1690*. New York: Longman.

Lockyer, Sharon (2006) 'A Two-pronged Attack? Exploring *Private Eye*'s Satirical Humour and Investigative Reporting', *Journalism Studies* 7(5): 765–781.

Lowrey, Wilson (2006) 'Mapping the Journalism–Blogging Relationship', *Journalism: Theory, Practice, Criticism* 7(4): 477–500.

Lucas, Martin and Wallner, Martha (1993) 'Resistance by Satellite: The Gulf Crisis Project and the Deep Dish Satellite TV Network.' In Tony Dowmunt (ed.), *Channels of Resistance: Global Television and Local Empowerment*. London: BFI Publishing in association with Channel Four Television, pp. 176–194.

McChesney, Robert W. and Scott, Ben (eds) (2004) *Our Unfree Press: 100 Years of Radical Media Criticism*. New York: New Press.

McKay, George (1996) *Senseless Acts of Beauty: Cultures of Resistance since the Sixties*. London: Verso.

McKay, George (ed.) (1998) *DiY Culture: Party & Protest in Nineties Britain*. London: Verso.

McLeary, Paul (2007) 'How Talking Points Memo Beat the Big Boys on the US Attorney Story', *Columbia Journalism Review*, 15 March. Available at: http://www.cjr.org/behind_the_news/how_talkingpointsmemo_beat_the.php 23 March 2007).

McQuail, Denis (1994) *Mass Communication Theory: An Introduction*, 3rd edn. London: Sage.

McReynolds, Louise (1991) *The News under Russia's Old Regime: The Development of a Mass-circulation Press*. Princeton, NJ: Princeton University Press.

Manning, Paul (2001) *News and News Sources: A Critical Introduction*. London: Sage.

Mano, Winston (2007) 'Popular Music as Journalism in Zimbabwe', *Journalism Studies* 8(1): 61–78.

Marliere, Philippe (1998) 'The Rules of the Journalistic Field: Pierre Bourdieu's Contribution to the Sociology of the Media', *European Journal of Communication* 13(2): 219–234.

Marx, Karl (1844/1975) 'Economic and Philosophic Manuscripts of 1844: Estranged Labour.' In *Karl Marx, Frederick Engels: Collected Works. Volume 3: Marx and Engels, 1843–44*. New York: International, 1975, pp. 270–282. Original work published 1844.

Marx, Karl (1887/1996) *Capital: Volume 1. Karl Marx, Frederick Engels: Collected Works. Volume 35: Karl Marx*. New York: International, 1996. Original work published 1887.

Mathes, Rainer and Pfetsch, Barbara (1991) 'The Role of the Alternative Press in the Agenda-building Process: Spill-over Effects and Media Opinion Leadership', *European Journal of Communication* 6: 33–62.

Matheson, Donald (2004) 'Weblogs and Epistemology of the News', *New Media and Society*, 6: 443–468.

Matheson, Donald and Allan, Stuart (2007) 'Truth in a War Zone: The Role of Warblogs in Iraq.' In Sarah Maltby and Richard Keeble (eds), *Communicating War: Memory, Media and Military*. Bury St Edmunds: Arima, pp. 75–89.

Media Center (2005) *Synapse*, April.

Media Center (2007) 'Our Commitment.' Available at <http://www.mediacenter.org/pages/mc/about/our_commitment/> (20 Oct. 2007).

Media, Culture and Society (2003) Special Issue: Alternative Media, 25(5).

Media History (2001) Special Issue: Alternative Media, 7(2).

Media International Australia (2002) Special Issue: Citizens' Media (103).

Meehan, Eileen R., Mosco, Vincent and Wasko, Janet (1993) 'Rethinking Political Economy: Change and Continuity', *Journal of Communication* 43(4): 105–116.

Meikle, Graham (2002) *Future Active: Media Activism and the Internet*. London: Routledge.

Mele, Christopher (1999) 'Cyberspace and Disadvantaged Communities: The Internet as a Tool for Collective Action.' In Marc A. Smith and Peter Kollock (eds), *Communities in Cyberspace*. London: Routledge, pp. 290–310.

Mercer, John (2004) 'Making the News: *Votes for Women* and the Mainstream Press', *Media History* 10(3): 187–199.

Mill, John Stuart (1844/1968) *Essays on Some Unsettled Questions of Political Economy*. Clifton, NJ: A.M. Kelley.

Minority Press Group (1980) *Here is the Other News: Challenges to the Local Commercial Press* (Minority Press Group Series, no. 1). London: Minority Press Group.

Montgomery, David (2002) 'I on the News: With Digicam and Laptop, "Independent" Journalism Rewrites the Rules, if not its Reporting', *Washington Post*, 22 April, col. 1.

Moorhouse, H.F. (1994) 'From Zines Like These? Fanzines, Tradition and Identity in Scottish Football.' In Grant Jarvie and Graham Walker (eds), *Scottish Sport in the Making of the Nation: Ninety Minute Patriots?* Leicester: Leicester University Press, pp. 173–194.

Morris, Brian (2004) *Kropotkin: The Politics of Community*. Amherst, NY: Humanity Books.

Morris, Douglas (2004) 'Globalization and Media Democracy: The Case of Indymedia.' In Douglas Schuler and Peter Day (eds), *Shaping the Network Society*. Cambridge, Mass.: MIT Press, pp. 325–352.

Mosco, Vincent (1996) *The Political Economy of Communication: Rethinking and Renewal*. Thousand Oaks, Calif.: Sage.

Mouffe, Chantal (1992) 'Democratic Citizenship and the Political Community.' In Chantal Mouffe (ed.), *Dimensions of Radical Democracy: Pluralism, Citizenship, Community*. London: Verso, pp. 225–239.

Murphy, Jarrett (2005) 'Village Voice Media, New Times Announce Merger: Deal to Combine Two Largest Alt-weekly Chains Would Require Justice Department Approval', *Village Voice*, 24 October.

Murray, John (1994) *The Russian Press from Brezhnev to Yeltsin: Behind the Paper Curtain*. Aldershot: Edward Elgar.

Nair, P. Thankappan (1987) *A History of the Calcutta Press: The Beginnings*. Calcutta: Firma KLM Private.

Navasky, Victor (2003) 'I.F. Stone', *The Nation*, 21 July. Available at: http://www.thenation.com/doc/20030721/navasky (1 Oct. 2007).

Nel, François, Ward, Mike and Rawlinson, Alan (2007) 'Online Journalism.' In Peter J. Anderson and Geoff Ward (eds), *The Future of Journalism in the Advanced Democracies*. Aldershot: Ashgate, pp. 121–138.

News Hounds (2006) 'News Hounds Manifesto'. Available at <http://www.news hounds.us/2004/07/02/news_hounds_manifesto.php > (19 Oct. 2006).

Nigg, Heinz and Wade, Graham (1980) *Community Media: Community Communication in the UK, Video, Local TV, Film, and Photography*. Zurich: Regenbogen.

Norris, Pippa (1999) *Critical Citizens: Global Support for Democratic Governance*. Oxford: Oxford University Press.

O'Connor, Alan (ed.) (2004) *Community Radio in Bolivia: The Miners' Radio Stations*. Lewiston: Edwin Mellen Press.

Open Society Institute (2007a) 'Media, Arts and Culture.' Available at <http://www.soros.org/initiatives/issues/media> (22 Oct. 2007).

Open Society Institute (2007b) 'Monks, Media, and the Military: The Protests in Burma.' Available at <http://www.soros.org/initiatives/bpsai/events/saffron_20071005> (22 Oct. 2007).

Open Society Institute (2007c) 'Assistance to Media Outlets.' Available at <http://www.soros.org/initiatives/media/focus/assistance> (22 Oct. 2007).

Ostertag, Bob (2006) *People's Movements, People's Press: The Journalism of Social Justice Movements.* Boston, Mass.: Beacon Press.

Outing, Steve (2006a) 'Innovative Thoughts from CitJ's Gurus', *Poynter Online*, 6 April. Available at <http://www.poynter.org/content/content_view.asp?id=97298> (8 March 2007).

Outing, Steve (2006b) 'CitJ's National Networks: Will They Bloom?', *Poynter Online*, 6 April. Available at <http://www.poynter.org/content/content_view.asp?id=96566> (8 March 2007).

Parthasarathy, Rangaswami (1989) *Journalism in India: From the Earliest Times to the Present Day.* New Delhi: Sterling Publishers Private Ltd.

Peacey, Jason (2004) *Politicians and Pamphleteers: Propaganda during the English Civil Wars and Interregnum.* Aldershot: Ashgate.

Peck, Abe (1985) *Uncovering the Sixties: The Life and Times of the Underground Press.* New York: Pantheon.

Peck, Chris (2007) 'JTM: The Next Newsroom', *Journalism That Matters*, 11 July. Available at <http://www.newshare.typepad.com/jtmnextnewsroom/files/next-newsroom-plan.pdf> (20 Oct. 2007).

Perez, Juan Carlos (2007) 'Online Ad Spending had Healthy Growth in 2006', *InfoWorld*, 7 March. Available at <http://www.infoworld.com/article/07/03/07/Hnonlineadspending_1.html> (10 March 2007).

Peter A. Mayer Advertising (2007) Available at <http://www.peteramayer.com/> (12 Nov. 2007).

Peters, John Durham (1989) 'John Locke, the Individual, and the Origin of Communication', *Quarterly Journal of Speech* 75(4): 387–399.

Peters, John Durham (2001) 'Witnessing', *Media, Culture and Society* 23(6): 707–723.

Philo, Greg (1999) *Message Received: Glasgow Media Group Research, 1993–1998.* New York: Longman.

Pickard, Victor W. (2006) 'United Yet Autonomous: Indymedia and the Struggle to Sustain a Radical Democratic Network', *Media, Culture and Society* 28(3): 315–336.

Pilling, Rod (2006) 'Local Journalists and the Local Press: Waking up to Change?' In Bob Franklin (ed.), *Local Journalism and Local Media: Making the Local News.* London: Routledge, pp. 104–114.

Platon, Sara (2002) 'Re: The Sad Decline of Indymedia.' Pers. comm. (email).

Platon, Sara and Deuze, Mark (2003) 'Indymedia Journalism: A Radical Way of Making, Selecting and Sharing News?', *Journalism* 4(3): 336–355.

Preston, Paschal (2001) *Reshaping Communications: Technology, Information and Social Change.* London: Sage.

Project for Excellence in Journalism (2007a) 'Alternative Weeklies', *State of the News Media Report – Newspapers*, 12 March. Available at: http://www.journalism.org/node/7225/> (23 Oct. 2007).

Project for Excellence in Journalism (2007b) 'Online: Citizen Media.' In *The State of the News Media 2007: An Annual Report on American Journalism.* Available at: <http://www.stateofthemedia.org/2007/narrative_online_citizen_media.asp?cat=8&media=4> (13 March 2007).

Pye, Lucien (1964) *Communication and Political Development.* Princeton, NJ: Princeton University Press.

Quail, John (1978) *The Slow Burning Fuse: The Lost History of the British Anarchists.* London: Paladin.

Rauch, Jennifer (2007) 'Activists as Interpretive Communities: Rituals of Consumption and Interaction in an Alternative Media Audience', *Media, Culture and Society* 29(6): 994–1013.

Raymond, Joad (1996) *The Invention of the Newspaper: English Newsbooks 1641–1649*. Oxford: Clarendon Press.

Reed, Liz (1989) The British Counter-culture, 1966–73: A Study of the *underground press*. New York: St Martins.

Reed, T.V. (2005) *The Art of Protest: Culture and Activism from the Civil Rights Movement to the Streets of Seattle*. Minneapolis, Minn.: University of Minnesota Press.

Ricardo, David (1817/1971) *On the Principles of Political Economy and Taxation*. Harmondsworth: Penguin.

Ritter, Alan (1980) *Anarchism: A Theoretical Analysis*. Cambridge: Cambridge University Press.

Rodriguez, Clemencia (2001) *Fissures in the Mediascape: An International Study of Citizens' Media*. Cresskill, NJ: Hampton Press.

Rodriguez, Clemencia (2002) 'Citizens' Media and the Voice of the Angel/Poet', *Media International Australia* 103: 78–87.

Rodriguez, Clemencia (2003) 'The Bishop and his Star: Citizens' Communication in Southern Chile.' In Nick Couldry and James Curran (eds), *Contesting Media Power: Alternative Media in a Networked World*. Lanham, Md.: Rowman and Littlefield, pp. 177–194.

Rodriguez, Clemencia and El Gazi, Jeanine (2007) 'The Poetics of Indigenous Radio in Colombia', *Media, Culture and Society* 29(3): 449–468.

Roggenkamp, Karen (2005) *Narrating the News: New Journalism and Literary Genre in Late Nineteenth-Century American Newspapers and Fiction*. Kent, Ohio: Kent State University Press.

Rojas, Peter (2002) 'Pirates of Peercasting', *Guardian* (Online supplement), 25 July: 6.

Rosen, Jay (1996) *Getting the Connections Right: Public Journalism and the Troubles in the Press*. New York: Twentieth Century Fund.

Rosenberg, Bernard and White, David Manning (eds) (1957) *Mass Culture: The Popular Arts in America*. Glencoe, Ill.: Free Press.

Ross, Karen (2006) 'Open Source? Hearing Voices in the Local Press.' In Bob Franklin (ed.), *Local Journalism and Local Media: Making the Local News*. London: Routledge, pp. 232–244.

Rugh, William A. (2004) *Arab Mass Media: Newspapers, Radio, and Television in Arab Politics*. Westport, Conn.: Praeger.

Rushton, Dave (1993) *Citizen Television: A Local Dimension to Public Broadcasting*. London: John Libbey.

Sabin, Roger and Triggs, Teal (2001) *Below Critical Radar: Fanzines and Alternative Comics from 1976 to Now*. Hove: Slab-O-Concrete.

Said, Edward (1981) *Covering Islam: How the Media and the Experts Determine How We See the Rest of the World*. New York: Pantheon.

Said, Edward W. (1982/1985) 'Opponents, Audiences, Constituencies and Community.' In Hal Foster (ed.), *Postmodern Culture*. London: Pluto, pp. 135–159. Original work published 1982.

Salcetti, Marianne (1995) 'The Emergence of the Reporter: Mechanization and the Devaluation of Editorial Workers.' In Hanno Hardt and Bonnie Brennen (eds), *Newsworkers: Toward a History of the Rank and File*. Minneapolis, Minn.: University of Minnesota Press, pp. 48–74.

Salerno, Salvatore (1989) *Red November, Black November: Culture and Community in the Industrial Workers of the World*. Albany, NY: State University of New York Press.

Salter, Lee (2006) 'Democracy and Online News: Indymedia and the Limits of Participatory Media', *Scan* 3(1). Available at: <http://scan.net.au> (10 Aug. 2007).

Sampedro Blanco, Victor F. (ed.) (2005) *13-M: Multitudes On-Line*. Madrid: Catarata.

Scan (2006) Themed issue: News and the Net – Convergences and Divergences, 3(1). Available at <http://scan.net.au> (10 Aug. 2007).

Schiller, Dan (1996) *Theorizing Communication: A History*. New York: Oxford University Press.

Schlesinger, Philip (1989) 'From Production to Propaganda?', *Media, Culture and Society* 11(3): 283–306.

Schneider, Gary (2005) *The Culture of Epistolarity: Vernacular Letters and Letter Writing in Early Modern England, 1500–1700*. Newark, Del.: University of Delaware Press.

Schramm, Wilbur (1964) *Mass Media and National Development*. Stanford, Calif.: Stanford University Press.

Schudson, Michael (1978) *Discovering the News: A Social History of American Newspapers*. New York: Basic Books.

Schudson, Michael (2001) 'The Objectivity Norm in American Journalism', *Journalism: Theory, Practice and Criticism* 2(2): 149–170.

Scott, Keeley (1999) 'Spotlight: TV-12', *Airflash*, July: 12–13.

Seldes, George (1929) *You Can't Print That! The Truth behind the News, 1918–1928*. New York: Payson and Clarke.

Shaaber, Matthias A. (1929) *Some Forerunners of the Newspaper in England: 1476–1622*. Philadelphia, Pa.: University of Pennsylvania Press.

Shah, Hemant (1996) 'Modernization, Marginalization, and Emancipation: Toward a Normative Model of Journalism and National Development', *Communication Theory* 6(2): 143–166.

Shapiro, Barbara J. (2000) *A Culture of Fact: England 1550–1720*. Ithaca, NY: Cornell University Press.

Shore, Elliot (1985) 'Selling Socialism: The Appeal to Reason and the Radical Press in Turn-of-the-Century America', *Media, Culture and Society* 7(2): 147–168.

Shore, Elliot (1988) *Talkin' Socialism: J.A. Wayland and the Role of the Press in American Radicalism, 1890–1912*. Lawrence, Kan.: University of Kansas Press.

Sibeko, Alexander (1983) 'The Underground Voice.' In Armand Mattelart and Seth Siegelaub (eds), *Communication and Class Struggle, Volume 2: Liberation, Socialism*. New York: International General, pp. 203–207.

Siklos, Richard (2005) 'The *Village Voice*, Pushing 50, Prepares to be Sold to a Chain of Weeklies', *New York Times*, 24 October.

Skilling, H. Gordon (1989) *Samizdat and an Independent Society in Central and Eastern Europe*. Columbus, Ohio: Ohio State University Press.

Skuncke, Marie-Christine (ed.) (2005) *Media and Political Culture in the Eighteenth Century*. Stockholm: Kungl. Vitterhets Historie och Antikvitets Akademien.

Smith, Adam (1776/1994) *An Inquiry into the Nature and Causes of the Wealth of Nations*, edited by Edwin Cannan. New York: Modern Library, 1994. Original work published 1776.

Smith, Culver H. (1977) *The Press, Politics, and Patronage: The American Government's Use of Newspapers, 1789–1875*. Athens, Ga.: University of Georgia Press.

Smith, Owen F. (2005) 'Fluxus Praxis: An Exploration of Connections, Creativity, and Community.' In Annmarie Chandler and Norie Newmark (eds), *At a Distance: Precursors to Art and Activism on the Internet*. Cambridge, Mass.: MIT Press, pp. 116–138.

Social Science Research Council (2007a) 'The Public Sphere.' Available at <http://www.ssrc.org/program_areas/ps/> (22 Oct. 2007).

Social Science Research Council (2007b) 'Necessary Knowledge for a Democratic Public Sphere.' Available at <http://programs.ssrc.org/media/> (22 Oct. 2007).

Solomon, William S. (1995) 'The Site of Newsroom Labour: The Division of Editorial Practices.' In Hanno Hardt and Bonnie Brennen (eds), *Newsworkers: Toward a History of the Rank and File*. Minneapolis, Minn.: University of Minnesota Press, pp. 110–134.

Sommerville, C. John (1996) *The News Revolution in England: Cultural Dynamics of Daily Information*. New York: Oxford University Press.

Sosale, Sujatha (2003) 'Envisioning a New World Order through Journalism: Lessons from Recent History', *Journalism: Theory, Practice and Criticism* 4(3): 377–392.

Sparks, Colin (1985) 'The Working-class Press: Radical and Revolutionary Alternatives', *Media, Culture and Society* 7: 133–146.

Spiers, John (1974) *The Underground and Alternative Press in Britain: A Bibliographical Guide with Historical Notes*. Brighton: Harvester Press.

Spurr, David (1993) *The Rhetoric of Empire: Colonial Discourse in Journalism, Travel Writing and Imperial Administration*. Durham, NC and London: Duke University Press.

Sreberny-Mohammadi, Annabelle and Ali Mohammadi (1994) *Small Media, Big Revolution: Communication, Culture, and the Iranian Revolution*. Minneapolis, Minn.: University of Minnesota Press.

Stavitsky, Alan G. (1994) 'The Changing Conception of Localism in U.S. Public Radio', *Journal of Broadcasting & Electronic Media* 38(1): 19–33.

Stein, Laura (2001) 'Access Television and Grassroots Political Communication in the United States.' In John Downing, Tamara Villareal Ford, Geneve Gil and Laura Stein, *Radical Media: Rebellious Communication and Social Movements*. Thousand Oaks, Calif.: Sage, pp. 299–324.

Strangelove, Michael (2005) *The Empire of Mind: Digital Piracy and the Anti-capitalist Movement*. Toronto: University of Toronto Press.

Streitmatter, Rodger (2001) *Voices of Revolution: The Dissident Press in America*. New York: Columbia University Press.

Sutherland, James (1986) *The Restoration Newspaper and its Development*. Cambridge: Cambridge University Press.

Swithinbank, Tessa (1996) 'World Exclusive!', *New Internationalist*, February: 28–30.

Switzer, Les and Adhikari, M. (2000) 'Preface.' In Les Switzer and Mohamed Adhikari (eds), *South Africa's Resistance Press: Alternative Voices in the Last Generation under Apartheid*. Athens, Ohio: Ohio University Center for International Studies, pp. xv–xvii.

Tacchi, Jo (2000) 'The Need for Radio Theory in the Digital Age', *International Journal of Cultural Studies* 3(2): 289–298.

Theobald, John (2004) 'Radical Media Critics: The Four Generations.' In *The Media and the Making of History*. Aldershot: Ashgate, pp. 19–53.

Thompson, E.P. (1966) *The Making of the English Working Class*. New York: Vintage.

Thompson, John B. (1991) 'Editor's Introduction.' In Pierre Bourdieu, *Language and Symbolic Power*. Cambridge: Polity Press, pp. 1–31.

Toynbee, Jason (2001) *Creating Problems: Social Authorship, Copyright and the Production of Culture* (Pavis Papers in Social and Cultural Research, no. 3). Milton Keynes: Open University, Pavis Centre for Social and Cultural Research.

Traber, Michael (1985) *Alternative Journalism, Alternative Media* (Communication Resource no. 7). London: World Association for Christian Communication.

Triggs, Teal (1995) 'Alphabet Soup: Reading British Fanzines', *Visible Language* 29(1): 72–87.

Trinkle, Dennis A. (2002) *The Napoleonic Press: The Public Sphere and Oppositional Journalism.* Lewiston, NY: Edwin Mellen.

Tusan, Michelle Elizabeth (2003) 'Writing *Stri Dharma*: International Feminism, Nationalist Politics, and Women's Press Advocacy in Late Colonial India', *Women's History Review* 12(4): 623–649.

Tusan, Michelle Elizabeth (2005) *Women Making News: Gender and Journalism in Modern Britain.* Urbana, Ill.: University of Illinois Press.

van de Donk, Wim, Loader, Brian D., Nixon, Paul G. and Rucht, Dieter (eds) (2004) *Cyberprotest: New Media, Citizens and Social Movements.* New York: Routledge.

van Vuuren, Kitty (2002) 'Beyond the Studio: A Case Study of Community Radio and Social Capital', *Media International Australia* 103: 94–108.

Vargas, Lucila (1995) *Social Uses and Radio Practices: The Use of Participatory Radio by Ethnic Minorities in Mexico.* Boulder, Colo.: Westview Press.

Vatikiotis, Pantelis (2004) 'Communication Theory and Alternative Media', *Westminster Papers in Communication and Culture* 1(2): 4–29.

Wall, Melissa (2005) '"Blogs of War": Weblogs as News', *Journalism: Theory, Practice and Criticism* 6: 153–172.

Wall, Melissa (2006) 'Blogging Gulf War II', *Journalism Studies* 7(1): 111–126.

Waltz, Mitzi (2005) *Alternative and Activist Media.* Edinburgh: Edinburgh University Press.

Weibull, Lennart (2003) 'The Press Subsidy System in Sweden: A Critical Approach.' In Nick Couldry and James Curran (eds), *Contesting Media Power: Alternative Media in a Networked World.* Lanham, Md.: Rowman and Littlefield, pp. 89–107.

Weigert, Andrew J. (1981) *Sociology of Everyday Life.* New York and London: Longman.

'What is Indymedia?' (2006) *The Indypendent*, 2 November.

White, Shirley A., Sadanandan Nair, K. and Ascroft, Joseph (eds) (1994) *Participatory Communication: Working for Change and Development.* Thousand Oaks, Calif.: Sage.

Wiener, Joel H. (ed.) (1988) *Papers for the Millions: The New Journalism in Britain, 1850s to 1914.* New York: Greenwood Press.

Will, Brad (2006) 'Fragments of a Shattered Hope: Brazil Makes War on Sohno Real Squatters', *Brad Will in Boog City*, 25 April. Available at: http://bradwillboogcity.blogspot.com/ (28 Oct. 2006).

Williams, Lisa, Gillmor, Dan and MacKay, Jane (2007) 'Frontiers of Innovation in Community Engagement: News Organizations Forge New Relationships with Communities', *Centre for Citizen Media.* Available at <http://citmedia.org/frontiers/> (8 March 2007).

Williams, Raymond (1963) *Culture and Society: 1780–1950.* Harmondsworth: Penguin.

Williams, Raymond (1967) *Communications.* Revised edn. New York: Barnes and Noble.

Williams, Raymond (1970) 'Radical and/or Respectable.' In Richard Boston (ed.), *The Press We Deserve.* London: Routledge and Kegan Paul, pp. 14–26.

Williams, Raymond (1978a) 'The Press We Don't Deserve.' In James Curran (ed.), *The British Press: A Manifesto.* London: Macmillan, pp. 15–28.

Williams, Raymond (1978b) 'The Press and Popular Culture: An Historical Perspective.' In George Boyce, James Curran and Pauline Wingate (eds), *Newspaper History from the Seventeenth Century to the Present Day*. London: Constable, pp. 41–50.

Williams, Raymond (1979) *Politics and Letters: Interviews with New Left Review*. New York: Schocken.

Williams, Raymond (1980a) 'Advertising: The Magic System.' In *Problems in Materialism and Culture: Selected Essays*. London: Verso, pp. 170–195.

Williams, Raymond (1980b) 'Means of Communication as Means of Production.' In *Problems in Materialism and Culture: Selected Essays*. London: Verso, pp. 50–63.

Williams, Raymond (1980/1989) 'The Writer: Commitment and Alignment.' In Robin Gale (ed.), *Resources of Hope*. London: Verso, 1989, pp. 77–87. Original work published 1980.

Willis, Fran (2006) 'Citizen Journalism: The Next Generation of Local News and Advertising', presentation to Growing Audience Seminar, Newspaper Association of America, 5 June. Available at <http://www.naa.org/conferences/gas/program.html> (9 March 2007).

Willis, Paul (1978) *Profane Culture*. London: Routledge and Kegan Paul.

Wolfe, Tom (ed.) (1973) *The New Journalism*. New York: Harper and Row.

Woodstock, Louise (2002) 'Public Journalism's Talking Cure: An Analysis of the Movement's "Problem" and "Solution" Narratives', *Journalism: Theory, Practice and Criticism* 3(1): 37–55.

Workers' Life (1928/1983) 'The Worker Correspondent.' In Armand Mattelart and Seth Siegelaub (eds), *Communication and Class Struggle, Vol. 2: Liberation, Socialism*. New York: International General, 1983, pp. 153–157. Original work published 1928.

Zhao, Yuezhi (1998) *Media, Market, and Democracy in China: Between the Party Line and the Bottom Line*. Urbana, Ill.: University of Illinois Press.

INDEX